MW01278633

Indomitable
CANADIAN FILIPINOS

Indomitable
CANADIAN FILIPINOS

Edited by Eleanor R. Laquian
Introduction by Hon. Dr. Rey D. Pagtakhan

The contents of this publication are mainly articles from *CanadianFiipino.Net*, a nationwide, online biweekly newsmagazine for Filipinos in Canada, published by Maple Bamboo Network Society, based in Vancouver, B.C

CanadianFilipino.Net is owned, managed, and operated by the Maple Bamboo Network Society, a non-profit society powered by 100% volunteers. This digital publication has been made possible through the support of Canadian Heritage and the Canadian Filipino community.

Social Sciences and Humanities
Research Council of Canada
Conseil de recherches en
sciences humaines du Canada
Canada

FriesenPress

One Printers Way
Altona, MB R0G 0B0
Canada

www.friesenpress.com

Social Sciences and Humanities
Research Council of Canada
Conseil de recherches en
sciences humaines du Canada

Canada

This book is published with partial funding from a Social Science and Humanities Research Council (SSHRC) Insight Grants Number: 435-2019-1203.

Cover design: Leo O. Cunanan Jr.

ISBN
978-1-03-915900-6 (Hardcover)
978-1-03-915899-3 (Paperback)
978-1-03-915901-3 (eBook)

1. HISTORY, CANADA

Distributed to the trade by The Ingram Book Company

Acknowledgements

Starting a new website in a crowded field of millions competing for the most hits and likes is a daunting task. Putting together a book from about a thousand CFNet articles published over five years is even more so. However, the CFNet editor and staff accomplished this task. The **CFNet Editorial Board** read reams of published articles to choose the ones that best tell the story of Filipino immigration to Canada.

Kudos to managing editor **Rachel Ramos-Reid**, who, with the help of **Emmy Buccat,** MBNS director in charge of fundraising and social media director, **Iona Santos Fresnoza,** newsletter coordinator, and **Arlene Wright,** webmaster, came up with a master list of over a thousand titles published. Many thanks are due to those who toiled:

For continuing this task, CFNet editor **Eleanor R. Laquian,** who, for the last five years, has steered and shaped the CFNet website into what it is today—an eloquent, timely, engaging, and well-documented biweekly newsmagazine for Filipinos in Canada.

UBC Professor **Nora C. Angeles,** for her thought-provoking CFNet column *RESPECT*, her boundless energy, her ideas on how to promote Filipino contributions to Canada's progress, for her concluding chapter, which opened opportunities for future researchers, and for sharing her SSHRC grant to publish this book.

Hon. Dr. Rey D. Pagtakhan, retired lung specialist and the very first Filipino MP (1988–2004), for his prodigious coverage of the COVID-19 pandemic in his CFNet column *Medisina at Politika*, and for his introductory chapter on what this book is all about.

Carlito Pablo, founding member of Maple Bamboo Network Society, whose idea to project a better Filipino community image in the media gave rise to the Board of MBNS, publisher of CFNet.

Eleanor Guerrero-Campbell, MBNS co-founder and MBNS board adviser, together with UBC professor **Dr. Aprodicio A. Laquian,** founding editor of CFNet and CEO of MBNS, for putting the MBNS and CFNet in motion.

Clay Campbell, CFNet first legal counsel and **Melissa Briones,** current legal counsel, for their guidance of CFNet as it navigates "thorny" legal issues in its coverage of news and views.

Finally, special thanks go to all CFNet staff and contributors in Canada, especially **Manolo Abella,** economist, formerly at ILO in Geneva, now a Vancouver resident and **Jo Flach** in Toronto, CFNet lifestyle guru. And to our contributors in the Philippines for religiously keeping us up to date on what is going on in their neck of the woods.

Special thanks also go to **Leo Orpilla Cunanan Jr**, artist and publisher of *Dahong Pilipino*, for designing the cover of *Indomitable Canadian Filipinos* that shows we are Canadians but Filipinos at core—as symbolized by a small, white sampaguita, Philippine national flower and symbol of hope, on a red maple leaf. And to **Veronica G. Caparas** for producing the index.

We are grateful to our "hero" MBNS Director **Emmy Buccat** whose computer skills saved this book from an "untimely death."

And to our readers, who inspire our publication to rejuvenate itself every first and sixteenth of the month, we owe deep gratitude—for without **you**, we wouldn't have bragging rights to over five million hits in only our fifth year of publication. May you ever remain our loyal readers and friends. **The CFNet Editorial Board**

Table of Contents

ACKNOWLEDGEMENTS VII

FOREWORD XIII

CHAPTER 1: INTRODUCTION 1

CHAPTER 2: FILIPINOS ON THE MOVE 8
Dynamics of Filipino Migration to Canada: An Overview............................... 9
A Decade of the Filipino Community Coming of Age..................................... 17
Will PM Trudeau's Promise of Kinder Immigration Come True?..................... 22
Canada's Immigration Policy: Policy and Performance................................... 24
Troubling Trends: The Alarming Backlash against Immigrants and Refugees in Canada 30
Migration Is Not a Problem to Be Solved but a Process to Be Managed............ 34
Needed but Not Wanted: Temporary Foreign Workers in Canada 40
What Canada Day 2020 Can Mean to Canadian Filipinos............................... 43
On Canada Day, a Look at People-to-People Connections in Canada-Philippine Relations............ 47
Will You Still Remember, Mommy?*(Maalala mo pa kaya, Inay?)*..................... 49

CHAPTER 3: OUR PHILIPPINE HERITAGE 52
The Filipino Family in Canada 54
Filipino Traits I'd Pass On to My Children 56
Mixed Marriages: Odd Couples No More 58
What I Would Show My Grandchildren about Their Philippine Heritage 61
Filipino Cultural Traits and the Canadian Workplace..................................... 65
Filipino Indigeneity and Indigenous Peoples of Canada 68
Finding Oneness in Filipino Community.. 71
Taal Volcano Eruption Shows *Bayanihan* in Canada 72
Bayanihan Spirit Moves Filipino Associations.. 74
Watching Filipino Movies: A Peek at Philippine Culture 76
Lent in Canada: Delta Parish Adopts Salubong 78
Celebrating All Saints' Day in the Philippines 82
Pasko na, Sinta ko, Paano ang Pasko sa Pandemyang ito? 84
Filipino *Belen* Tradition Brings Baby Jesus to Vancouver Homes................. 87
Sambayanang Pilipino Introduces All-Tagalog *Simbang Gabi* 90

The Essence of Christmas...92

The Role of Food in Filipino Culture...95

Kape Tayo, or Connecting Cultures Through Coffee 96

CHAPTER 4: WHEN SUCCESS MEETS FILIPINOS 99

Canada Proclaims Filipino Heritage Month...100

Criteria for CFNet's Selection of Outstanding Filipinos in Canada.........................103

CFNet's Outstanding Filipinos in Canada, 2021...104

CFNet's Outstanding Filipinos in Canada, 2022...118

Filipinos in Small Towns Making a Difference...138

Yvonne Clark, First Filipino MLA of Porter Creek, Yukon 138

Edwin Empinado on Safeguards for North Gateway Pipeline 140

Restaurateur Estela Aguilar Chow Helps the Poor in Ontario and the Philippines............141

Rowena Santos, Lisa Abarquez Bower Elected to Municipal Councils in Ontario............142

First Filipino in City Council of Whitehorse...143

Cardeno's Grill Brings Pandesal to Small Town in Ontario..........................145

Newcomer Junifer Torralba Launches Online Grocery in Fredericton 146

De Leon's Grill Caters to NWT Legislature..148

Chef Audie Banania Gives Back to Community 149

Filipinos Reelected in Municipal Elections 151

Tony Flores Advocates for Persons with Disabilities....................................152

Boxer to Entrepreneur: Rey Fortaleza's Game Plan......................................153

Gemma Dalayoan: 2019 University of Manitoba Distinguished Alumni for Community Service.156

Quiambao, Laxamana Honoured for Global Cooperation Work 157

Toronto Filmmaker Patrick Alcedo Wins Recognition for Works 159

Lawyers Ho and Gatchalian Named to Highest Courts of Nova Scotia and Alberta in 2021 160

Filipino Hospitality at Baldwin Village Inn, Toronto's Urban Oasis 161

CHAPTER 5: THE BEST OF TWO WORLDS 163

For 1.5 and Second Generation Canadian Filipinos, the Best of Two Worlds....................164

Living Hyphen: Untangling the Knots of Our Identity 167

Learning (to be) Beyond the Book 170

Young Filipinos Create Individual Identities 172

My Filipino Identity..175

Reflections of a Second Generation Canadian Filipino on "Filipino Identity" 177

On What It Means to Be a Filipino 179

Making the Next Day Better in Vancouver...181

Second Generation Filipinos in Trudeau's Post-National Canada 182

Two Lands, One Heart...185

CHAPTER 6: THE LIFE-UPENDING COVID-19 188

The COVID-19 Pandemic: More Than a Two-Year Viral Journey—Lessons, Insights, What's Next..191

Lessons from the Pandemic...195

Bayanihan in the Time of Social Distancing...199

Introducing RESPECT: Filipino Workers in Pandemic 200

CHAPTER 7: AGEING IN CANADA 204

Is There Life after Sixty-Five for Filipinos in Canada? 205

Why I Prefer to Grow Old in the Philippines..206

Why Canada Is the Best Place for Ageing...208

Being a Senior Is More Fun in the Philippines..210

How Catholic Filipinos Deal With Death 212

MAD Divides the Catholic Church 215

If There's a Will . . . Or, How to Plan for the Inevitable 220

Why You Should Write Your Will...223

Searching for Lola...226

Pondering Our Mortality: Is Quality of Life Possible in Ageing? 228

CHAPTER 8: EARNING THEIR KEEP 232

Filipino Values Contribute to Canada's Rich Asian Heritage 233

The Philippines Deepens Economic Relations with Canada 235

The CDWCR Story: Caring for Caregivers 237

Canadian Filipino Authors Featured in 2017 LiterASIAN Festival 241

Progress of Filipino Businesses in Canada...244

Introducing a New Breed of Filipino Entrepreneurs 246

Filipino Community Hubs in Saskatoon...248

Macario "Tobi" Reyes in Vancouver Property Development: How Does He Do It?....................250

Victoria Filipino Canadian Association's Legacy of Service...252

Gelaine Santiago Champions Filipino Artisans 257

CHAPTER 9: ISSUES TO PURSUE 261

A Website for Thought and Action 262

Canadian Filipinos Will Thrive under Two Flags...263

Dual Citizenship: All Pros and No Cons 265

Is Education an Equalizer for Filipinos in Canada?..271

Filipinos Now Third-Largest Immigrant Group in Canada...273

Gender Equality: An Unfinished Global Task..276

Beyond Apology: A Call for Vigilance against Racism..278

Foreign Domestic Workers/Caregivers: Able and Available to Meet Canada's Labour Needs........282

Stereotyping and Racialization: A Constant Canadian Filipino Struggle...........................287

Everyone Should Try to Avert a Climate Meltdown...288

Safeguard our Collective Multicultural Identity...290

Why are Canadian Filipinos Underrepresented in Canadian Politics?...............................293

Sorting Out Ticklish Situations in the Political Engagement of Canadian Filipinos..........295

Filipino Food: Why Has It Not Gone Mainstream?..298

Heart in Two Places: An Immigrant's Joy and Sorrow..300

CHAPTER 10: FILIPINOS IN CANADA AS NATIONAL, TRANSNATIONAL, AND GLOBAL CITIZENS 302

APPENDIX A... 320

The *CanadianFilipino.Net* (CFNet) Team 320

Contributors 325

APPENDIX B... 333

The Maple Bamboo Network Society, Publisher of *CanadianFilipino.Net*....................... 333

INDEX 337

Foreword

In the fall of 2015, a small group of us dreamed the idea that would eventually become *CanadianFilipino.Net* (CFNet). We did it because we could not accept that our Filipino community, after being in this country for over a hundred years (the first documented Filipino arrived in Canada in 1861), now so large and contributing significantly to Canadian workplaces, community organizations, and institutions, could be so under the radar.

We wanted to change that and raise the profile of Filipinos in Canada through CFNet, by writing about their identity and culture, achievements, issues, struggles, and needs, their hopes and dreams. We hoped that in doing so, Filipinos in Canada would gain the recognition and respect they deserved, that their needs would be given more attention by government, and that their issues would be clarified and discussed among themselves, for stronger and connected community advocacy across the country.

In July 2016, CFNet was officially launched. Five years later, after more than 120 online twice-a-month editions that produced over a thousand articles, editorials, interviews, and features, the Filipino presence is being felt in Canada.

The election of Rechie Valdez as MP for Mississauga–Streetsville in Ontario, making her the second Filipino MP in Canada after Dr. Rey Pagtakhan of Winnipeg, Manitoba, was an event noticed and written up in media across Canada. Canadian Filipino performers and artists are enjoying mainstream audiences and success. Filipino food is achieving acceptance at Filipino food festivals, food trucks, restaurants, and even the first Jollibee outlet in Vancouver, becoming the talk of the town.

That the month of June is now celebrated throughout Canada as Filipino Heritage Month bears witness to Canada's recognition of the Canadian Filipino community.

CFNet may have helped in increasing this profile, as shown by how viewership has shot up through the years, growing to five million hits by over eighty thousand unique visitors throughout Canada by 2021.

But the reality is that our community is finally coming of age, and CFNet has been privileged to document its flowering as much as contributing to it by writing about it. CFNet unearthed the largely hidden achievements of the first generation, and profiled the rise of the 1.5 and second generations. It witnessed the improvement of immigration policy for caregivers through the strong advocacy of the community including CFNet.

Today, the future of our community is ensured by a well-educated and highly engaged 1.5 and second generations. Their CFNet stories depict them employing the power of their dual identity as Filipinos and Canadians, leading to global citizenship.

Some issues remain, for sure—the rise of Asian discrimination and the continued non-recognition of educational credentials of many Filipino immigrants, for example. But the Filipinos' proven refusal to accept defeat will prevail.

Kudos to the staff of *CanadianFilipino.Net*, contributors and supporters, and its publisher, the Maple Bamboo Network Society—all volunteers in the campaign to shine a light on the Filipinos' indomitable spirit. Thank you for your persistence, dedication, and hard work. Your reward is the satisfaction of knowing your work is bearing fruit.

By Eleanor Guerrero-Campbell, Co-founder, Maple Bamboo Network Societyand *Canadian Filipino.Net*

Chapter 1:
INTRODUCTION

By Hon. Rey D. Pagtakhan, PC, OM, LLD, ScD, MSc, MD

[About the author: Dr. Pagtakhan—widely published in medical journals and textbook chapters—is a retired lung specialist and professor of paediatrics and child health, former member of parliament, parliamentary secretary to the prime minister, and cabinet minister, and recipient of academic, governmental, professional, and community awards and honours. He graduated from the University of the Philippines, trained at the children's hospitals of Washington University and University of Manitoba, and spent a sabbatical year as visiting professor at the University of Arizona. With abiding interests in medicine, politics, and community volunteerism, he writes the column *Medisina at Politika* for *Pilipino Express* and *CanadianFilipino.Net (CFNet)* and volunteers on the Advisory Council of Immigration Partnership Winnipeg and the Board of St. Paul's College Foundation at the University of Manitoba.]

"It is and will continue to be a long and hard grind for every Filipino who has a spot to claim in the Canadian landscape, but success can certainly be had and be rightfully deserved by those who do not hesitate to take that journey."

Rachel Ramos-Reid
CFNet Managing Editor
2022

Purpose and Scope

The first Filipino migrated to British Columbia in 1861, six years before Canada's Confederation in 1867 and a century earlier before the first wave of Filipino migration to the country started cautiously in the 1960s. Today, 70 years since the onset of the first migration wave, close to a million Filipinos across the country call Canada home. In grateful celebration, the Canadian Filipino community is pleased to share their contemporary Canadian story.

This is where *CanadianFilipino.Net* (CFNet) comes in with its novel history book, **Indomitable Canadian Filipinos,** telling the broad story about the past seventy years of Filipino immigration to Canada from a uniquely Filipino viewpoint on Canadian life.

How can one best judge if it is, indeed, one-of-a-kind, a novelty?

University of Manitoba history teacher Dr. Jon G. Malek provides a guide on how to answer such a question. When he accepted the invitation from the Canadian Historical Association to do a "summary history of the Filipino community in Canada," he posted in his *Pilipino Express* column, *It's All History*, these twin guidelines in the form of interrogatives: 1) How can one best represent the lives, activities, and experiences of those who have come to call Canada home? and 2) What broad story should be told?" When he released in December 2021 his booklet, *Filipinos in Canada,* he wrote: "History is something that is lived, experienced, remembered, and shared."

Aptly, this CFNet book is a virtual window into the experiences of the first, first-and-half, and second generations of Canadian Filipino migrants across the vast geography of the country from the Arctic North to the Atlantic Eastern Shores and the Pacific West Coast. It mirrors that broad Filipino-shared immigrant story of aspirations, sacrifices, triumphs and search for a better life. It reflects the arduous path travelled; the heritage and cultural values summoned to anchor one's fortitude; the unyielding confidence and strong work ethic marshalled and applied; the indomitable spirit mustered to conquer adversity; and the rewards of success harvested at the end of an audacious journey.

Sources of Contents

The main source of contents for the book came from the news, views and features on people, places, events, activities and issues faithfully recorded in real time on CFNet by its nationwide Canadian Filipino corps of volunteer staff, correspondents and contributors. Written in engaging prose and occasionally poetry, materials were sufficient to help inform the contemporary history of the fast-growing community from a uniquely Filipino viewpoint of Canadian life. The editorial team 1) reviewed over a thousand articles from July 2016 to July 2022; 2) distilled the varied Filipino lived experiences to a little over a hundred illustrative examples; and 3) segmented them into eight thematic book chapters (Chapters 2 to 9).

The emerging new knowledge from the 'laboratory' of Canadian Filipino social scientist Dr. Leonora C. Angeles of the University of British Columbia provided one unique additional source. She is embarked on a study to know how "the dynamism of Canadian Filipinos in navigating the changing landscapes of citizenships and national identities" might impact governments, business and civil society and influence relationships between Canada and the Philippines and Canadians and Filipinos. To avail of this emerging new knowledge, CFNet invited Professor Angeles to share her research work (Chapter 10).

Contents and Chapters

Readers can expect to see the fruits of their labour while on their own journey from chapter to chapter. **Chapter 2** sets the tone and elegantly treats the readers not only to the exponential growth of regular Filipino migration waves but also to the demographic and socioeconomic dynamics during its first six decades from 1950 to 2010, with the seventh decade from 2011 to 2022 dubbed as "A Decade of the Filipino Community Coming of Age." **Chapter 3** highlights the twin realities that Canadian Filipinos "have integrated into Canadian life with ease" while retaining the "positive elements of their Filipino culture and value system."

Chapter 4 profiles Canadian Filipinos who have distinguished themselves in their chosen fields to help inspire new migrants and younger generations. CFNet has invited the achievers and the accomplished of the community to share their names and stories of success so as to continually update its roster.

Chapter 5 focuses on the "young generations grappling to define their identity as Filipinos growing up as Canadians." Filled with amazing contents, let me quote from two. Carissa Duenas in **Two Lands, One Heart** *writes*: "I am profoundly lucky. I have two homes. One holds my past, the other my present. Together, they have enriched my life." Beautiful and imbued with optimism and great hopes. It eloquently portrays the collective sentiment of Canadian Filipinos.

Prod and Eleanor Laquian's **Young Filipinos Create Individual Identities** reflects their confidence in the youth as the future: "Among Filipinos in Canada today, there are two distinct groups that will eventually become the face of Canadian Filipinos of the future: (1) Filipinos who arrived young in Canada with their immigrant parents and grew up here (1.5 generation), and (2) those who were born and raised in Canada by Filipino parents (second generation). Together, this demographic will define the roles that Filipinos will play in Canada's diverse society of today. They are the true global citizens of the future."

Chapter 6 speaks about the COVID-19 pandemic—how a virus unseen by the naked eye has brought havoc and upended life around the globe. The Canadian Filipino community can feel rightfully privileged by being at the forefront of dedicated public health service 1)) as health care providers attending to direct needs of citizens and 2) as providers of health information via CFNet to keep the community and others continually informed. **Chapter 7** calls attention to the need for conversations not only about health concerns but also about practical, spiritual, and psychological aspects of ageing, including open intergenerational dialogue.

Chapter 8 assures readers that Canadian Filipinos arrive in the country "ready to serve in every aspect of life in Canada," with hard work, commitment to excellence and adaptability their standards for personal growth and participation in nation-building.

Chapter 9 reminds readers about some of the unfinished community agenda "close to a Canadian Filipino's heart" such as the need for an orderly and fair process of accreditation of foreign-obtained professional credentials and trade skills and for a clear path to Canadian citizenship for temporary migrant workers.

Chapter 10 is Professor Angeles' acceptance of CFNet's invitation to share the thrust of her Social Sciences and Humanities Research Council research project, "Postnationalism and Canada-Philippine Bilateral Relations: Trends, Patterns, Limits, and Possibilities of Postnational Citizenship and Transnational Linkages for Development" – a natural link to this book.

Dr. Angeles delineates three forms of citizenship from the viewpoint of social science – namely, national, transnational, and postnational – and posits that differences in perspectives and citizenship focus "have implications for individual, community and international development."

She asserts that Canadian Filipinos, many of whom have taken up dual citizenships, would make interesting research subjects because "they intensify economic and cultural globalization and engage in dense transnational activities as citizens, migrants, and temporary or permanent settlers in foreign lands (and therefore) their identities, sense of nationalisms, attachments and loyalties are also changing."

She wants to know more about "the dynamism of Canadian Filipinos in navigating the changing landscapes of citizenships and national identities" and how it might "impact governments and civil society organizations." She envisions gaining new insights into community development planning and how it may influence both country-to-country and citizen-to-citizen relationships.

Impact and Importance

Filipino community in its entirety: Until now, most books on Filipinos published in Canada had been limited to Filipinos in a province, city or specific occupation. Important as they are, the need to expand inquiries more widely and more inclusive of geography and occupations has become an imperative in light of the fast-growing community.

Dr. Jon Malek, while researching for his above-noted introductory booklet, had keenly observed that "very few works had been published in Canada about the Canadian Filipino community **in its entirety.**" He singled out *Seeking a Better Life Abroad: A Study of Filipinos in Canada (1957–2007)* by Eleanor Del Rio-Laquian and Aprodicio A. Laquian as one of the few.

Now a vintage book, *Seeking a Better Life Abroad* provided a natural groundwork for *Indomitable Canadian Filipinos* which encapsulates the contemporary history of the Canadian Filipino community in its entirety.

Admittedly, many intervening developments have transpired in the Canadian Filipino community since the publication and distribution in Manila of the Laquians' pioneering book a decade-and-half ago. The magnitude of Filipino migration to the country has remarkably increased. The 1.5 and second-generation Canadian Filipinos have more actively participated in Canadian affairs. And there has been heightened awareness about Filipino heritage, culture and traditions since Canada's Parliament declared "June, every year, as Filipino Heritage Month" nationwide.

To Canadians in general, *Indomitable Canadian Filipinos* offers **1)** an opportunity to better understand Canadian Filipinos as a community with their own unique perspective on Canadian affairs and impact on Canadian society; **2)** a comprehensive coverage of Canadian news and views as seen from the perspective of Canadians with Filipino heritage; and **3)** information on the community across the country and beyond the first generation. Thus, one can anticipate greater **inter**cultural and **intra**cultural understanding and collaboration.

To Canadian Filipinos, knowing or knowing more about their own contemporary history would show them the depth and richness of their Filipino heritage and the jewel box of Filipino values of which they can take pride. They would become more confident when engaged in conversations with their non-Filipino friends, neighbours, and co-workers about the scope of Filipino heritage, culture, traditions and work ethic, and more assured when they dialogue with the fast-growing 1.5 and second generations who grapple with their identity.

Overall, when Canadian Filipinos become an increasing part of the national conversation – the availability of this book to many Canadians will help that happen – it will reinforce national consciousness that Filipinos are a significant part of Canada's national identity and prosperity. When their community's contributions to the varied spheres of our nation's life—cultural, economic, environmental, political, and social—are made known to the greater whole, the vibrancy of the community will be duly acknowledged. Greater things then become more forthcoming.

Intergenerational adjustments within Canadian Filipino families will proceed with more ease. Any lingering perception that the Canadian Filipino community is fragmented and non-visible on issues of national dimension would be laid to rest.

Informative and inspiring: The book could serve as a motivational tool for role modelling and a reference source for governments, industry sectors and educational institutions. Historians, social scientists and policy-makers stand to gain new insights on universal human values and to envision future research projects. Most certainly, the book commends itself as a legacy for future generations of Canadian Filipinos. Just as it is hoped readers would find this book informative, inspiring, and entertaining.

Sharing a Realized Community Dream

The quote at the beginning of this *Introduction* captures the Filipinos' indomitable spirit – the sense of hopefulness, resilience and unyielding confidence that Filipinos share in common –– a distinctive Filipino attribute not lost on the editorial team when choosing the title for the book. Indeed, Filipinos are impossible to keep down for long. They will surely shine in no time and eventually find the better life they have come to seek in Canada.

It is within this same spirit that Canadian Filipinos have long nurtured the aspiration to have a book published in Canada about their contemporary history that is national in scope, drawn from their collective experience, and written through their uniquely Filipino lens. That longing has now been met with this novel *Indomitable Canadian Filipinos.*

Mabuhay!

Chapter 2:
FILIPINOS ON THE MOVE

The history of Filipino immigration to Canada began in 1861, when Benson Flores arrived on Bowen Island, BC, as reported by the 1911 Canadian Census. But large scale Filipino migration happened only in the last seventy years, with the majority arriving after 2000. Their story starts in this chapter, with a brief history of their journey (1950–2022), as part of the global Filipino diaspora. It explains the aspirations, trials, and triumphs of a people seeking opportunities for a better future for themselves and their children.

Since the 1960s, when Filipinos started arriving in major waves, the Canadian Filipino community has continued to grow exponentially. A 2017 report by Statistics Canada about the results of the 2016 Census noted that Canadian Filipinos had the highest growth rates among visible minority groups from 2006 to 2016.

All these numbers show that Filipinos make a major contribution to the cultural diversity of Canada. This contemporary history of close to a million Filipinos in Canada tells how they have fared as Canadians in their adopted country.

Dynamics of Filipino Migration to Canada: An Overview[1]

By Eleanor del Rio-Laquian and Aprodicio A. Laquian

Part One: 1950–2010

The first major wave of Filipino migrants to Canada arrived in the 1960s. In 1964, there were only 770 Filipinos in Canada. In 1965, however, 1,467 Filipinos came to Canada—mainly nurses and doctors from the United States, to apply for their US visa extension. They liked what they saw and migrated to Canada instead. After 1965, the flow of Filipino migrants gradually increased until 1993, when almost twenty thousand Filipinos immigrated in that year alone.

The 2006 census reported 410,695 Filipinos in Canada. In 2007, the Philippines became the number-one source of temporary foreign workers in the country. In 2009, Filipinos became the second-largest among recent ethnic immigrant groups in Canada. That year, Canada admitted some 35,500 Filipinos (20,500 permanent residents and 15,000 temporary workers). Considering the number of Filipino migrants to Canada over the past forty-five years, it is safe to assume that there are now more than five hundred thousand Filipinos in the country including those who were born here.

When considering Canadian immigration policies, it is important to keep in mind that Canada's manpower needs primarily dictate the entry of foreigners to this country. Thus, the number and types of Filipinos admitted to Canada over the years have depended mainly on what Canada considered necessary for its economic and social development—not its commitment to helping refugees or achieving multiculturalism.

In our analysis of Filipino migration to Canada, we found the year 1980 a convenient cut-off point for dividing Filipino migrants into the first wave of earlier migrants and the subsequent wave of later migrants. Our studies show significant changes in their demographic and socioeconomic characteristics, as follows:

---

1   Paper presented at the *Bayanihan sa Canada* Conference, sponsored by the Philippine Consulate General, on October 16, 2010 in Vancouver, BC.

1. There has been a downward shift in the level of educational, professional, and technical qualifications of Filipino migrants to Canada.

The first wave of Filipino migrants to Canada included many professionals and technical people, such as doctors, nurses, lawyers, engineers, teachers, etc. A 1972 nationwide survey by Eleanor found that 82.2 percent were college graduates (72.1 percent had at least a bachelor's degree and another 10.1 percent had post-graduate degrees). They were mostly young and female. The entry of highly educated Filipinos was due to the point system that favoured professionals and college graduates. However, as Filipinos started coming under the family reunification program, the educational level of Filipino migrants declined because sponsored family members like young children and grandparents had lower qualifications.

In 1981, Canada established the Foreign Domestic Movement (FDM) program, followed in 1992 by the Live-in Caregiver Program (LCP). Both programs required a minimum Grade 12 education for entry to Canada. This had the effect of lowering the educational and professional qualifications of Filipino migrants even further.

Another interesting demographic fact is that Filipino immigrants have an unbalanced sex ratio. According to the 2001 census, the sex ratio among Filipinos was 57.6 percent females to 42.4 percent males. These proportions barely changed in the 2006 census (57.2 percent females to 42.8 percent males).

By 2006, some eighty-five thousand Filipino domestic workers and care-givers (98 percent of them female) were in Canada. They made up about 93 percent of all domestic workers and caregivers in the whole country. A significant number of them had higher than the Grade 12 education required by the LCP, although many had graduated from lesser-known schools and colleges in the provinces.

2. Filipino immigrants have the highest educational levels among visible minorities in Canada, but they have the second-lowest level of per capita income among all Canadians.

Although Filipinos had higher educational levels than foreign-born and non-foreign-born Canadians, they had much lower incomes. According to the 2001 Census, Filipinos had an annual income of $32,748, compared to $43,989 for non-foreign-born and $37,957 for foreign-born Canadians.

One possible reason for the lower income of Filipinos is that their high educational qualifications are not recognized in Canada, making it difficult for them to find good jobs. Filipinos mainly hold jobs where they receive regular salaries. Not many Filipino-Canadians have gone into business. In fact, despite the efforts of Canadian provinces to attract investors from the Philippines, very few Filipinos fall into the "investor" category.

A 2006–07 study we conducted among Filipino entrepreneurs in British Columbia found that most of them were "accidental entrepreneurs" who saw an opportunity to open a *sari sari* (general grocery) store or restaurant and went into the venture with little project study or preparation. Not surprisingly, many of these businesses did not last long.

Canada's immigration programs to recruit service workers, of course, account for the lower incomes of Filipinos. The great majority of domestic workers and caregivers (CDWs) usually receive the minimum wage of ten dollars per hour or less.

Still, because most CDWs are "overqualified" for caregiving jobs, most of them have progressed quite well after leaving the program. We conducted a study this year of five hundred CDWs who were members of the Vancouver Committee for Domestic Workers and Caregivers Rights (CDWCR). The 2010 study revealed the following:

1) All the CDWs who came as temporary workers between 1986 and 2000 have become Canadian citizens, and 40 percent of those who came after 2001 achieved permanent resident status three years after arrival;

2) After arriving in Canada, 71.6 percent of the CDWs surveyed took additional education and training to enhance their career and earning capabilities;

3) Among earlier CDWs, more than half earned from $20,001 to $30,000 per year, and 37.8 percent earned between $30,001 and $60,000 per year; and

4) About 81.1 percent of the earlier CDWs now own cars, 98.7 percent have credit cards, and 36.5 percent own their homes.

3. The main reasons for coming to Canada have changed for Filipino migrants.

In our studies of Filipino migrants in 1972 and 2006, the most important reason given for moving to Canada had been "to seek better economic opportunities." Among the earlier migrants, the second-most important reason given was "attraction of travel and adventure." This contrasted sharply, however, with the second-most important reason given by recent migrants, which was "dissatisfaction with job and conditions in the Philippines."

Interestingly, while not one of the earlier migrants gave the welfare of their children as a reason for migration, we found that about 18.8 percent of recent migrants said they "wanted a better future for [their] children" because they considered the quality of education in the Philippines to have deteriorated.

From the survey responses, Filipinos who migrated before 1980 were mainly pulled and attracted by the prospects of a better life in Canada. However, it seems that recent migrants have been "pushed" by what they perceived as the deteriorating economic, social, and political conditions in the Philippines.

4. Filipino immigrants have integrated seamlessly into Canadian society.

A CBC program early this year noted that Filipinos have come into BC "under the radar." This is not surprising, because with their high educational and professional qualifications, ability to speak English, capacity for hard work, and uncomplaining nature, Filipinos have integrated into mainstream Canadian society very well. Many Filipinos accepted jobs far below their qualifications, went back to school to learn new skills and trades, and made sure they did not get into trouble with the law. They energized Canadian churches, volunteered in community affairs, paid their taxes regularly, and proudly refused to go on welfare. They tended to integrate into mainstream Canadian communities.

Filipino-Canadians do not form geographical enclaves similar to the Chinatowns, Little Indias, or New Saigons of other immigrant groups. As soon as they are able to save enough money for a down payment on a home, Filipinos move to the best neighbourhood they can afford.

5. The majority of Filipino immigrants have settled in large, urban areas, but in recent years, many are going to smaller rural and frontier settlements.

Early Filipino immigrants flocked to large cities—the 2001 Canadian Census revealed that of the 308,580 Filipinos in the country at the time, Toronto had 45.5 percent, Vancouver, 19.9 percent, Winnipeg, 10.1 percent, and Montréal, 6.2 percent. In the 2006 Census, the percentage of Filipinos in large cities declined slightly to 41.8 percent in Toronto, 19.2 percent in Vancouver, 9 percent in Winnipeg, and 5.7 percent in Montréal. The Canadian Census of 2011projected that the proportion of Filipinos living in smaller cities and towns would likely increase because Canadian authorities give extra points to immigrants if they choose to go to less-populated regions. This trend is already discernible in current settlement patterns. For example, despite the intense cold, about a hundred Filipinos now live in Iqaluit, the capital of Nunavut. Canadian authorities appreciate the fact that unlike other immigrant groups, most Filipinos have stayed where they first landed.

6. Filipino immigrants join social organizations, but they lack unity.

Filipinos in Canada are great joiners. Our 2006 survey found that about 67.1 percent of the respondents were members of at least one organization. In 2006, there were 535 Filipino associations formally registered with the Philippine Embassy in Ottawa. The most common of these were associations based on places of origin in the Philippines, such as the Bicolano Pagtitipon Association in Calgary, Anac ti Batac in Winnipeg, Circulo Pampanguenoin Vancouver, etc. There were also patriotic and nationalist associations like the Knights of Rizal, sports and athletic associations, professional associations, alumni groups, artistic and cultural groups, etc.

A major problem faced by Filipinos in Canada is that they lack unity. It is a common joke that every time a Filipino association holds an election, another association is born (because the losing candidates form their own group).

7. Filipino Canadians have a low level of political participation.

Filipinos have not been a major factor in Canadian politics. With more than half a million Filipinos in the country, it is surprising that only fifteen Filipinos have been elected to political office in the past forty-five years.

Many reasons account for this. First, most Filipinos in Canada are more focused on improving their lives, getting their children educated, and preparing for a comfortable future. Second, getting into politics in Canada is very different from how it is back home. In Canada, one has to start at the bottom, work with a political party, run for a lower-level position, and slowly come up the political ladder. Most Filipino-Canadians do not have the time for all that. Third, with the possible exception of Winnipeg, Filipinos are not concentrated in specific ridings. As such, they do not form identifiable bailiwicks that serve as power bases for politicians. Finally, the most important factor is their lack of unity. Without a solid organizational base to support them, Filipino candidates find it difficult to get elected.

8. Many Filipino migrants maintain emotional ties with the Philippines, but the majority plan to spend the rest of their lives in Canada.

Most members of the first wave of Filipino migrants to Canada have now reached retirement age. It is not surprising, therefore, that our 2006 survey found at least thirty-four senior citizen associations all over the country. The great majority of these associations are social in nature, but there are also seniors housing cooperatives, educational and training centres, mutual support societies, and associations devoted to arts and cultural activities.

Asked about their retirement plans, about 28.4 percent of the respondents in our 2006 survey said they would spend the rest of their lives in Canada. Another 39.7 percent said they would stay in Canada but visit the Philippines frequently in what they called a "six months here, six months there" plan (depending on Canada's harsh winters). Only about 5.6 percent wanted to return to the Philippines and spend the rest of their lives there.

However, there is a difference between earlier and later migrants when analyzing emotional ties to the Philippines. Most earlier migrants want to spend the rest of their lives in Canada (only 2.1 percent of them intend to return to the Philippines).

The main reason for wanting to stay in Canada is that their children and grandchildren are here, and they want to be near them. Some also say they have been away from the Philippines too long and they have very few relatives and friends still living there. A few are concerned about the peace and order conditions in the Philippines, expressing the fear that they may be kidnapped or robbed if they are seen as wealthy *balikbayans*.

Later Filipino migrants tend to have closer emotional ties to the Philippines (about 8.4 percent planned to return to the Philippines). They travel to the Philippines more often and keep abreast of news about the country through the Internet or Filipino community newspapers. Some of them have taken out dual citizenship. Others invest in condos and other properties in the Philippines. Professionals participate in medical and social development missions. They send remittances to family regularly, and donate funds when calamities strike their towns or provinces of origin.

9. A new breed of Filipino-Canadian is emerging all over the country.

Our studies have shown that a new breed of Filipinos has begun to emerge all over Canada. These are Filipinos who were either born in Canada or who came as young children and grew up here. With the educational and training opportunities in Canada, they have become lawyers, doctors, engineers, dentists, and other professionals. Quite a number have become successful entrepreneurs—especially in the fields of information technology, finance, real estate, and entertainment.

Perhaps the dramatic change in the lives of Filipinos in BC can be illustrated by what has been happening in the hotel industry. In the early 1990s, most Filipinos working in Canadian hotels were chambermaids, dishwashers, janitors, and cleaners. At present, however, Filipinos in the hotel industry have taken over managerial positions in sales, human resources management, food and beverage, etc.

The change can also be seen in the banking sector, where before, Filipinos tended to be clerks or tellers, but now, they are personal banking advisers, financial analysts, supervisors, and branch managers.

The second generation of Filipino-Canadians may be divided into three groups. First, there are the children of domestic workers and caregivers who were separated from their parents (usually the mother) for many years. Some have lost their ability to speak Pilipino or their parent's dialect. In some cases, their parents discouraged them from speaking their native language so they would not have a foreign accent that could hamper their performance in school or in finding a job. Some encounter difficulties adjusting, and they tend to drop out of school and end up in low-level jobs at fast food chains.

Secondly, there are young Filipinos whose parents came to Canada because of extreme dissatisfaction with conditions in the Philippines, who have taken more activist roles in community life in Canada. Members of this group have intense interest in Filipino affairs. They actively support reformist causes and movements to alleviate poverty, eradicate corruption, and achieve equity and social justice. This group is rather small, but extremely active in pursuing their causes. Members are also very well organized and highly vocal in their advocacy.

Finally, there are Filipino Canadian youngsters who are the most interested about their historical and cultural heritage. They want to learn Pilipino and attend formal classes. They attend lectures on Filipino history, culture, and the arts, and attend showings of Filipino music, dances, and movies. They have a sincere desire to be directly linked to their Filipino identity, even as they grow up quintessentially Canadian.

10. *Filipinos have contributed significantly to Canada's development.*

The half a million or so Filipinos in Canada have significantly contributed to their adopted country's development economically, socially, and culturally. They have worked hard, taking on even menial and low-paying jobs. They have paid their taxes regularly. They have energized churches and rendered community services. Most important of all, they have contributed a great deal to Canada's economic development by providing an educated, highly motivated, and skilled work force.

About two thirds of the Filipino migrants to Canada came during their most productive ages (twenty-five to forty-five). They came skilled, educated, highly motivated, and ready to join the work force upon arrival. This means the feeding, clothing, skills training, and social upbringing of these Filipino migrants were essentially paid for by the Filipino people before they left the country.

If it is assumed that about six thousand dollars per year had been "invested" by Philippine society in the development of these migrants, then the Philippines, an underdeveloped country, has given about 511.8 million dollars as a manpower "gift" to Canada since the 1960s. This gift is much more than the 500 million dollars the Philippines has received from Canada, a technologically advanced country, over the same period.

Part Two: 2011–2022

A Decade of the Filipino Community Coming of Age

By Rachel Ramos-Reid

In this contemporary history of Filipinos in Canada, 2011 to 2022 is the decade when the Filipino community came of age. It is when Canadian Filipinos emerged from under the radar to assume their rightful place as Canadians in Canada's diverse society.

It's a long, hard grind for the average Filipino to make ends meet in the Philippines. Is it the same when that average Filipino moves out and lands on Canadian soil? What about the children who come after them? Do they suffer their parents' fate?

Canadian Filipinos continue to increase in numbers in Canada: From about half a million in 2010, they doubled in number to almost one million in 2020. Filipinos in Canada currently make up 2.4 percent of the population of the country (35,151,728), up from 2 percent in 2011. They grew from being the fourth-largest group in 2011 to the third-largest group in 2016.

The last decade or so shows that for Filipinos in Canada, it is still a challenge, in spite of all the good that Canada has to offer. But many have started to reap the fruits of their labour. Some first-wave immigrants have attained success, despite non-recognition by Canadian employers of their professions acquired outside Canada. Others who sacrificed careers to get their children educated are proudly watching them succeed as consolation for their hardships.

Giving an anecdotal picture of how Filipinos have fared in Canada in the last decade, *CanadianFilipino.Net* (CFNet) reports about successful Filipinos in Canada many of whom are 1.5 and second-generation Canadian Filipinos.

Politics

Most recent is the election of **Rechie Valdez**, daughter of Filipino immigrants, as Member of Parliament for the riding of Mississauga–Streetsville in Ontario in September 2021. In her acceptance speech, Valdez declared, "This is a 'we' moment. We did this together . . . . Today, we made history and herstory, as you helped elect the first Filipina in parliament." A political neophyte who has not held any political or elected positions in the past, Valdez fills the federal Filipino representation vacuum left by Dr. Rey Pagtakhan, who retired in 2004.

Dr. Rey Pagtakhan, aside from having enjoyed an illustrious political career, is himself a story of a first-wave immigrant's success. He was among the first Filipino professionals to succeed in Canada. Pagtakhan graduated from the University of the Philippines, did postgraduate training and studies at the children's hospitals of Washington University in St. Louis in the US and the University of Manitoba in Winnipeg, and joined the medical faculty at the University of Manitoba in 1971. He was elected MP after twenty-one years living in Canada.

After serving as a Winnipeg school trustee, Pagtakhan ran in the 1988 federal election in the riding of Winnipeg North, won and served as parliamentary secretary to the prime minister, and cabinet minister as secretary of state for science, research, and development until his retirement in 2004. He continues to keep himself up to date on medical advancements and to play an active role in the Filipino community.

Science

Another Canadian Filipino in the field of medicine is Toronto's public health officer, **Dr. Eileen de Villa,** who serves more than two million Torontonians as their chief public health officer. "I was raised in a household where the general teaching was, 'you've been a very fortunate person; you've been afforded a great opportunity,' and the expectation [was] to give back," de Villa shared with the *Toronto Star* prior to her 2017 appointment.

Fleeing the Philippines in 1972 soon after the declaration of martial law, de Villa's family planted the seeds of de Villa's public health advocacy. The young Eileen de Villa listened to dinner conversations about political unrest and martial law atrocities in the Philippines, the birthplace of her parents and brother as well as the home of the de Villas' extended family.

Five-year-old **Phil de Luna** moved from the Philippines to Windsor, Ontario with his parents in the late 1990s. De Luna's career path, which eventually led him to specialize in clean energy, is one that is deeply rooted in his own personal experience as a son of immigrant parents.

"Moving to Canada and not having much money growing up, my parents always told me that education was the one thing they could give me, since they couldn't give me much in terms of material things," the scientist shared exclusively with CFNet. De Luna earned degrees in quick succession until his appointment as program director of the National Research Council of Canada's Energy Materials Challenge Program in 2019.

Law

In the legal profession, **Bernette Ho** holds the distinction of being the first Philippine-born lawyer appointed to the Court of Appeal of Alberta, the highest court in the province while **Gail L. Gatchalian,** QC, appointed as Justice with the Supreme Court of Nova Scotia, is the first female Canadian Filipino to be appointed to a provincial supreme court.

Ho was only six months when she immigrated with her parents in 1971 to Cochrane, Albert. She earned her degrees from the Universities of Calgary and Alberta and called to the Bar in 1996.

Gatchalian, daughter of Dr. Celso Gatchalian who immigrated from the Philippines, graduated from the Dalhousie University with a bachelor of science degree with honours in 1993 and a bachelor of laws from the University of Toronto in 1996.

Ho's life story pays homage to her Filipino heritage, from growing up supporting her parents' restaurant business in Calgary (one of the first in the city) to how family values prepared her for her law career. She "credits her parents for teaching her and her siblings the value of hard work and the importance of family and always being there for one another."

Steve Coroza, son of Filipino immigrants, was appointed in 2020 as Justice of the Court of Appeal for Ontario. Born and raised in Ontario, Coroza is the first and only Canadian Filipino to be appointed to the Court of Appeal for Ontario, and before this, the Ontario Superior Court of Justice and the Ontario Court of Justice.

Dulce Amba Cuenca, CFNet contributor and columnist of *That's the Law,* is a lawyer at the Professional Institute of the Public Service of Canada. The PIPSC is a union with over sixty thousand federal public service professionals working for the Canadian government. Cuenca left the Philippines as a lawyer but re-established her law career in Canada by initially volunteering.

CFNet's own honorary legal counsel **Melissa Remulla-Briones** is licensed to practice law in both Canada and the Philippines. Remulla-Briones fast-tracked her legal career upon arriving in Canada in 2011. She told CFNet, "I thought my legal background would easily translate to employment in that field. I was wrong. No law firm would give me the time of day."

Remulla-Briones went back to school, continued to challenge the Federation of Law Societies of Canada's National Committee on accreditation exams, writing a total of eight exams, and finally received accreditation in November 2017.

Arts

"Resilient" is an oft-repeated adjective to describe Filipinos, but "innovative" is probably one that would rightfully describe a few Filipino immigrants' journey to Canada.

Hailing from Paete, a town in the province of Laguna that is famous for its skilled woodcarvers, brothers **Antonio and Ross Baisas** won first place in the 2018 international ice-carving competition at the Boardwalk Ice on Whyte Festival in Edmonton. In 2021, they again dominated Winterlude's first-ever virtual national ice-carving competition held virtually across Canada. Antonio won the top prize, with his creation *Pit Stop*, and Ross won second prize with *Adrenaline Rush*. The brothers initially came to Canada to work at casinos in Québec, carving ice, fruit, vegetables, and other decorative food items.

Business

A lack of "Canadian work experience" did not deter go-getters **Marvi Yap** and **Anna Maramba**, who were crowned "multicultural moguls" by no less than the *Financial Post*. Yap and Maramba, brought up by their parents to be independent, resourceful, and accountable, are behind a successful niche advertising agency that links mainstream brands to the ethnic consumer.

Both were born and raised in the Philippines. Despite earning university degrees there, the pair found themselves doing odd jobs in Canada—from bagging frozen bagels from 11 p.m. to 6 a.m. to delivering the *Toronto Star* in the early morning, to working in a dingy mailroom.

The *eureka* moment came during a subway ride, seeing an ad and figuring out what the idiomatic expression on the ad, "breaking the bank," meant. "That's when it hit us," Maramba said of this serendipitous moment. "We thought, let's start a multicultural agency to cater to people just like us!"

Community Volunteerism

Paul Ong is a Filipino achiever with a heart. He arrived in Winnipeg in his twenties with his siblings and parents in 2010. In 2015 he started to host his annual "Concert for a Cause" which has been ongoing for the last five years.

Now a community tradition and source of pride, the concert has benefited charities that include the Children's Heritage Fund, Military Family Resource Centre, Siloam Mission, Sistema Winnipeg, Hands of Hope, and CancerCare Manitoba Foundation with over eighty-five thousand dollars of accumulated donations.

Paul holds a Bachelor of Science in education psychology *(magna cum laude)* from De La Salle University in Manila and a master's in education from the University of Manitoba. He is vice principal at Garden Grove School in Winnipeg. His recent concert show was on March 16, 2022 at the Manitoba Centennial Concert Hall.

Will PM Trudeau's Promise of Kinder Immigration Come True?

By Prod Laquian

January 1, 2017 – In June 2016, Prime Minister Justin Trudeau hosted the Tres Amigos Summit in Ottawa with US President Barack Obama and Mexican President Enrique Peña Nieto. During the summit, the three North American leaders reiterated their common respect for diversity.

President Obama paid homage to the universal values of equality, tolerance, diversity, and the natural and legal rights of people to participate in a pluralistic society. Trudeau added, "That's what Canadians believe in because that is what we are."

This latest statement from the Canadian prime minister reinforces the Liberals' election promise of kinder and more humane immigration policies under the upcoming Trudeau government. For Canadian Filipinos, this is good news.

The Philippines has been the primary source of recent immigrants to Canada, having surpassed India in 2010 and China in 2012. In fact, according to the 2011 Canadian Census, more than 50 percent of Filipinos in Canada arrived in 2000 and after. From only 770 Filipinos in Canada in 1965, their numbers have now reached more than 800,000. With 30,000 or more admitted each year, they may exceed a million by 2020.

It is important, therefore, to understand how the new immigration policies promised by the Liberal government under PM Trudeau will solve their problems and improve their lives. The past decade under the Conservative Party was not good for Filipino immigrants. Although Canada accepted more Filipinos during that period, the government drastically changed immigration policies by accepting more temporary foreign migrants rather than permanent residents. This was done through the Live-in Caregiver Program, the Provincial Nominee Program, and, largely, through the Temporary Foreign Workers Program. There was an undertone of racism in these policies. Liberal Canada has traditionally regarded immigration as a nation-building measure. Under the Conservatives, however, immigrants were mainly viewed as temporary workers to occupy low-paying, menial jobs that Canadian citizens don't want.

Thus, the Harper government reduced the number of economic migrants and those coming under the family reunification and the live-in caregiver programs. Instead, it accelerated the entry of temporary foreign workers whose chances of becoming permanent residents depended on the pleasure of their employers.

The recent victory of the Liberal Party under Prime Minister Justin Trudeau promises to change the Conservatives' negative immigration policies. PM Trudeau has announced that the multicultural policies adopted during his father's administration would be restored. More permanent residents, including those under the family reunification program would be accepted. The processing of the applications for permanent residence by live-in caregivers would be accelerated. The immigration of foreign temporary workers, including caregivers, would be reconsidered, to avoid the exploitation of workers from less developed countries. Thus, the more positive policies of the Liberal government under PM Trudeau should significantly improve the lives of Canadian Filipinos—because the majority of caregivers and temporary foreign workers in low-paying jobs are from the Philippines.

If Filipino caregivers are to continue coming to Canada, it would ease their immigration if they were allowed to come as landed immigrants instead of as temporary workers. Canada would need more caregivers in the not-too-distant future because of its ageing population. Unless their situation is changed by such policies, these undervalued Filipino caregivers are in danger of becoming a permanent underclass in Canadian society. Hopefully, the Liberals promise of "sunny ways" will let the sun shine on their lives again.

Canada's Immigration Policy: Policy and Performance

By Eleanor Guerrero-Campbell
(Dr. Rey D. Pagtakhan, in conversation with Eleanor Guerrero-Campbell of CanadianFilipino.Net*)*

Prime Minister Justin Trudeau made a number of commitments on immigration in his election campaign. Photo by the PMO.

November 6, 2016 –November 4 this year is the one-year anniversary of the federal government under the leadership of Prime Minister Justin Trudeau, who, a year ago, campaigned on the slogan, "Strong Middle Class." In observance of this anniversary, *CanadianFilipino.Net* has chosen to focus this month's issue on how Canada has delivered on its immigration policy as promised in the election platform.

To assess the government's performance, we sought the parliamentary insights of Dr. Rey D. Pagtakhan, the first-ever Canadian Filipino elected to parliament and appointed cabinet minister in two prior Liberal federal governments. His parliamentary career spanned nearly sixteen years, and he once chaired the House of Commons' Standing Committee on Citizenship and Immigration.

We also asked one of our MBNS board members, Eleanor Laquian, to give our readers a brief account of the transformative changes in the history of Canada's immigration policy. She, with her husband, Aprodicio Laquian (founding chair of our editorial board), not long ago published the well-researched book *Seeking a Better Life Abroad: A Study of Filipinos in Canada, 1957 to 2007*, Her account is included here to serve as a background for the development of Canada's immigration policy.

Eleanor R. Laquian (ERL): In the last fifty years, the process by which Canadians allow foreigners to settle in their country has undergone major transformations—from "white Canada forever" to multiculturalism—reflected in the Immigration Acts of 1952, 1976, and 2002. Each new law has opened the door a little wider for immigrants—but not without resistance from militant doorkeepers opposed to non-European immigrants.

Unlike Australia, Canada never officially adopted a "white-only" immigration policy, though early in its history, it was not particularly welcoming to non-whites—except as cheap labour, to do the hard work Canadians did not want to do.

In the 1800s, Chinese labourers were brought in to work on the railroads. People from India were recruited to work in agriculture. Japanese trades people were admitted as fishermen and craftsmen. They were not always welcomed by certain white groups. Whenever the migrant numbers increased too rapidly, there were explicit racist reactions.

In 1907, there were anti-Chinese and anti-Japanese riots in Vancouver, where Asians were beaten up by "white hooligans," who also burned down their camps. In 1914, the SS *Komagata Maru* sailed from Hong Kong to Vancouver, carrying 376 passengers from the Punjab, British India. The passengers were denied entry, and the ship was forced to return to India.

Many died on this trip. Some historians have concluded that "the history of Canada, rooted as it is in the two founding nations theory, has been characterized by explicit, systemic, and institutional racism."

Through the years, however, Canada's robust economic development, low fertility rate, and need for more people to meet labour needs created a more positive view of immigrants. In 1971, the federal government, under Liberal Prime Minister Pierre Elliot Trudeau, adopted its multiculturalism policy, which recognizes and respects the diversity of its society in languages, customs, and religions. Canada then became the first country in the world to adopt multiculturalism as an official policy. A pan-Canadian value was guaranteed in Section 27 of the *Canadian Charter of Rights and Freedoms* when it was enacted in 1982. Section 27 is referenced in the *Canadian Multiculturalism Act* that became law in 1988 under the leadership of Conservative Prime Minister Brian Mulroney.

Still, there remains a militant and vocal segment of the Canadian population that advocates a pragmatic policy based primarily on Canada's manpower needs, not on humanitarian and nation-building ideals. Thus, the Conservatives under the Harper government promoted the Temporary Foreign Workers Program, which squeezed all it could get out of cheap labourers and then discarded them after four years to return to the poverty of their own country, older and wiser, yet not better off than when they left. Many of these Conservative lawmakers were voted out of power in the fall of 2015, when the majority of Canadians believed the promises of a young, rapidly rising Liberal political leader.

Eleanor Guerrero-Campbell (EGC): During the election campaign of 2015, the Liberal Party's Justin Trudeau promised to bring back the "sunny ways" of his father's government, with reforms to bring about a kinder and more humanitarian immigration policy. Has he delivered on this?

Rey D. Pagtakhan (RDP): Fulfilling an election promise is a crucial test of political integrity. It strengthens the citizenry's faith in our parliamentary system of democracy. This is particularly true when the elected governing political party has the majority in parliament and therefore could be expected, without legislative difficulties, to adopt regulations, enact laws, and pass the needed budgetary appropriation to transform election promises into performance.

Yes, the Trudeau government has delivered on the major promises in its immigration election platform and work is progressing well on the remainder, except on remittances. Since it has been in office for only a quarter of the usual four-year term for a federal government, I trust we will see fulfillment of all promises by the end of its present mandate.

EGC: By the time this issue of *CanadianFilipino.Net* appears online, the Trudeau government would have been in office for a little over a year. What, specifically, has it done with respect to its election promises?

RDP: On the issue of refugees, Minister John McCallum said: "Our government will continue to renew and expand Canada's refugee resettlement program." The Interim Federal Health Program that provides temporary health benefits to refugees and refugee claimants—discontinued by the previous government—"has now been fully restored." The Prime Minister's pledge to assume a major role in the global challenge posed by the Syrian refugee crisis is a humanitarian act *par excellence*—supported by the great majority of Canadians, received with deep gratitude by the refugees, and duly acknowledged by global leaders. Indeed, it was a great achievement to swiftly resettle twenty-five thousand Syrian refugees in Canada.

On the one promise, which is close to the hearts of immigrant communities, the IRCC Minister spoke with pride: "I am also proud that we made great progress in reducing processing times for spouses and families. Reuniting spouses and families quickly and efficiently will continue to be a priority going forward."

EGC: These changes are laudable. While on this point, how close are we to realizing, one, the elimination of the thousand-dollar Labour Market Impact Assessment fee for Canadian families in need of caregivers to help their family members with disabilities, and, two, the development of a system of regulated companies to hire caregivers on behalf of families and protect them from employers?

RDP: Still in progress, but deeply committed. The Minister spoke on these issues while in Manila meeting with the Philippine Canadian Chamber of Commerce and again in his 2016 Annual

Report, where he said: "The Government of Canada will make it easier and simpler for Canadian families to hire foreign workers to help them care for their loved ones; . . . will work with the provinces and territories toward developing a system of regulated companies to hire caregivers on behalf of families . . . [and] to make it simpler for families to hire caregivers and protect caregivers by allowing them to change employers in case of abuse."

He re-affirmed that "the government will also seek to modify the Temporary Foreign Workers Program to eliminate the thousand-dollar Labour Market Impact Assessment fee to hire caregivers for family members with disabilities. It's something we're in the process of doing."

EGC: How about the promises respecting temporary foreign workers and international students?

RDP: Two programs encompass the temporary foreign workers, namely, one, the Temporary Foreign Worker Program, which allows an employer, following approval through a Labour Market Impact Assessment, "to fill acute labour shortages on a temporary basis by demonstrating that there is a need for a foreign worker to fill the job and that no qualified Canadians or permanent residents are available;" and two, the International Mobility Program, which "facilitates the entry of foreign nationals holding work permits that are not subject to an LMIA, and whose primary objective is to advance Canada's broad economic and cultural national interests." In 2015, IRCC admitted 73,111 individuals to Canada under the TFW Program and 176,772 under the IMP, of whom 43,573 work permit holders (17.43 percent) subsequently obtained permanent residency—an increase of just under 2 percent from the preceding year.

Of international students, the Minister said: "International students bring with them new ideas and cultures that enrich the learning environment within Canadian educational institutions. They also make a major economic contribution—international students spend more than 11.4 billion dollars in Canada annually, are well prepared for the Canadian labour market, and can integrate quickly into Canadian society, primarily due to their Canadian educational credentials."

This is a notable acknowledgement coming from the Minister, and it reflects the value the government attaches to these students. Last year, Canada received nearly 188,000 international student applications—an increase of 6.4 percent—and issued 125,783 new study permits. A total of 5,829 international study permit holders became permanent residents.

The report also reiterated that "reforms will be explored for the Canadian Experience Class Program to reduce barriers to international students." Moreover, "the Government of Canada will move to restore the residency time credit given to international students and other temporary residents to make it easier to become a Canadian citizen."

The Minister does not think every immigrant-applicant needs to undergo a Labour Market Impact Assessment process. In Manila last August, he told his audience he would "make it easier for them to come in under Express Entry and do more to court younger university students from the Philippines, to see if they would like to come and become students in Canada . . . and for successful university students to then become permanent residents." I add that provincial nominee programs maybe an avenue to permanent residency for international graduates following completion of their studies. However, why not treat temporary foreign workers and international students with equal preference for permanent residency status? If the former are qualified enough to help with Canada's acute labour needs, they should be qualified enough to pursue their dream of a better life in Canada.

EGC: I cannot agree more. On the last remaining promise: what is the latest on remittances? The remittance industry is a multi-billion enterprise worldwide.

RDP: I have not ascertained any progress nor heard of any first step taken on this promise. Naturally, Canada would like its workers to have access to safe and low-cost transfer services when sending money overseas to help family members, to not be gouged by high fees. Whether the Government of Canada has motivated Canada Post and our chartered banks to encourage competition or consulted with the provincial governments to regulate the industry is not known. Since it is a truism that absence of evidence is no evidence of absence, the Canadian government may well be on top of the issue but not quite ready to make any announcement yet.

EGC: Let me conclude with the similar questions that Prod and Eleanor Laquian of our CFNet board asked at the start of our series. He, in fact, entitled his editorial "Will Trudeau's Promise of Kinder ImmigrationPolicy

Come True?" and she, in her introduction to our series, asked, "Has he delivered on this (a kinder and humanitarian immigration policy)?"

RDP: What we have seen to date is the balancing of the three dimensions of Canada's immigration policy: economic, social, and humanitarian. It is no longer dominantly manpower-driven; it has become once more a vital nation-building tool. The IRCC minister has sent clear signals of the laudable direction he has embarked on. At the same time, vigilance remains in order, in light of current world events in Europe and south of the border. Even more important is for Canada to sustain its confident optimism in the generosity and decency of our people and in their determination to work hard and succeed. 🍁

Troubling Trends: The Alarming Backlash against Immigrants and Refugees in Canada

By Eleanor R. Laquian

November 19, 2018 – Canada has an enviable global reputation as a liberal and progressive country, with its recognition of same-sex marriage, LGBTQ rights, gender parity, and, most recently, legal recreational cannabis. But a sudden influx of asylum-seekers from the US has contributed to the negative view of refugees in Canada.

Canada is known as a safe and peaceful country, with a national policy of diversity, a stable multiethnic democracy, and robust economy. It is considered one of the top ten countries in the world, as a staunch defender of human rights with a solid record on core civil and political rights protections, guaranteed by its *Charter of Rights and Freedoms.*

Although its founders were French and Anglo-Saxons, Canada today has no official religion, race, or culture. Every Canadian, regardless of faith or ethnic origin, is as Canadian as everybody else. Tolerance that comes with multiculturalism is what unites Canadians—at least, that's what liberal Canadians like to believe.

With the rise of populism, nationalism, protectionism, and racism in the United States and Europe, Canada is the only country in the West that still welcomes immigrants and refugees with open arms. Recent polls and studies, however, show that more and more Canadians now feel it's time to close the door and put away the welcome mat.

Canada's current population is estimated at about thirty-seven million, and it is ageing rapidly—so that by 2036, seniors could represent more than 25 percent of its total population. With low fertility rates, high divorce rates, and longer life spans, Canada has been welcoming skilled professional migrants to meet the required labour for Canada's economic growth and development.

However, with the arrival in the last two years of thousands of Middle Eastern refugees and irregular border crossings of asylum-seekers from the United Sates, sensitive questions have arisen from the resulting immigration crisis: Is Canada's refugee policy too lenient? Out of control? Should Canada's immigration be based solely on merit, as with the current point system, or more on compassionate and humanitarian grounds, as recently announced by its Liberal Prime Minister?

Recent Changes in Canadian Attitudes Toward Immigrants and Refugees

In *Documenting Hate*, a documentary from CBC's *The Passionate Eye*, aired in October 2018, Dr. Barbara Perry, an expert on hate crime, was quoted as saying Canadians should be concerned about the rise of hate groups in this country. Most of these groups are organized around ideologies against religion and race—with anti-Muslim and anti-Jewish sentiments being the most common, followed by hate against immigrants, Indigenous people, women, LGBTQ communities, and other minorities.

Statistics show that hate crimes are on the rise in Canada. Criminal incidents motivated by hate reported to police rose by 3 percent from 2015 to 2016, for a total of 1,409 crimes. According to Perry, most of these hate crimes documented by police are by individuals who are not part of hate groups. Of these crimes, 43 percent were deemed violent offences, which included assault, uttering threats, and criminal harassment—accounting for a 16 percent increase from the previous year.

In a 2017 survey, the majority of Canadians indicated that they agree that Canada should accept fewer immigrants and refugees. The Radio-Canada poll released in March 2017 showed 74 percent said they also support screening for anti-Canadian values as a way to keep terrorism out of the country.

This is in sharp contrast with an October 2016 study of Canadian values by pollster Angus Reid, which showed that while about 68 percent of those polled said they wanted minorities to do more to fit into the mainstream, the same number also said they were nonetheless happy with how the immigrants were integrating themselves into the community. Further, 79 percent of Canadians believe immigration policy should be based on the country's economic and labour needs rather than on the needs of migrants to escape poverty and corruption in their home countries.

In an analysis of the survey, Reid wrote that Canadians' commitment to multiculturalism is not increasing, and that the United States and European nationalist movements have affected Canadian attitudes toward immigrants and refugees. He also expressed his concern over the increasing number of illiterate refugee immigrants who can affect the fabric of Canadian society and compromise the current quality of life for Canadians in general.

A 2017 poll found 37 percent of Canadians said too many refugees were coming to Canada, up from 30 percent in 2016. The 2017 poll also asked respondents about their comfort levels with surface diversity, like around people of different races and religions—a question that was also asked in 2005–06. This year, 89 percent said they were comfortable around people of a different race, down from 94 percent in 2005–06.

In affluent enclaves of Vancouver, the ramblings among white condo owners (known as mainstream Canadians) against having their strata documents and bylaws translated into Chinese for the benefit of Chinese residents are becoming louder and more forceful in 2018. White owners demand that the Chinese residents learn English or have their children translate the documents themselves instead of using strata funds for the translation and printing of strata documents into Chinese.

While Jews and Muslims are targeted in the US and Europe, Chinese people and Muslims are getting the hate in Canada. Anti-Chinese sentiment is strongest in Richmond, BC, where more than 50 percent of the city's population is Chinese. They were blamed for traffic congestion, unaffordable housing, and the rising cost of living.

Racist flyers were circulated that claimed wealthy Chinese immigrants use Canadian social services without paying taxes, because only the unemployed wives and children live in Canada while the husbands work and live in China. The poll of the Asia-Pacific Foundation of Canada found that 46 percent of Canadians said they felt threatened by the growing Chinese presence in their country.

The University of Toronto and the McGill Institute for the Study of Canada partnered with Ipsos Observer in a January 2017 study to ask 1,522 Canadians about their views on immigration. Almost a third said the government should discriminate against Muslims when selecting foreigners to move to the country, and a third wanted to discriminate against people of colour to prioritize white immigrants. More than 65 percent think immigrants have a responsibility to behave "more like Canadians."

With the influx of illegal asylum-seekers crossing the border from the United States, immigrants and asylum-seeking refugees have become hot topics of discussion in Canada. The border situation may get more complicated. Poor migrants, fearful that if they reach the US, they may not be wanted, may end up crossing another border illegally to seek asylum in what they assume is a more welcoming Canada.

In fact, illegal migrants in the US who perceive Canada as a better option than deportation—which they face if they remain in the US—have already resorted to crossing the porous US-Canada border to illegally seek asylum in Canada since late last year. This has upset many Canadians whose farms and woodlands have been overrun by throngs of Haitians and Nigerians as they try to find their way to the nearest refugee office to file their asylum claims.

Overnight, what used to be polite and hushed debates among Canadians over racism have suddenly become open, vocal, and often belligerent. These days, when it comes to immigration, asylum-seekers, and refugees, many polite Canadians are no longer polite. Hateful words are shouted at bearded men of colour on the streets, Syrian refugees have been pepper-sprayed as they come out of their mosques. Women wearing hijabs in public places have been told, "Go back where you came from; your head scarves are not wanted here." Hostile protestors have confronted asylum-seekers at border crossings in Québec.

If openly talking about this unfortunate backlash against immigrants and refugees will clear the air of resentment and bitterness, then let the conversation and debate continue. Hopefully, dialogue will help Canadians better understand the problems and benefits of immigration and arrive at a solution for the common good of all. But will it?

Current Editor of CanadianFilipino.Net *Eleanor R. Laquian has written four best-selling books and co-authored four others with husband Prod Laquian. She has served in various capacities at the University of British Columbia's Institute of Asian Research—as manager of administration and programs, editor and chair of the publications committee, and primary researcher of the Asian Immigration to Canada project. She has a degree in journalism and literature from Maryknoll College in the Philippines and a master's degree in public administration from the University of the Philippines.*

Before coming to UBC, she worked with the UN Food and Agriculture Organization, the World Health Organization, and the UN Information Center. She was a researcher and bureau manager of The New York Times *in Beijing, China from 1984 to 1990.*

She was the first and only Filipino to conduct a nationwide survey of Filipinos in Canada, in 1972. She did the survey for her master's thesis at UP. It was published as A Study of Filipino Immigrants in Canada, 1952–1972. *She updated the survey in 2005 for a book, co-authored with her husband Prod, and titled* Seeking a Better Life Abroad: A Study of Filipinos in Canada, 1957–2007, *published by Anvil Publishing and distributed by the National Book Store in Manila in 2008. She and Prod have visited over a hundred countries all over the world for work and pleasure. They immigrated to Canada in 1969. They have been married for over sixty years and have two children (George, married to Brenda Jamer, and Helen, married to Dan Flagg) and three grandkids (Elizabeth, Maya, and Jack).*

Migration Is Not a Problem to Be Solved but a Process to Be Managed

By Manolo I. Abella

January 1, 2019 – In an earlier article, Eleanor Laquian drew our attention to growing dissatisfaction among Canadians about the country's policies on immigration and multiculturalism. Which some blame for the rising xenophobia in what has always been seen as a peaceful and hospitable society.

She cited the findings of several opinion surveys that indicate that the majority of Canadians are now apprehensive about the growing numbers of people of colour, the growth of hate crimes, the displacement of local workers in the labour market, and the fiscal burden imposed on the rest of society by those who come only to take advantage of Canada's socialized health services and highly subsidized public education system. These concerns have armed some politicians—the most recent one from Québec—with arguments for reducing Canada's admission of new immigrants.

There is a strong undercurrent of suspicion that the wave of new refugees—especially from Muslim countries—will not integrate with the rest of Canadian society, because they hold values completely at odds with that of the majority.

Canada's Points System: A Model

In this article, I argue that Canada's immigration policy has been looked upon as a model by many countries. The roots of the problems Eleanor cited may lie not so much in the number and origins of the people we admit, but in how we manage their social and economic integration once they have come in.

Canada is widely credited with having a liberal, progressive, and well-managed migration system. Under our Constitution, immigration is a shared responsibility between the federal and provincial governments. The federal government sets annual targets for the admission of permanent residents following consultations with broad sectors of society. For example, the Conference Board of Canada recently advised that Canada's immigration rate should increase to 1 percent of the population by 2030 in order to replicate its population growth rate of recent decades and ensure modest labour force and economic growth. The admission target for 2017 was in the order of three hundred thousand, of which about two of every three are economic immigrants, one of every 4 are family reunification, and one of every eight are protected persons or refugees. Canada pioneered the now widely imitated "points system," which aimed to make decisions on immigration admissions not discretionary but based solely on a set of objective criteria, such as age, educational attainment, work experience in occupations in demand, employment offer, language skills and adaptability, and whether or not one has a support system (i.e., relatives) in Canada.

The United Kingdom, Australia, New Zealand, and the Republic of Korea have since fashioned their own versions of the points system. Despite some shortcomings, a number of features of Canada's seasonal agricultural worker program—such as the organization of employer cooperatives to supervise non-exploitative recruitment, adequate housing for the workers, and the provision of health and medical services—have been followed by other countries.

Over the past decade, Canada's provincial governments have taken a more prominent role in managing immigration. They have been credited with the flexibility that characterizes Canada's temporary foreign worker programs, which were intended to attune admissions more closely to the needs of the provincial economies. Last year, some 286 thousand work permits were issued to temporary workers. Many Filipinos have found their way to Canada through these programs, which include a path to permanent residency. About one out of every five temporary workers have succeeded in gaining permanent residency through this path.

How Immigrants Fare in Canada

How well have immigrants fared in Canada? Canada shows the most equality among the thirty-six OECD (Organization for Economic Cooperation and Development) countries in terms of employment rates of native-born and immigrant-born populations. The disparity in rates of labour force participation between Canadian-born and immigrant-born females is lowest among OECD countries, and the difference among males is negligible.

Immigrants do face challenges integrating into the Canadian labour market. Censuses have revealed that earning disparities between foreign- and the native-born Canadians have worsened over time. Although their earnings have increased over time, the foreign-born have not kept pace with native-born Canadians. In 1980, recent immigrant men with employment income earned eighty-five cents for each dollar received by Canadian-born men. By 2000, the ratio had dropped to sixty-seven cents, and by 2005, to sixty-three cents. The corresponding ratios for recent immigrant women were eighty-five, sixty-five, and fifty-six cents, respectively.

As a recent study points out, it makes a lot of difference *when* one lands in Canada, since economic opportunities can change from one period to another. Those who entered Canada at the beginning of the 1990s faced very poor economic conditions, which had an impact on their employment earnings. Later cohorts of immigrants fared better, especially skilled immigrants, who were disproportionately concentrated in occupations in the IT sector—specifically engineering and computer-related occupations. As a result, they were also disproportionately impacted by the collapse of that sector at the beginning of this decade, and their earnings profile during 2000–08 reflects this reality.

The experience suggests the complexity of managing immigration, even before looking at how one can address the question of how to deal with state obligations to give temporary refuge to those seeking protection as defined by the UN Convention on Refugees. Canada is a signatory to this UN convention, and thus accepts sharing the burden of giving asylum to persons needing protection.

Dealing with Refugees and Asylum-Seekers

Over the past ten years, violent conflicts in some countries have displaced many millions of people, forcing them to seek safety in other parts of their own country (so-called "displaced persons"), while others have been forced to cross borders into neighbouring countries—or beyond—to seek asylum (so-called asylum seekers and refugees). The UNHCR reported that there were 25.4 million refugees all over the world in mid-2018, of whom 85 percent were being hosted by developing countries—principally those bordering countries afflicted by violent civil strife like Syria, Afghanistan, South Sudan, and Somalia.

Turkey alone now hosts some 4 million Syrian refugees, while Pakistan and Iran still host over 3 million Afghans, many years after the Russian occupation. The burden of hosting these refugees has fallen heavily on some of the world's poorest countries, like Ethiopia and Bangladesh, and some of the smallest, like Lebanon (1.5 million refugees) and Jordan (2.7 million refugees).

North America has so far escaped the refugee burden. Although many Indo-Chinese refugees did find their way to the US and Canada during the 1970s, in recent years, their refugee admissions have been insignificant compared to those of other countries. In 2016, the US accepted some eighty-five asylum-seekers as refugees, a tiny fraction compared to the million or so who were admitted into Germany.

Last year, Canada received less than 0.2 per cent of the overall refugee population in the world, according to UNHCR. In 2017, the Canadian government established a target of 43,500 refugee admissions in recognition of an emerging refugee crisis. It immediately provided refuge to 25,000 Syrians. Of the 47,425 refugee claims referred to the Refugee Protection Division of Immigration and Citizenship, about a third came from countries where Islam is the dominant religion.

How have Muslim refugees fared in Canada? A 2016 national survey conducted by Environics Institute in partnership with the Tessellate Institute, the Canadian Race Relations Foundation, the Inspirit Foundation, the Olive Tree Foundation, and Calgary-based Think for Actions revealed what it is like to be Muslim in Canada, and how this has changed compared to a previous survey conducted in 2006. According to its report, "The results show that Muslims as a whole are embracing Canada's diversity, democracy and freedoms, and feeling more positive about the country than a decade ago. This is despite continuing to experience discrimination due to religion and ethnicity well above levels experienced by the Canadian population-at-large."

The government has been tracking the earnings of all refugees since 1981. A recent report showed that government-assisted refugees on average earned less than twenty thousand dollars a year in their first decade in the country, when many families rely on provincial welfare and other government benefits to get by. However, after twenty-five to thirty years in Canada, the average refugee is earning roughly fifty thousand a year, about five thousand dollars more than the average Canadian. The study also shows the earnings gap between government-assisted refugees, who initially do worse than privately sponsored refugees, basically disappears over the long run.

Managing the Process of Integration

Statistics on comparative economic performance only suggest how far policies and programs succeed in the integration of immigrants and refugees. However, they are much more reliable than opinion surveys, which only capture sentiments of people at certain points in time—sentiments which tend to change very quickly, as they are greatly influenced by daily events. A "terrorist attack" in one corner of a city can influence opinions across the country, but may not have any lasting effect on how people live their lives.

Integration is a two-way street requiring efforts both of the immigrants as well as of the host community for success. Experience has everywhere demonstrated that language acquisition is a very basic requirement—hence support for language instruction is fundamental to success. The involvement of local communities in creating opportunities for personal contacts (e.g., cooking sessions popularized in Italian towns), for employment of immigrants (e.g., job-targeting in Sweden), for accessing social services (e.g., multilingual telephone services in Australia), and enabling recognition of qualifications (e.g., the mentoring system in France) are only a few of the many good examples of how migrant integration can be managed.

If our leaders can avoid the temptation to engage in "identity politics" despite the influence of our southern neighbour, Canada can easily overcome the concerns of its citizens about the growing presence of the "alien."

The world's most dynamic places are multicultural cities like London, New York, San Francisco, Rome, Istanbul, and Bangkok because diversity stimulates competition, innovation, and cooperation.

Manolo Abella, a Filipino economist, was formerly the director of the International Migration Programme of the International Labour Office (ILO) based in Geneva and a member of the advisory board of the Centre for Migration Policy and Society (COMPAS) at the University of Oxford. He also served on the board of the Migrating Out of Poverty Programme of Sussex University. He has been actively involved in international efforts to develop a multilateral framework for the management of labour migration and spent many years writing, speaking, and rendering advice to governments on policies and best practices. He heads the working group that developed under the World Bank's and the ILO's auspices the methodology for measuring what workers pay to migrate, which is being considered for inclusion as one of UN's Millennium Development Goals. He now lives in Vancouver, BC.

Needed but Not Wanted: Temporary Foreign Workers in Canada

By Manolo I. Abella

November 16, 2016 – Temporary foreign worker programs (TFWP) or "guest worker" schemes are an example of contradictions in liberal democratic states that are looking for compromises in achieving conflicting social and economic objectives as well as meet divergent interests of different groups in their societies.

In order to achieve greater productivity and economic efficiency, have a more equal distribution of income, enhance social cohesion and feelings of national identity, and maintain national security and public order, policy-makers have to make difficult choices on ends to pursue and on instruments to use. Because it is in their interest to have ample supply of workers at low or stable wages, business pressures their governments to have a wider door open for foreign workers. Trade unions, fearing loss of jobs of their members and negative effects on wages, prefer to close them.

Commitment to equal treatment for all workers often runs up against concerns of taxpayers over the cost of extending public services to all newcomers, like schools, medical care, and social safety nets like unemployment insurance, when economies are susceptible to sudden downturns. With growing concerns over ethnic tensions and public safety, citizens pressure their governments to tighten doors and be more discriminate in allowing entry and stay.

Except for inherently "time-bound" jobs, such as in construction or in agriculture, TFWPs are hard to justify for most jobs that are inherently continuous.

The very term "temporary" already indicates a denial of equal rights to job security, treatment in social security, mobility in the labour market, access to promotion, and, in many instances, to be reunited with their families. However, temporary schemes have been easier to sell to the voters, because they are perceived—rightly or wrongly—to be, on balance, highly beneficial.

TFWPs offer flexibility and speed in meeting fluctuating demands for labour, to minimize the risks of crowding out native workers and maximize net fiscal benefits, since guest workers may pay taxes but not bring their families.

Most states have adopted immigration policies that essentially aim to "keep the skilled" and "rotate the unskilled." Most countries, developed as well as developing, including the Philippines, are guided by the same philosophy in their approach to immigration. Interestingly, Canada's TFWP was originally used to bring in highly skilled foreign workers. The traditional countries of immigration (US, Canada, Australia, and New Zealand) slightly differ from others to the extent that they still give priority to "family reunification" for permanent residence. The wider trend in the recent past has been to use immigration much like a water tap, to be in sync with cyclical fluctuations in their economies, rather than to fill its historic role in constructing societies. Canada's annual admission of temporary foreign workers rose from less than fourteen thousand in 1995 to over ninety-four thousand in 2014.

Although ageing societies like many in Europe recognize their inevitable need for more immigrants if they are to sustain their standards of living, far-right political parties have driven the discourse on immigration away from these long-term considerations to easily exploitable concerns over losing control over borders and rising social costs as the numbers of refugees and irregular migrants, in some places, explode.

The Brexit vote is an outstanding example of where such paranoia can lead to self-inflicted damage to economies. The consequence has also been to disregard the fact that most newcomers work "hard and scared" because they want very much to stay and build their lives in countries where they can feel safe and secure.

In Canada, we are fortunate that immigration has not aroused the same toxic debate and passions as in other countries. The House of Commons committee that has been tasked by the new government with making recommendations for Canada's temporary foreign worker program announced last September some proposals that are, in my view, very hopeful.

The most important is the proposal to eliminate the tying of work permits to the employer. This policy, followed by many labour-importing countries, has a devastating effect on the power of the worker vis-à-vis his or her employer, with predictable consequences on conditions of employment. Change in this policy will most probably involve requiring a new employer (or the worker) to pay back the original employer for any of the cost incurred for recruitment and travel.

The second-most important recommendation is the opening of a pathway for temporary workers to obtain permanent residence. And the third is the proposal to end the "cumulative duration" rule that makes certain workers ineligible for new work permits if they have been in Canada for four years. Whether this is envisaged to have retroactive effect to benefit those who have completed four years and have applied for an extension was not clarified by the House of Commons committee, however. This is a major concern for many temporary migrants who have already settled in the country with their families.

And finally, the fourth-most important recommendation is for Immigration, Refugees and Citizenship Canada (IRCC) to provide multiple entry visas for seasonal workers.

How many of these recommendations will find their way into Canada's immigration policy remains to be seen, but recent statements by the Minister of Immigration give reason for optimism. The Minister has been quoted saying Canada needs more immigrants and proposing to raise the admission level next year to 320 thousand. Favoured categories are family reunification and economic migrants with skills needed in the country.

Over the past decade, Filipinos have led the increase in admissions as permanent immigrants. According to Statistics Canada, from 2006 to 2015, some 321,742 Filipinos arrived in Canada as permanent residents. We have become the largest group of entrants over the years. While only 18,400 were admitted in 2006, the number rose to 50,816 in 2015.

It is highly unlikely that Canada will abandon or even give lower priority to its Temporary Foreign Worker Program in the future, because it is the easiest path to responding to businesses' clamour for more workers, but the reforms being proposed will eventually remove many of the real differences between temporary and permanent admissions.

Keep in mind that migration is not a problem to be solved, but a process to be managed. Vigilance and active engagement of Filipino communities in Canada in the task of improving migration management is making a difference.

What Canada Day 2020 Can Mean to Canadian Filipinos

By Eleanor R. Laquian

July 1, 2020 – On July 1, Canada celebrates a national holiday to mark the 153rd anniversary of the confederation that created Canada as a country in 1867. The almost one million Filipinos in Canada can take this opportunity to demonstrate that they are at home in Canada, where they now belong , while asserting their Filipino identity and making their community visible in positive ways.

A good way to start is to familiarize themselves with Canada's Charter of Rights and Freedoms, which explains the following fundamental benefits and freedoms guaranteed to any person living in Canada, whether a Canadian citizen, a permanent resident, or a newcomer:

- freedom of conscience and religion;
- freedom of thought, belief, opinion, and expression, including freedom of the press and other forms of media communication;
- freedom of peaceful assembly;
- freedom of association;
- the right to live and seek employment anywhere in Canada;
- legal rights (to life, liberty, and personal security);
- equality rights for all;
- the official languages of Canada;
- minority language education rights;
- preservation and enhancement of Canada's multicultural heritage;

Photo by Government of Canada.

The Charter is enshrined in the Constitution, the supreme law of Canada, which explains how the government operates and affirms the social values Canadians believe are essential in a free and democratic society. However, the rights and freedoms in the Charter are not absolute. Section 1 of the Charter says that Charter rights can be limited by law so long as those limits can be shown to be reasonable in a free and democratic society.

Section 33, the "notwithstanding clause," gives Parliament and provincial and territorial legislatures limited power to pass laws that may limit certain Charter rights—namely fundamental freedoms, legal and equality rights.

With the emergence of COVID-19 in March 2020, restrictions on the freedoms of movement and association were imposed by the government to control the spread of the virus. These restrictions succeeded in flattening the curve.

The pandemic also shows the valuable contributions of Filipinos in this critical time, because they are highly represented in the essential areas of healthcare and the service industry, making them frontline workers who risk their own lives to make everybody else safe, fed, clean, and healthy.

Canadian Filipinos in Pandemic

This pandemic has demonstrated that Filipinos are capable of making Canada a safe and better place with their competence, talents, skills, compassion, and hard work. It has also proven that Filipinos are fully committed Canadians ready to risk their lives for the good of all.

It is therefore time for Canadian society to accept them as citizens with the same rights and freedoms as other Canadians. Their whole family—and future generations—are here to stay for good.

Filipino immigrants came to seek a better life for themselves and especially for their children. They need to have the means to make themselves upwardly mobile. Canada can make it happen by making it easy for them to have their educational credentials acquired outside Canada recognized in Canada. Otherwise, there is a risk they and their future generations will become a permanent underclass in a prosperous Canada they helped to build.

For over fifty years, Canada has benefitted, through its immigration programs, from the cheap but quality labour of Filipino caregivers and temporary workers, by taking advantage of their desperate need to escape from dire conditions back home and secure a better future for their children.

It's time for a just and compassionate Canada to make up for its unkind and short-sighted treatment of these migrants—even though they voluntarily accepted the cruel conditions of their immigration to Canada.

Need to change their Low-status image

Filipinos can help change their current low-status image in Canada by getting into occupations commensurate with their educational and professional training. While there are conditions and pressures that may make them accept jobs below their qualifications, they could try to get recertification, new training, or change careers altogether.

They should do this now, to give the next generation a brighter future. Since things will never be the same as they were before the pandemic, now is the time to start the changeover of how Filipinos are perceived and treated in Canada. But they must do it themselves.

Canadian Filipinos can start the changeover by using Canada's *Charter of Rights and Freedoms* to their advantage. For example, with the right to live and seek employment anywhere in Canada, they can move to a smaller town that may have more opportunities and needs for their particular services. Or, with their multicultural Filipino talents and skills, such as the gifts of gab and persuasion, they can create new jobs and promote their Filipino values of service and reciprocity.

In keeping with the Canadian values that Trudeau's Liberal government has shown with its Canada's Emergency Response Benefits, Filipinos know that being Canadian means helping to make Canada a just and caring society, a country where democracy and social justice are the norm in practice. The extra children's allowance, rent subsidy, wage support for unemployment, special grants to students and seniors with disabilities were only some of the benefits Canadians received from the government at the height of the COVID-19 pandemic.

To help build the country with fellow Canadians, Filipinos are gladly paying back whenever they can. Despite the hardships, they appreciate the opportunities available to them to do better. Many of them are already doing this, as seen in Filipino restaurants offering free meals to those in need, Filipino mom-and-pop businesses making free personal protective equipment for frontline workers, and Filipinos laid off by COVID-19 volunteering as drivers/service providers for charitable institutions like food banks and making themselves useful in true Filipino *bayanihan* fashion.

It is the undervalued and low-income Filipinos who will lead the changeover, because they are the largest group affected. They have proven in this pandemic that they deserve a fair shake. They have earned it by what they did and what they are doing now.

On Canada Day, a Look at People-to-People Connections in Canada-Philippine Relations

By Prod Laquian

July 1, 2018 – Since the 1960s, when Filipinos started moving to Canada in large numbers, they have integrated seamlessly into Canadian mainstream society, never calling attention to themselves. In fact, in 2012, when Census Canada revealed that Tagalog (the Philippine national language) was the fastest-growing non-official language in Canada, it was news to most Canadians, even to Filipinos.

As Canada has deepened its engagement with Asia after the unraveling of the North American Free Trade Agreement (NAFTA) and other trade disruptions brought about by the seemingly isolationist US Trump administration, the human connections, rather than trade, provides the strongest link between Canada and the Philippines.

The Human Connections

The first group of Filipino immigrants were predominantly highly educated women who passed the qualifying board exams of their respective professions to get a license to practice in Canada.

For Filipinos, an important feature of Canadian immigration has been the family reunification program. It allowed families to immigrate together, stay together, and build strong family ties.

Succeeding waves of Filipino migrants included caregivers—again, mostly women—and skilled temporary foreign workers. Because the educational requirements for these types of immigrants were lower than those required for professionals, the overall average educational level of Filipino migrants dipped, though many primary migrants who arrived during that time exceeded the educational qualifications demanded by Canada's points system based on merits.

The admission of so many caregivers was not a purely Canadian humanitarian gesture, though. This short-sighted Live-in Caregiver Program with racist implications, ruined many a Filipino family because of years of separation of mothers from their own children.

The Temporary Foreign Workers Program of 2002, also with racist undertones, adversely affected Filipino migration to Canada. It admitted TFWs to work in hotels, fast food chains, service industries, construction firms, and on farms. Problems arose. In response, the government issued regulatory monitoring systems supposedly to "weed out" unscrupulous employers.

The surge in number of Filipinos in Canada remained unnoticed for almost five decades. When the Philippines became the primary source of new migrants in 2010, a CBC radio documentary observed that Filipinos had come in "under the radar."

Studies of Canadian Filipinos found that a major factor in their easy integration into Canadian society is their ability to speak English. Compared with other Asians, Filipinos are fairly "globalized" and westernized in outlook, having been a colony of Spain for three hundred years and of the United States for fifty.

It is interesting, however, that not many have taken out dual citizenship, even though the Philippines has allowed it since 2003. Some explained that it was because their families were already in Canada, and they want to stay together. And they send money remittances to support their families back home and thus help the Philippine economy to grow.

The Philippine Embassy and Consulates General in Canada are encouraging more Canadian Filipinos to apply for dual citizenship citing the many advantages of being a citizen of two countries. As more and more Filipinos are becoming global citizens, this people-to-people relationship may soon become a major factor in Philippine relations with Canada and other countries.

Will You Still Remember, Mommy? (Maalala mo pa kaya, Inay?)

By Dulce Amba Cuenca

Image by RENE RAUSCHENBERGER from Pixabay.

It's been four years since we said goodbye.
You went abroad to take care of two kids as old as Kuya and I.
I counted the days, weeks, months, and years.
Each passing day, my longing for you swelled through my tears.
Will you still remember the shape of my face?
Will you feel the same when we embrace?
Will you still know exactly when to hug me when I cry?
Will you still have all the answers each time I ask how and why?

Will you still sing to me each night,
to lull me to sleep and make everything alright?
Will you still remember the sound of my laughter?
Especially when we pretend we're riding a roller coaster?
Will it matter that I have not hugged you in so long?
Will you be upset that I am now a bit headstrong?
I hear Lola use that word to proudly describe me.
She says I am growing up to be like my mommy.
Will you mind that I'm now eight years old instead of four?
Will you mind that I can now sleep on my own, unlike before?
Will it matter that my hands are bigger, my hair longer?
The great news is that I have gotten so much stronger!
Finally, we will be together again, as a complete family.
Soon ,we will be together—you, me, Kuya, and Daddy.
Imagining you with the kids you care for often makes me cry.
I longed for that day when we would never have to say goodbye.
Will you still remember that spot on my tummy,
Where I tickle easily?
Will your giggle sound the same as we laugh ourselves silly?
Will you know how much milk to add in my cup
when I ask for more?
Will you still know how to kiss my boo-boo
so it won't hurt anymore?
Will you still help me collect colourful shells from the seashore?
Will you still know how to hold my hand when we cross the street?
Will you still know how to calm my heart's every fearful beat?
Will you notice that my hair got curlier?
That I got heavier, taller, and my voice got fuller?
Will you be proud that I now know how to ride a bike?
Will you be upset to know that I am now a bit shy,
and that sad movies make me cry?
Will you notice that the mole on my left cheek got bigger?
Will you notice that I have two new front teeth?
Will you notice that I have a scar on my knee
that I got from climbing a tree?

Soon, we can hug and kiss for real, and not through our phones.
It was hard to time our chats and calls from different time zones.
Will you still have the same scent, the same laugh?
Will the same things make you sad or glad?
Mommy, will it all even matter?
All I want is for us to be together.
I still and will remember, feel, and know, my child dearest.
For my love is deeper and stronger than I can ever express.

Dulce Amba Cuenca is a lawyer in British Columbia and was also admitted to the Philippine Bar prior to immigrating to Canada in 1996. She has worked in the field of human rights and employment and labour law since 2006, travelling across BC and the Yukon, representing workers and human rights complainants. She is a grateful immigrant who got her first job in Canada in 1996 by volunteering. She served as trustee of the Richmond Public Library Board for eight years and was a member of the Board of Richmond Cares Richmond Gives. She also volunteers with Access Pro Bono. She believes that volunteerism completes an immigrant's integration in the community because it unites people from diverse backgrounds to work toward a common goal.

Chapter 3:
OUR PHILIPPINE HERITAGE

Chapter three deals with Filipino culture, values, and traditions that Filipinos bring with them to preserve and share with other Canadians. It highlights the fact that while Filipinos have integrated into Canadian life with ease, they have also retained positive elements of their Filipino culture and value system as they straddle both Eastern and Western cultures.

This chapter offers an opportunity for Canadians in general to understand Canadian Filipinos as a community with their own perspective on Canadian affairs and their impact on Canadian society.

In 2021, Canada observed the fiftieth anniversary of multiculturalism as an official government policy. Simply put, multiculturalism celebrates the country's cultural diversity. On October 8, 1971, then Prime Minister Pierre Trudeau announced the policy, making Canada the first country in the world to do so.

In 1982, the policy received constitutional recognition. It came when the *Canadian Charter of Rights and Freedoms* provided that the charter shall be "interpreted in a manner consistent with the preservation and enhancement of the multicultural heritage of Canadians." Multiculturalism was enshrined into law with the adoption of the *Canadian Multiculturalism Act* in 1988.

Five decades to the day after Prime Minister Pierre Trudeau pronounced multiculturalism as a policy, his son, current prime minister Justin Trudeau, commemorated the event by noting that the "diversity of Canadians is a fundamental characteristic of our heritage and identity. For generations, newcomers from all over the world, of all backgrounds, ethnicities, faiths, cultures, and languages, have been coming to Canada with the hopes of making it their home," Justin Trudeau said in an official statement on October 8, 2021.

"Today," the Prime Minister continued, "in addition to First Nations, Métis, and Inuit peoples, people from more than 250 ethnic groups call Canada home and celebrate their cultural heritage with pride—they are at the heart of our success as a vibrant, prosperous, and progressive country."

"As we continue to build a more inclusive and open country, we recognize that a multicultural society is a work in progress," Trudeau reminded us in his statement. The Prime Minister went on to note that only by appreciating differences among peoples as a source of strength can Canada be able to build a "truly inclusive, vibrant, and multicultural society."

Filipinos proudly share their culture with other communities as it becomes part of the Canadian mosaic. And *CanadianFilipino.Net* serves as a platform for them to share their values and traditions.

This chapter deals with the Filipino family in Canada, and how it has changed, although the same Filipino traits are passed onto children in Canada as in the Philippines. There are also articles on Filipino feasts and holidays—and traditional ways of celebrating them—and how Filipino hospitality and *Bayanihan* are practised in Canada just as they were in the Philippines. Some Filipino religious rituals have been adopted by parishes in Canada, where priests and parishioners are mostly Filipinos.

The Filipino Family in Canada

By Prod Laquian

June 1, 2017 – The family, the basic social unit, is the foundation of social life for most Filipinos. Parents consider it their duty to provide for the material and educational needs of their children while children, in turn, are expected to obey and respect their parents—and to take care of them when they grow old as well as grandparents and other elders of the family.

Characteristics of the Traditional Filipino Family:

- Equality between husband and wife
- Authority—whether patriarchal or matriarchal, adults rule
- Extensive—includes all relatives of the father and mother; in addition to blood ties, there are relationships through ritual kinships
- Christian—the majority of Filipinos are Christian
- Based on church teachings, marriage has monogamy as its foundation—marriage is often within one's social class, religion, or local grouping
- Functions as a social, economic, educational, religious, recreational, and political unit

The Changing Filipino Family in Canada

Family relationships played an important role in the early migration of Filipinos to Canada. In a 1972 survey by Eleanor Laquian of Filipino immigrants, 75 percent stayed with relatives upon arrival—or with friends or friends of friends. Only 9.8 percent stayed in hotels, and the rest in employer-provided facilities.

Laquian's 2005 study—which updates her 1972 findings—tried to verify whether the idealized Filipino notion of "the family that migrates together, stays together" has endured in Canada.

In general, the new study found that family ties were strongly maintained initially. This was especially so if the members lived near each other, could visit often, helped each other as needed, and celebrated special occasions together.

With the passage of time, however, extended family ties tended to weaken, and the nuclear family of only parents and children became the norm—especially among second generation Canadian Filipinos. This becomes more evident when Filipinos move away or marry non-Filipinos who do not share the cultural values of the elder Filipinos.

The slow unravelling of family ties is reflected in the family cycle. For grandparents sponsored to babysit grandchildren, the problem starts when their babysitting assistance is no longer needed. Some return to the Philippines; others end up, sadly, in nursing homes, because it is difficult for working adult children to look after their young family and old folks at the same time. Most family homes are rarely equipped for the disabled.

In the case of retired parents who spent the best years of their lives giving their children a better future in Canada, the solution is not simple. They want to remain in Canada, but worry about ageing and living in a retirement home. They are disappointed when their children and grandkids seldom visit their "empty nests." They feel they are losing their family when their children are too busy to phone and their grandchildren leave to study far away from home.

Some families are able to stay together, despite problems such as family separation, quarrels over money and inheritance, dependency of family back home, young generations' growing pains, clash of cultural values between the young and the old, borrowing and lending money, and conflict between parents and non-Filipino in-laws. For others, family members eventually go their separate ways, keeping in touch only by Facebook, Twitter, blogs, and the occasional email.

As the Filipino immigrant ages, the problem of growing old in Canada without the care and support of extended family becomes more acute. This is now being felt by first wave Filipino immigrants as well as domestic workers and caregivers who arrived in the 1980s under the Foreign Domestic Workers Movement andwere unable to bring their families to Canada.

For many Filipinos in Canada, however, the slowly weakening family ties means freedom from the restrictive tendencies and mores of the traditional clan. This gives them independence to pursue their own goals in their own ways and directions. They become self-confident and rely on their own capabilities. As they become individualistic in a universalistic democratic system, they develop other relationships and interests—at work, in church, in the neighbourhood and the community. Their new friendships and social ties make it easier for them to integrate into Canada's diverse society, where the common good is a strong goal. The younger generation of Filipinos in Canada may develop new patterns of familial relationships—especially if they marry non-Filipinos, which is becoming quite common.

Filipino Traits I'd Pass On to My Children

By Helen Flagg, as told to Eleanor R. Laquian

June 1, 2017 – Helen was only two when her parents took her to the US, and three when they immigrated to Canada. Because her parents worked in international organizations, she grew up aware that people are of many different nationalities and that it's all right to be different.

When she was a kid, Helen said she used to wonder why she had so many *tito* (Spanish for uncle) and *tita* (Spanish for aunt). When she was planning her wedding, she had to explain the invitation list to her future American in-laws, who wondered why her parents seemed to have so many siblings. She had to point out who was the real uncle or aunt by blood and who was related by ritual ties.

Asked what Filipino traits she would pass on to her children, Helen said: "There are so many good ones! Respect for elders and family is the number one Filipino trait I try to teach my children. I want them to know their place and their role in the family—they are not the boss; they are learning from parents, grandparents, and adult role models. My husband and I care for them and make sacrifices for them, and, in turn, they grow up to be good people and take care of us and their family and their community. Not that our kids are perfect, but they know 'the look' (that parental glare, which the kids call the 'stink eye') when they see it, and they know how to behave.

"The number two Filipino trait that I find important to pass on to children is the concept of *utang na loob* (debt of gratitude). I try to teach my kids about the importance of reciprocity and establishing a mutually beneficial social relationship. The kids need to learn that society is give-and-take, and that they are interdependent in their community. This trait also has overtones of gratitude, respect, and social obligations, and is tricky to teach to kids because it is not common in Western culture. But it is well worth the effort to teach them.

"At number three is hospitality. I try to teach my children to be welcoming and gracious to visitors and respectful of guests. I want them to be considerate of the needs of others— like giving up their room when Lolo and Lola come to visit, or letting a playmate take the first turn with a toy if they are at our house, or not showing up empty-handed when invited to a friend's house. I guess most people associate hospitality and generosity with Filipinos. I like that, and I am proud of it.

"My number-four favourite concept is *hiya* (shame). I can think of many choices I made because I didn't want to bring embarrassment or shame to myself or my family. I certainly would like my kids to consider, 'What would my mother think?' when they are faced with a tough decision. To say that someone is *walang hiya* (no sense of shame) is derogatory indeed. I think a lot of people could benefit from being more conscious of *hiya* and try to maintain dignity and decency. So much of today's reality TV shows fall under the category of 'Have you no shame?' or 'Yikes, what would your mother think if she saw you?'"

Since Helen's kids are growing up in a Western culture, which puts a premium on being assertive and outspoken, she worries that her kids would be at a disadvantage if they follow the Filipino trait of always being accommodating to preserve social harmony.

She finds the Filipino trait of always saying "yes" even when they mean "no" a disadvantage. She said it may save face in the Philippines, where everybody knows the rules, but those rules don't apply in North America, where yes is *yes* and *no* is no. Thus, she teaches her children to say what is really on their minds. She encourages them to speak frankly but politely.

Helen says that whether they realize it or not, American Filipino children and Canadian Filipino children are heirs to a wealth of traditional values and beliefs, even as they grow up in a Western society, that has its own specific values and traditions. As they mature, they develop their own personal values that they use as guiding principles in their own lives. 🖌

Mixed Marriages: Odd Couples No More

By Jo Leuterio Flach

July 16, 2017 – Toronto is probably the most culturally diverse city in the world. It is crowded with people with different color skin and thousands of restaurants of various cuisines. Today, any combination of couples walking down the street does not even rate much of a second glance.

But in the late sixties, when Venket and Letty Rao wed, an interracial union was perhaps a novelty. Marriage to a non-Filipino was often referred to as *"halo-halo,"* (Tagalog for "mixed") says Venket.

Originally from India, he met his future Filipino wife on campus while both were pursuing post-graduate studies at the University of Oregon, Portland. Although he was Hindu and she Catholic, they had the same social and family values, and hit it off right away.

Around the same time, in Toronto, Filipina Norma Moya Solaria, newly married to up-and-coming lawyer Marvin Flancman, felt lingering looks cast her way at the family functions and Jewish celebrations they attended. "I felt as though I was in an aquarium."

On the other hand, the same curiosity was palpable when she and Marv went to the Philippines for a visit. At a family gathering, a cousin asked, diffidently, "How does it feel to be married to a Canadian?" to which she replied with a smile, "Just the same way you feel to be married to a Filipino."

In addition to the notion that "men are from Mars and women are from Venus," complications may arise in a marriage due to different cultural values and traditions.

But luckily, centuries of Spanish rule, the American occupation, and intermittent visits from Chinese traders have made it almost natural for Canadian Filipinos to love or marry non-Filipinos or people of different ethnicities .

Apparently, in Europe, a "mixed marriage" refers to a union between citizens of different countries. Elsewhere, it also describes a relationship between people of different races. This may mean varied cultures, behavioural patterns, family dynamics, and religions—which could spell trouble for the couple.

On the other hand, it can mean opportunity! It can open up a new world and change one's outlook. One only has to have an open mind, a sense of adventure, and an appreciation of differences. And there are differences. With some tolerance and understanding, these are easily overcome.

I married a German. We met at the University of Toronto during "International Night. He is 6'2', very fair and blond, while I am, of course brown and to put it nicely, petite – an odd couple. But people notice mostly that he is very tall. He is a Berliner, and I grew up in Quezon City/Manila, so our interests are quite urban.

Early in our marriage, my parents and his mother were visiting. We took them to the theatre one evening. During intermission, I noticed that his mother was holding a glass of bubbly and my parents were not! Knowing that my mom would especially have enjoyed that, I asked, "Where are their drinks?"

My dear husband replied, "I asked if I could get them a drink and they said, 'No, it's alright.'"

I was furious! "You should have asked them again. You should let them know that you really mean it!"

To Peter, who is very direct, "no" means no—but often, for Filipinos, "no" means "ask me again" or "maybe."

I learned to be more straightforward since then. We are a very nice people, and, as Peter's mother observed, "It's nice to be nice." But, very often, we are too accommodating, and say "yes" when we should say "no."

Thus, it comes as a surprise when a demure Filipina stands her ground and pushes back. This often results in very lively debates in our household!

I grew up the eldest of seven children. I was always looked after; I never did any housework. I came and went as I pleased. Even after I had learned to drive, I always had a driver sitting next to me.

My mother was adamant that if I did not find the right man, she'd rather I not marry, and stay home. Even after I got a job, I continued to live at home quite contentedly.

On the other hand, Peter was the only child of a widowed mother. He had summer jobs. He was taught to be self-reliant. As soon as he could, he supported himself and made his own way. He was very close to his mother, and they were good friends. Family is very important to him, and he was only too happy to be welcomed to my big immediate family and hordes of relatives.

We have a traditional marriage. I stayed home, and he went to work. My life became more structured. I took care of the children. I learned to cook and keep house.

It was important to Peter that the children, armed with a good upbringing and a good education, become self-reliant. They took summer jobs and learned to manage their money.

They lived on campus when they attended university. They so valued their independence that they couldn't wait to live on their own.

It comes as no surprise that our children are also married to non-Filipinos, and non-Canadians. There are five nationalities in our family, five different languages.

My eldest son is married to a Latvian and lives in Vancouver, my other son is married to an English-Canadian and lives in Hong Kong, and my daughter is married to a Swede and lives in Stockholm.

We remain close, visit each of them every year, get together for Christmas or a beach holiday and they visit each other in between.Our seven grandchildren, ages seven to thirteen, are very good friends.

While we would prefer to have them live closer, we accept that this is our world now. Intermarriages increase greater ethnic tolerance and social networks. After all, we started the whole thing!

My family and friends in the Philippines are now Peter's, and his friends in Germany are mine. The Flancmans and Raos' children are also married to non-Filipinos. It is not a novelty anymore. 🐚

What I Would Show My Grandchildren about Their Philippine Heritage

By Prod Laquian

Known as the eighth wonder of the world, the two-thousand-year-old Banaue Rice Terraces were carved by Ifugaos using only simple tools and their bare hands. Photo by Department of Tourism, Government of the Philippines.

June 16, 2017 – My grandchildren Elizabeth, Maya, and Jack are my pride and joy. Elizabeth and Jack were born in Boston and are growing up in the US with my daughter Helen and her American husband, Dan Flagg. Maya is what Vancouverites call "born and bred in Vancouver," living with my son George and his Canadian wife, Brenda Jamer.

None of my grandkids have been to the Philippines yet, but I dream of their eventual visit there. I would like to show them how beautiful the country is.

They should see their *Lola's* hometown of Pila, Laguna, with its verdant rice fields turning golden when the palay ripens and the towering coconut trees that compete with Mounts Banahaw and Makiling in touching the ever-blue skies. I would also take them to my hometown of Apalit, to get a glimpse of Mount Arayat and see the Pampanga River, where I learned how to swim as a boy.

A country with more than seven thousand islands, the Philippines has inviting beaches everywhere. I'll fly the kids to Iloilo (where Eleanor's mother came from), Bohol, and Cebu to enjoy white sandy beaches, calm blue waters, sweeping ocean views, and luxurious, world-class resorts. The kids would love watching the colourful sunset after sun-drenched days. I would also show them Iloilo's beautiful Miag-ao church, a UNESCO heritage site—and other churches built during the Spanish times.

In Manila, I'll take the kids to the Luneta Park, enjoy a sumptuous breakfast of *agahang magbubukid* with them at the Manila Hotel, and then board the double-decker sightseeing bus for a leisurely ride along Roxas Boulevard. I'll point out all interesting landmarks, like the Jose Rizal monument, the Baywalk, the Rizal Memorial Stadium, where their *Lola* first learned how to swim, the old Malate church next to the Aristocrat restaurant, where we used to celebrate special occasions, the Central Bank of the Philippines, and all those five-star hotels with fantastic ocean views. After this, I'll take them to Intramuros for a brief history lesson on the

Philippines under Spain. I'll show them Fort Santiago and the old San Agustin church within the walled city.

On a Sunday, I'll take the kids to the farmers' market in Cubao and let them sample a variety of tropical fruits like *atis, balimbing, caimito, camachile, chico, duhat, macopa,* and *siniguelas.* I will point out fresh vegetables that grow only on Philippine soil. I will show them colourful and fragrant flowering plants, unique shrubs, and beautiful, wild orchids. I'll buy them souvenir handicrafts made from bamboo and coconuts. We'll go five-star-hotel-hopping for lunch, merienda, and dinner, so they can see that the services and amenities in these hotels are far better than their counterparts in other parts of the world.

Between meals, the kids and I will shop in malls like the SM Mall of Asia, Mega Mall on EDSA, the Glorietta in the Ayala Center, and the Trinoma north of Manila. Or we can take in a movie in Eastwood City, where the seats recline like La-Z-Boy lounge chairs. Or I'll take them to a Filipino restaurant serving traditional Filipino foods, cooked the way they should be as in Abe's in the Greenbelt and the Barasoain on Amorsolo Street in Makati. We'll attend shows at the Cultural Center of the Philippines for a taste of Filipino creativity in song, dance, painting, and the various visual arts and exhibits.

To get a feel of the pulsating everyday life in Manila, I'll take the kids on an airconditioned "hop-on, hop-off" tour of the city, with touristy stops for shopping, leisure, and entertainment in Manila, Makati, and Pasay City. This will be an exhausting tour, so, after a hectic day, I'll take them to a spa for pampering, rest, and relaxation, including a soothing massage for their tired feet and a drink of calamansi or buko juice, for a taste of something new.

For a sight they will see only in the Philippines, I'll fly the kids to Baguio, and from there, take an airconditioned motor coach for a breathtaking tour of the Banaue rice terraces in the Cordillera Mountain range. Eleanor and I first visited these rice terraces in the early 1960s, when the drive up the mountain from Baguio was difficult and dangerous, on narrow, serpentine roads. Now, there are airconditioned buses and even a luxury hotel in Banaue for tourists wanting to see this wonderful UNESCO heritage site.

I'm proud of these rice terraces, because they show the ingenuity of our Filipino forebears. They tamed and reshaped their environment to enable them to grow rice for their subsistence. Scholars believe that rice has been planted on these terraces for about two thousand years. The rice terraces are prominent national symbols of the Philippines, because they were built by Filipinos by hand, without foreign assistance or influence. There is nothing else in the Philippines that can top their beauty and grandeur.

I love both the natural and manmade beauty of the Philippines—its mountains, forests, and beach resorts— its fruits, flowers, and home-cooked foods. I am proud of its history, and our forefathers' fight for freedom against foreign invaders. Most of all, I'm proud of the people's adaptability, creativity, generosity, optimism, perseverance, resilience, resourcefulness, and warmth. I hope my grandkids will observe these traits during their visit—especially when they spend a weekend with Eleanor's relatives in Pila, Laguna to attend the town fiesta. Surrounded by caring family and friends there, they will clearly understand and appreciate their rich and unique blend of Asian and Western heritage.

President/CEO of Maple Bamboo Network Society (MBNS) and founding editor of CanadianFilipino.Net ***(CFNet)***

Prod Laquian is professor emeritus of community and regional planning at the University of British Columbia. He was a former director of the UBC Centre for Human Settlements. After retiring from UBC in 2000, he was a professor and acting director of the Massachusetts Institute of Technology's special program in urban and regional studies in Cambridge, Masachusetts.

He was also resident scholar at the Woodrow Wilson Center for International Scholars in Washington, DC, a consultant on China, at the Asian Development Bank and coordinator of a study of basic urban services in seven hundred cities and towns in sixteen Asia-Pacific countries funded by United Cities and Local Governments in Barcelona, Spain.

He has a Bachelor in public administration, cum laude, from the University of the Philippines, and a PhD in political science, with a major in urban studies, from MIT. He has authored twenty books and numerous articles on urban planning, governance, and delivery of urban infrastructure and services (water, sewerage, transport, sustainable energy, solid waste management, and affordable housing).

Before joining UBC in 1991, he was the UN Population Fund's country director in the South Pacific. From 1984 -1990 he was UN Population Fund's country director for China, Outer Mongolia and North Korea.

Filipino Cultural Traits and the Canadian Workplace

By Eleanor Guerrero-Campbell

June 16, 2017 – To secure a job and succeed in the Canadian workplace, Filipinos will do well to take certain traditional Filipino traits to work, and restrain a few others.

Many traditional Filipino traits will easily carry the Filipino forward in the Canadian workplace environment. Filipinos are known for their hard work, loyalty, and stability. They are family-oriented and practise a strong faith. These traits spell reliability and trustworthiness to an employer. Generally, Filipinos are known for their caring qualities, which make them suitable in nursing, caregiving, social services, and customer service.

Also, Filipinos generally have good interpersonal relationships. This makes them good team players. Generally self-effacing and modest, they do not want to be seen as showing off or calling attention to themselves ("*mahiyain*"). They are fun-loving, and quickly become well-liked in their workplaces.

According to a Survey of Workplace-Related Internationally Trained Immigrants Cultural Traits conducted by Eleanor Guerrero-Campbell in 2008, Filipinos have a strong respect for authority. As with many Asian cultures, they have a hierarchical style of leadership (versus an egalitarian style)

A study in 2007 by Lionel Laroche and Don Rutherford (Recruiting, Retaining and Promoting Culturally Different Employees.) provides a distinction between 'hierarchical' and 'egalitarian' cultures and how the difference in styles impacts performance in the workplace.

In hierarchical societies, dependence of subordinates on superiors is accepted as the norm on both sides—roles are clearly defined and distinct. Individuals are unlikely to question the boss's decisions. The employee's task is to follow orders and please the boss. In less hierarchical or more egalitarian societies (as in Canada), a consultative style, equality of status, and interdependence between layers of power are considered desirable.

In the hierarchical leadership style, respect for authority—"*hiya*"—and other Philippine cultural traits, when pushed to an extreme, may produce negative results for Filipinos in the workplace. Filipinos should be aware of possible consequences.

Over-respect for authority, including calling supervisors "sir" and "ma'am" may indicate subservience or passivity, which is disconcerting in Canada, where relations are more egalitarian between supervisors and supervised. An employee from a hierarchical culture may expect the boss to give him instructions, and does not see anything wrong with not offering ideas. In concert with not wanting to call attention to oneself, the Filipino may end up not actively participating in discussions. When the employee does not take the initiative but only implements decisions of the boss, he may seem disengaged and lacking ideas. It may be seen as lack of initiative and independent thinking, and may prevent the Filipino from advancing at work.

Employees in Canada are normally expected to provide input into their performance evaluations, such as comments about supervisory relation-ships. The input about their performance may be difficult for a Filipino who is modest about his abilities, and the comments about the supervisory relationship may also be difficult as that may mean 'criticizing' the boss.

In applying for work, Filipinos cannot let their sense of modesty get in the way of clearly explaining their achievements. The "we" culture of Filipinos (shared by many Asian cultures) may make a Filipino express his achievement in the form of "we did this" or "we did that," which make a recruiter in Canada's more individualistic culture wonder whether the Filipino is "hiding behind the team." Specifying which particular task you did doesn't mean you are bragging about your role. You are simply provid-ing specific information to the recruiter about your own achievements, skills, and experience.

The Filipino's desire to please can sometimes make it difficult for him to say no—even when there's good reason—to requests by supervisors or other team members. This can have a negative impact later, when it becomes apparent that saying no would have been the best course of action.

Filipinos could learn to be more assertive—i.e., the quality of being self-assured and confident without being aggressive. Assertiveness training and practice can go a long way to assist Filipinos moderate some cultural traits that, in excess, may hold them back in the Canadian workplace. Along with the many positive traditional Filipino cultural traits, assertiveness will help Filipinos succeed in any Canadian workplace.

(This article is based on research undertaken by EGC and Associates for the project "Hiring and Retaining Skilled Immigrants: A Cultural Competence Toolkit," developed for the BC Human Resource Managers Association of BC, 2008).

Eleanor Guerrero-Campbell is a city planner, community champion, and writer. She came to Canada in 1977 with a degree in English and comparative literature, and a master's degree in urban and regional planning, both from the University of the Philippines. She went on to work as a planner manager in Edmonton, Alberta and Surrey, Richmond, and Vancouver in British Columbia.

Guerrero-Campbell cofounded the Multicultural Helping House Society, where, as executive director, she established programs to assist newcomers in Canada.

As chief executive of the Minerva Foundation for BC Women, she managed leadership programs for women in various stages of their careers.

She currently co-convenes the City of Vancouver's Immigrant Partnership Program Committee on Access to Services.

Filipino Indigeneity and Indigenous Peoples of Canada

By Leonora C. Angeles

October 16, 2020 – If not for the COVID-19 pandemic, Canadians would have been seen wearing orange on September 30 in their workplaces, schools, and public places.

September 30 commemorates the impacts the Indian residential school system has had and continues to have on Indigenous people in Canada. It emphasizes that only through learning the truth of Canada's colonial history can we move forward toward reconciliation. As Filipinos, we need to understand this colonial history of conquest and Indigenous land dispossession as uninvited guests and immigrants arrived in Canada.

We can also use this as an opportunity to come to terms with our connections with this Canadian colonial history and our own history as colonized peoples from the Philippines. We have a lot to learn and share with Indigenous peoples in Canada, based on our solidarity and mutual experiences.

As a people, we have to come to terms with our own Indigenous roots. The majority of our Indigenous lowland, coastal, riverside, and upland populations (Poly-Austronesians, Indo-Malays) have interbred with non-Indigenous peoples—Chinese, Arabs, Indians, Japanese, Europeans, Americans.

One might argue we are among the first truly multicultural societies, being at the crossroads of East and West. Since the first millennium of global trade, our islands have been the gateway between the Pacific and Europe—the Old World—and the Americas—the New World.

Filipino men were also the first Asian group to arrive in the New World, or what is now Mexico, Canada, and the US, through the 250-year history of the Manila-Acapulco galleon trade.

The Philippines as a country is a colonial creation. It even bears the name of a former Spanish King. Had the Philippines not been consolidated as a colonial state by the Spaniards, foreigners would have less trouble recognizing the Indigenous among inhabitants of the Philippines today.

"Pilipino," used in reference to both language and people, is a term with colonial origins in Filipino, originally used by colonizers to refer to Spaniards born in the Philippines. The term was later used by nationalist leaders to refer to indigenous populations—or anyone born in the country.

Both "majority" groups (e.g., Tagalog, Kapampangan, Ilokano, and Bikolano) and "minority" groups (e.g., Aeta, Ati, Binukid, Igorot) are ethno-linguistic groups indigenous to what is now the Philippines. Philippine culture has often been labeled "authentic" but "not exotic." Our national and local cultures are of a hybrid, heterogenous nature of the indigenous and the foreign, which we now call "Philippine," "Filipino," or "Pilipino."

Our culture's diminished exoticism is partly to do with the easy recognition of European, American, Chinese, Indo-Malay, Austronesian-Polynesian, Arabic, Islamic, Judeo-Christian and Protestant elements in Philippine food, music, dances, religions, languages, and dialects.

Philippine culture has been compared to an onion. It is an apt metaphor for its varied cross-cultural, colonial influences, which can be peeled away. In peeling an onion, we reveal what is there: nothing but a sliver of green stalk. This green stalk core is not the indigenous in the Pilipino. Rather, the onion is its peeling, is its skin, and is its body and very constitution. The indigenous, authentic Pilipino, not-so-exotic "other" to the foreign eye, is a hybridized creation *sui generis*.

In this context, the search for the "authentic"—the "indigenous"—is both futile and meaningless. Worse, the assumption of Filipinos' lack of indigeneity has led to the denigration of Filipino culture—in particular the lowland Christian variety—by Westerners.

Filipino culture has also been denigrated by other Asians—and sadly, by some educated Filipinos themselves. Our culture has been called "bastardized," our cuisine "inauthentic," our designs and forms "derivative," "imitative," or a form of "mimicry." Such denigration only reveals our colonial orientation, lack of self-knowledge, confidence, and -respect, and anxieties or angst over our indigenous roots and identities.

We need to read what has now become "Filipino culture" as original, syncretic, and multicultural. It is based on the supersession and layering of the pre-colonial, the indigenous, the Asian, and the Western. All cultures are constructs which in themselves are syncretic, or still in-process or in-formation, dynamic.

In the language of the nation-state bureaucracy, the term "Indigenous peoples" is reserved for "tribal" or "ethnic" minorities. In this official, popular, and political (politically polite, but not anthropologically and historically accurate) usage, we misrecognize indigenous, lowland, Christianized Filipinos as non-Indigenous. And yet in Canada and in other contexts, religious conversion, intermarriages, and inter-relations are not used to exclude or deny Indigenous identities to urbanized, edu-cated, converted, intermarried Indigenous peoples.

As we commemorate the legacies of the Indian residential school system on Indigenous peoples in Canada, we should not also forget how colonialism in the Philippines has led to the erasure of our own Indigenous identities and roots.

We owe to ourselves and our future generations the desire to embrace and learn more about our own Pilipino indigeneity.

Leonora "Nora" Angeles is cross-appointed faculty at the University of British Columbia School of Community and Regional Planning and Institute for Gender, Race, Sexuality, and Social Justice. She taught at Queen's University, where she did her doctoral studies, at the University of Regina, and University of Saskatchewan before moving to Vancouver. She is president of the National Pilipino Canadian Cultural Centre (NPC3) for 2020, vice president of the University of the Philippines Alumni Association of BC, and member of the Company Erasga Dance board of directors and Critical Asian Studies editorial advisory board. She also helped convene the organization of Daloy-Puso Youth Network and the Filipino-Canadian Futures: Education, Leadership and Capacity-Building. She may be reached at nora.angeles@ubc.ca. 🐚

Finding Oneness in Filipino Community

By Prod Laquian

August 1, 2017 – *Bayanihan* is a valued tradition among Filipinos. In Philippine villages, its spirit draws farmers to join hands and help each other to plow the fields, plant and harvest the rice, maintain irrigation canals, or move a house. It inspires urban dwellers to get together and volunteer to patrol the neighbourhood to keep peace and order, or fight fires. Interestingly, when Filipinos migrate to Canada, the *bayanihan* spirit continues to permeate their community life through Filipino associations.

As they blend into mainstream Canadian society, Filipinos maintain active links with their *kababayan* (compatriots) through spontaneous or organized activities. They see each other in Catholic churches every Sunday. They buy Philippine groceries in the same *sari-sari* (variety) stores, or eat in Filipino restaurants. When they send money to family back home or ship *balikbayan* boxes to relatives, they go to Filipino agencies for money remittances and cargo delivery.

Filipinos are scattered in cities or towns—wherever they may choose to reside. But they prefer to deal with their compatriots in social linkages as part of Filipino cultural values, rooted in a reciprocal kinship system of trust. They seek out fellow Filipinos when needing the services of a physician, lawyer, dentist, realtor, car dealer, mechanic, insurance agent, plumber, or barber. The communal nature of Filipinos—their strong need to be part of a group—has led to a proliferation of Filipino associations.

The 2017 issue of *Dahong Pilipino* (*DahongPilipino.ca*) listed 161 associations in British Columbia alone. A 2006 Philippine Embassy listing of Filipino associations all over Canada included 535 associations registered with the Embassy. Others estimated the number to range from eight hundred to one thousand, because they claimed that when two or more candidates ran for a tightly contested presidency of an organization, the losers often formed a separate organization.

Ontario has the most Filipino associations. Based on the Philippine Embassy list updated under Ambassador Francisco Benedicto in 2006, Filipino associations were organized based on categories such as a member's place of origin in the Philippines or the Canadian city and town of residence.

Filipinos are joiners, and Filipino associations give them the opportunities to socialize, network, and benefit from mutual aid services. As the number of Filipinos in Canada increases, so does the number of Filipino associations. In Canada's diverse society, Filipinos find oneness in belonging and togetherness in the company of people with whom they share a common interest. 🖊

Taal Volcano Eruption Shows *Bayanihan* in Canada

By Staff

March 16, 2020 – Filipinos in and outside their native country, including Canada, are particularly proud of one of their ancient traditions, called *bayanihan*.

Bayanihan is a Tagalog word meaning how a community comes and works together to achieve a common goal, often to help members needing assistance. It's derived from the word "*bayan*," which literally means "town," and generally evokes a sense of a united people.

As the recent eruption of Taal Volcano in the Philippine province of Batangas proves, *bayanihan* is alive and strong among Filipinos in Canada. It did not take long before Canadian Filipinos responded to the January 12, 2020 eruption of Taal.

The Talisay Association of Manitoba was one of the first organizations that organized fundraising activities. Three days after the volcano eruption, the association of former residents in the Batangas town of Talisay started receiving donations at the Philippine Canadian Centre of Manitoba in the city of Winnipeg.

Lucille Nolasco of *Pilipino Express* in Winnipeg reported that Filipinos in the city organized different fundraisers, including dance mobs, Zumba classes, mini shows featuring local talents, and fundraising breakfasts in Filipino restaurants.

Community artist Jojo Alpuerto performs at the
Sagip Taal, Bangon Batangas event in Surrey, BC.

Marites Sison of *Philippine Reporter* in Toronto wrote that the Philippine Independence Day Council of Toronto scheduled a February 25 kick-off to its planned long-term fundraising for Taal victims. "This will be a long-term effort," PIDC president Ramon Estaris said.

According to Estaris, the latter phase of the group's effort will be to empower victims of the natural disaster to "rebuild their homes and livelihood."

The Praise Christian Family Church in Toronto also held a fundraising event on January 18 and 19.

Sison of *Philippine Reporter* noted that the Philippine Consulate in Toronto is encouraging Filipino organizations interested in offering assistance to directly contact non-profits in the Philippines.

Consul Edwin Mendoza said in a phone interview: "We have received some calls from concerned Filipino organizations, and we've told them that it's better to go directly to their local contacts."

The Lemery Club of Toronto held a *tiangge* (Tagalog for "sale") on January 26. Lemery is one of the towns in Batangas that was affected by the volcano eruption.

Migrante Canada and its chapters around the world issued calls for cash donations as part of Sagip Migrante, a program that responds to calamities in the Philippines. Migrante is an organization dedicated to immigrant and migrant workers' rights.

No community is too small to help, as was proven by Filipinos in Dawson Creek in British Columbia, where a fundraising dinner was held on January 26, 2020. Around 350 donors for volcano victims attended the dinner, organized by Gregg Apolonio with the support of Filipino and non-Filipino residents.

Also in BC, the Filipino Canadian Cultural Heritage Society (FCCHS) held Sagip Taal, Bangon Batangas, a fundraising event in Surrey, where local performers and bands entertained the crowd, emceed by Jojo Alpuerto and Tisha Newland.

One of the founding members of FCCHS is Mario Hernandez, a native of San Luis, Batangas. Hernandez was incidentally on a trip to the Philippines when Taal Volcano erupted. He opened his house for refugees, distributed relief goods, and provided water for residents in the industrial district of Canlubang, in the province of Laguna, which was affected by the disaster.

The Philippine Asian News Today reported that Surrey mayor Doug McCallum and member of parliament for Fleetwood Port Kells Ken Hardie attended the event and gave monetary donations.

Many non-Filipinos also generously donated funds and goods for the Taal Volcano victims, in sympathy for the Filipino community.

As of March 8, 2020, the Philippine Institute of Volcanology and Seismology (Phivolcs) has maintained Alert Level 2, the lowest in a five-step alert status by Phivolcs.

Bayanihan Spirit Moves Filipino Associations

By Eleanor R. Laquian

August 16, 2017 – An avid observer of how Filipinos behave in Canada once remarked that there were probably as many Filipino associations in Canada as there were islands in the Philippines.

The lists of such associations maintained by the Philippine Embassy and Consulates and those compiled by *DahongPilipino* (*DahongPilipino.ca*) show that there may be some truth to that comment.

Asked why there are so many Filipino associations in Canada, Greg V. Barcelon, a psychologist who immigrated to Canada in 1993, explained: "There are probably three factors that create this situation. First, Filipino behavior is coloured by our cultural past—the communal nature of Filipinos strengthens the us-against-them attitude, which explains our strong need to be part of a group. Second, our familiarity with inequality drives many of us to aspire for top positions, so we can say 'I'm somebody.' Lastly, our short-term orientation, shaped in part by our lack of control over our personal and national destiny in the past, accounts for self-interest rather than commitment to the greater good."

Filipino associations in Canada are formed around provincial or regional origins, university affiliations, or common interests. They are organized according to the following categories:

- Place of origin in the Philippines – Anac ti Batac, Mekeni Club, Bicolanos Pagtitipon
- Canadian city or province of residence – Filipino Winnipegers, Filipinos of PEI
- Patriotic and nationalist goals – Knights of Rizal, Philippine Independence Day Committee
- Professions – Fil-Can Medical Association, Filipino Lawyers of Ontario
- Sports –Filipino Bowling League, Filipino Lawn Tennis Association
- Arts and culture – Folklorico Filipino, Dimasalang Group
- Seniors – Diamond Society, New Era Society, Filipino Seniors of Mississauga
- School alumni – UPAA of Metro Toronto, Mapua Alumni of Canada
- Cause-oriented – INTERCEDE of Toronto, CDWCR of Vancouver
- Women – PINAY of Montréal, Women's Barangay of Alberta
- University-based – Filipino Students at UBC, Filipinos at York University
- Mutual aid – Fil-Can Neighbourhood Association, Ang Magkakapitbahay
- Trade –Phil-Can Trade Council, Filipino Chamber of Commerce Edmonton

A former Philippine consul general, Minerva Falcon, who used to attend four or five affairs of "hometown" Filipino associations per week, said she "welcomes the formation of these associations because it highlights the 'Philippine-ness' of Filipino-Canadians."

Current consul general Neil Ferrer says: "The proliferation of Filipino associations in BCmakes for an active and vibrant Filipino community in Canada. These associations, which mirror our rich culture and diversity, reflect Filipinos' enthusiasm to do well for the community and represent various causes in society."

Filipinos newly arrived in Canada can count on Filipino associations to help them. Volunteers help newcomers and respond quickly to requests for assistance—especially from people arriving from their own hometowns in the Philippines.

Newcomers who received support and friendship in community associations are often inspired to return the favour to other newcomers, and thus ensure that the Filipino *bayanihan* spirit continues to live in Canada.

Watching Filipino Movies: A Peek at Philippine Culture

By Mel Tobias

June 1, 2017 – When I delivered the opening remarks at the introduction of Filipino Movie Nights, a Filipino film series presented at the ExplorASIAN Festival of the Vancouver Asian Heritage Month, on May

18, 2017, I was hoping my comments would help the audience understand and appreciate Filipino movies for what they really are—a true reflection of Filipino life and culture.

The film series was sponsored by *Dahong Pilipino*, Anyone Can

Act Theatre (ACAT), and Tulayan(meaning "to bridge the gap"). Tulayanis a grassroots, community-powered group with a mission to link the ever-growing Filipino diaspora and create an inclusive environment to explore the histories, languages, and ever-evolving cultures of the Filipino people. It endeavours to cultivate opportunities for new connections and community-building through dialogue about history and fostering positive cultural identification.

Filipino movies are long. They run for two hours or more. Why? Movie producers know their market well. If the movie is short, like one hour and twenty minutes, the audience will feel short-changed. So it can be long and tedious, because the main message is repeated two or three times to satisfy the audience.

Acting in Filipino movies is generally heightened with high melodrama—some may find the style to be "overacting." But Filipinos are highly emotional, like the Spaniards and the Italians. They express their emotions with extra flair. There are, however, some Filipino actors who *under*act (depending on their roles), like Nora Aunor in *Himala* ("*Miracle*") and Jacqueline Jose in *Ka Rosa* who won the best actress award at the 2016 Cannes International Film Festival. "Under-acting" actors use their eyes, facial expressions, and body language to communicate emotions.

A Filipino melodrama on film punishes the wicked in the end. There is redemption, and good wins in the end, unlike some American movies—where you can get away with murder—and with no open endings, like in French movies.

The storyline is often a morality play with the following ingredients: guilt, fatalism, sexual repression and eroticism, double standards, religious influences, sacrifice, and acceptance of things that can't be changed. Some of the characters are victims of fate.

To sum it all up, a Filipino movie is a Filipino movie. To appreciate it, one must accept its origin in a developing country. Filipinos have their own conventions, stereotypes, and clichés—and a Filipino way of looking at survival, poverty, socioeconomic differences, and life in general. Filipino movies allow us to understand the complex Filipino culture and personality. It is cinema verité, cinema of truth.

While there are numerous escapist commercial Filipino movies, there are also many outstanding Tagalog movies that remain hidden or forgotten. Filipino art films win many awards, but 80 percent are not given a commercial release. Directed by serious Filipino filmmakers with social conscience, these films hold up a clear mirror reflecting Filipino society.

Mel Tobias was a movie critic, lifestyle, and entertainment editor, author, foreign correspondent, amateur actor, broadcaster, festivalier, impresario for the arts, proprietor of a vintage collectibles boutique, frustrated saloon singer, gourmet who knew where best to eat, and a collector of esoteric and nostalgia recordings and books. He was an avid fundraiser for charitable causes. He wrote about Filipino films. He passed away in 2017.

Lent in Canada: Delta Parish Adopts Salubong

By Leonardo B. Cunanan

April 1, 2018 – The Philippines is the most Catholic country in Asia, with over 80 percent of its population of more than a hundred million belonging to the Roman Catholic faith. For Filipinos, Ash Wednesday is a significant religious event, as it begins the forty-day period of Lent which culminates on Easter Sunday. On Ash Wednesday, Filipinos bear witness to their faith with a cross marked on their foreheads.

British Columbia's Immaculate Conception Parish in Delta is one of the most active Catholic parishes of the province, with a significant number of Filipino parishioners. Reverend Amador M. Abundo, the Filipino pastor of Immaculate Conception, explained how his parish is celebrating the Lenten Season, beginning with Ash Wednesday and leading to Holy Week from Palm Sunday to Easter Sunday. "We try to get everybody to share in the passion of our Lord in the spirit of penance on Ash Wednesday," he said.

Father Abundo has been in Canada for twenty-two years now, and has served in four different parishes in the Archdiocese as assistant pastor and pastor before he was assigned as pastor for Immaculate Conception in 2014. He is the first Filipino priest to be incardinated in the Archdiocese of Vancouver.

In his Delta parish, Ash Wednesday starts with a bonfire of blessed palms for ashes to be used to mark the faithful with the austere symbol of a cross on their foreheads, as a sign of conversion, penance, fasting, and human mortality.

People generally leave the marks on their foreheads all day as a sign of their faith. Far from being a mere external act, the Church has retained the use of ashes to symbolize that attitude of internal penance to which all the baptized are called upon during Lent. It is a sombre reminder that "you are dust and to dust you will return."

During Lent, Catholics are encouraged to fast, give up something they enjoy on Fridays, such as meats, and offer other personal sacrifices. At Immaculate Conception Parish, Holy Week 2018 started on March 25, Palm Sunday—or Passion Sunday—to celebrate the triumphant entrance of Christ into Jerusalem before his impending death on the cross. Before Mass, palms were distributed to the parishioners, who carried them in a ritual procession into the church. The priest blessed and sprinkled the palms with holy water. Many people fashioned the palms into small crosses or other items of personal devotion to take home.

Father Abundo explained that the readings and Gospel for Palm Sunday Mass were long because they covered the complete narrative, starting with the entrance of Jesus into Jerusalem riding on a donkey and being welcomed by adoring crowds, ending with his arrest, trial, and crucifixion.

Burning of last year's blessed palms for use on Ash Wednesday.
This ritual, called Silab-sala, *means "burning of sins," so that the faithful*
may share the passion of Christ with a cleansed heart.

On Wednesday, March 28, all priests in the Archdiocese of Vancouver participated in the Mass of Chrism, celebrated at the Holy Rosary Cathedral with Archbishop Michael Miller as celebrant, and concelebrated by diocesan priests and religious orders from all parts of the archdiocese. The priests renewed their vows, and the holy oils were consecrated.

On the evening of March 29, Holy Thursday, the three gifts Jesus imparted to His beloved bride, the Church, were celebrated: the Priesthood, the Eucharist (Mass of the Lord's supper), and a love that is stronger than death.

At the Immaculate Conception parish, Father Abundo re-enacted the washing of the feet of twelve disciples by Jesus as a sign of love and humility. Twelve members of the parish ministries and organizations were chosen to serve as disciples. After the Mass, the faithful could stay for the Adoration of the Blessed Sacrament until midnight or join a group for *Visita Iglesia*, visiting and praying at seven nearby churches—and then back to the parish for prayers.

Good Friday, March 30, was quiet as parishioners came for morning prayers at the church. There was no mass, but schoolchildren made the Stations of the Cross, joined by parents and other parishioners, in the morning. In the afternoon, at 3 p.m., the parishioners attended the Liturgy of the Passion of the Lord, the veneration of the cross, and communion, followed by the Novena to the Divine Mercy. After the services, the veils covering the crosses in the church were removed—while the veils covering the images were removed before the Easter Vigil. The parishioners were encouraged to observe fasting, abstinence, and meditation.

As Father Abundo explained, the focus of Holy Saturday, although there was no Mass and the altar was bare, was the Easter Vigil, which began at 9 p.m. and had four distinctive stages: Service of Light, Liturgy of the Word, Liturgy of Baptism, and Liturgy of the Eucharist. The New Fire and the Paschal Candle were blessed. The Paschal Candle is the central symbolic object in the celebration of the Vigil Liturgy, because it represents the Risen Lord. As part of the service, the people who completed the Rite of Christian Initiation of Adults (RCIA) course were baptized and confirmed. They were received into full communion with the Catholic Church.

Easter Sunday is a celebration of Christ's resurrection from the dead. A new activity, not normally done in Canada—but which is a tradition in Catholic churches in the Philippines—was introduced in the parish three years ago and is now part of the Easter Mass at Immaculate Conception parish. It is called "*Salubong*," or "meeting of the risen Christ with His grieving mother Mary."

Salubong starts with two separate processions coming out of two separate church doors at 7:30 a.m., one hour before mass. One procession, with the statue of the Risen Lord, is accompanied by men. The second procession of the statue of the Virgin Mary wearing dark clothes and a dark veil, is accompanied by women. Though the two processions head off in different directions, they eventually meet up in front of the church, where a high platform from where a child dressed as an angel lifts the mourning veil of the Virgin Mary as she meets up with the Risen Christ.

At the precise moment that the veil is lifted, the lead angel, joined by a chorus of other angels, sing alleluias, and the Easter Sunday celebration begins with the pealing of church bells.

The devotees experience a certain joy—a share in the gladness of the Blessed Virgin Mary upon meeting her son who had come back to life. Her tears of sorrow turned to joy—and a cause for celebration for those joining the procession and the glorious Easter mass at the church immediately after the "*Salubong*" procession. This ritual of *Salubong*, a beautiful religious and cultural tradition, is a Filipino contribution to Canada's diverse society.

Celebrating All Saints' Day in the Philippines

By Eleanor R. Laquian

November 1, 2017 – My father died when I was only ten, so I spent many an All Saints' Day at the old Manila North Cemetery (Sementeryo del Norte) where he was buried. This was in the 1950s, before memorial parks became popular. Days before November 1, my siblings and I would clean up the gravesite, repaint the tombstone white, arrange flowering plants around the grave, and polish the marble epitaph.

November 1 was called *Todos los Santos* then, or *Araw ng mga Patay* ("Day of the Dead"). Today, this holiday is commonly called *Undas* or *Undras*, from the Spanish word *honrar*, meaning "honour," since this is a day for honouring the dead.

Although *Undas* is a sombre occasion to reflect on the afterlife and remember departed loved ones, it is also a festive occasion, as families and friends troop to the cemeteries with flowers, candles, food, and drink for a day of celebrating the departed. Traffic is usually horrendous, and the cost of fresh flowers goes up five hundred times that day—with the white fragrant *azucena* as the bestselling flower.

Our family usually goes to the cemetery after lunch with baskets of food, flowers and candles, umbrellas, and folding chairs. Because public toilets in public cemeteries were notoriously horrid, we bring fruits to quench our thirst rather than liquids. Luckily, November is *lanzones* and *dalandan* season, so we bring lots of those. The native delicacy usually served in Laguna on this day is *sinukmani*, a glutinous rice cake similar to what they call *biko* in Manila. We bring this instead of sandwiches. We also bring boiled peanuts and corn on the cob, which are filling but do not make one thirsty. We always say the rosary as soon as we get there, because as the crowd gets bigger by the hour, the place begins to look and sound like a sprawling picnic park of noisy merrymakers.

Every gravesite is surrounded by people eating, drinking, chatting, or fanning themselves while listening to music on their portable radios. Their children collect candlewax drippings and have a contest as to who can make the biggest ball of wax by the end of the day.

Because the majority of Filipinos are Catholic, the observance of *Todos Los Santos* or All Saints' Day has been part of the Philippine religious tradition. It is not just for commemorating departed loved ones; it's also a time for family reunions. Those working in the cities and abroad return to their hometowns in the provinces to join the family for the cemetery visit.

People go to the cemeteries to bond, reminisce, and chat. Others go there to feast and party with guitars, stereos, and lots of food, to bring cheer to an otherwise sad occasion.

In some public cemeteries, city officials have had to ban loudspeakers, karaoke singing, loud radios, and even decks of cards from cemeteries, to show some respect for the dead and those still in mourning.

We usually stay until after dark, because that is when the cemetery turns eerily magical as a sea of a thousand flickering candles illuminate the darkening tombs. For some, their vigil lasts throughout the night. The following day, November 2, is All Souls' Day. This is mainly a church event, when prayers and Masses for the dead are offered. Tombs are blessed by the priest, by request, for a donation for church upkeep.

All Saints' Day in the Provinces

A tradition in the rural areas of the Philippines on the night of November 1 is called *pangangaluluwa* (from the Tagalog word *kaluluwa*, meaning "souls" walking about). As soon as it gets dark, groups of singers go from house to house singing mournful songs, asking for prayers to bring them to heaven from the purgatory where they have suffered long enough. They get rewarded with *sinukmani* (rice cakes) wrapped in banana leaves.

In the town of Pila, in the province of Laguna, prominent families have tombs in the church itself. After ten years in the Manila North Cemetery, my father's bones were moved to the San Antonio de Padua Catholic Church of Pila, where his parents were buried. The All Saints' Day observance in a Catholic church is very different from the mass movement of multitudes to cemeteries and fiesta-like celebrations we experienced in the Manila North Cemetery.

There are only a few gravesites inside the Pila Catholic Church, and most families visiting them know each other—many of them are even related. So, the atmosphere is more like a sombre family reunion instead of a carnival. There is no eating or drinking in the church—only candles, flowers, prayers, and quiet conversations. Photos of the departed in happier times adorn some graves. People go back and forth all day from their nearby homes.

San Antonio de Padua Catholic church in Pila, Laguna.

There are no night vigils. They go home at dusk to eat and await the *pangangaluluwa* at night. While waiting for the singers, the family gathers around to listen to stories about the departed loved ones. The older kids scare each other with ghost stories, whispering to younger ones, "I smell candles burning. Can you smell it?" or "Where's that flower smell coming from?" until a small kid cries from fright and all the kids are sent to bed. But nobody wants to sleep alone, so they all sleep under a big mosquito net, with a light on all night. Only the departed gets to sleep in peace that night.

Pasko na, Sinta ko, Paano ang Pasko sa Pandemyang ito?

(It's Christmas again, my dear—how will it be in this pandemic?)
By Adelaida Lacaba-Bago

December 1, 2020 – As far as I can remember, Christmas season in the Philippines is the most awaited celebration for young and old alike. It is the most festive, the longest, and the most memorable. The season is an endless

merrymaking series of Christmas parties in homes, schools, government and private offices.

It is also a time for family reunions, as Filipinos living abroad usually come home to spend the Christmas holidays in the country.

Christmas is a time for gift-giving—not only for family members and friends, but also for the garbage collectors, street sweepers, the mailmen, and other delivery and service persons who served families throughout the year. Those who are employed usually look forward to receiving a Christmas bonus and some other perks, like baskets of groceries or envelopes of cash from their bosses.

The buildup of excitement for the season starts with the first "-ber" month, and continues during the other months ending in "-ber." Usually, at the start of September, radio and television announcers begin the count-down to Christmas by launching the holiday season with Christmas carols. The caroling continues throughout October, November, and December, with the number of carols played increasing by the day.

By mid-November, some families start decorating their homes with Christmas lights and the lighted traditional *parol*, or Christmas lantern, beams and twinkles from many windows. Artificial Christmas trees are taken out of storage, decorated, and displayed in bay windows of big homes.

Local governments also decorate the streets with lights and huge, colourful lanterns hanging from lamp posts. Department stores, with elaborate Christmas displays, start selling Christmas decorations, as well as holiday houseware. Children go around the neighbourhood, singing Christmas carols, expecting gifts of money or refreshments for their efforts. Young adults form caroling groups as fundraisers. They go around well dressed, men usually in barong, to serenade, accompanied by guitars and/ or accordions, homes and stores in malls with carols for a worthy cause. By early December, news reports inevitably include the prices of favourite holiday foods, such as ham, *queso de bola* (cheese), canned fruit cocktail and all-purpose cream—essentials for Filipino-style fruit salad—apples, grapes, mayonnaise.

For Catholic Filipinos, the nine early morning Masses, or *simbang gabi*, are an integral part of Christmas. They are held at dawn, starting on December 16, and culminate on Christmas Eve with a Midnight Mass. Christmas is celebrated as the birth of the Redeemer so Catholic Filipinos consider it an occasion for hope, redemption, and thanksgiving.

A Pandemic Christmas

All the merrymaking and traditional rites were the marks of Christmases past, before the Coronavirus pandemic (*pandemya* in Tagalog) and successive catastrophic typhoons—accompanied by killer floods and landslides—struck the Philippines in 2019. In mid-November, three major typhoons, one after the other, ravaged the Luzon region with flooding that drove some homeowners in Manila to the rooftops for safety. Many lives and homes were lost.

In the face of these natural calamities, on top of the COVID pandemic scourge, will Filipinos celebrate the Christmas season in 2020? Yes, of course. It is certain that Filipinos will celebrate the holidays this year, despite these happenings—because Christmas in the Philippines is a meaningful event, and not just for fun. However, Christmas 2020 will be like no other.

This Christmas will be scaled-down. Many places in the country are still under COVID lockdown—all of Luzon has been declared in a state of calamity after the series of typhoons. As a response to the three pre-Christmas natural calamities, many groups of generous people are engaged in fundraising to provide help to the victims of these natural disasters.

In Metro Manila, it will be a sombre celebration, since all local governments have banned Christmas caroling. *Simbang gabi* will continue to be held at cock's crow, but with restrictions as to how many are allowed inside the church—to observe proper social distancing and avoid the spread of the COVID-19 virus.

The festive-sounding radio and TV stations have been muted somehow. There are no exciting countdowns till Christmas, and very few Christmas carols are played on the air. It will be a sad Christmas for the many who lost loved ones to COVID and the recent typhoons. There are still many who are suffering or dying from the virus.

Perhaps this is how it should be—a calibrated and restrained celebration in consideration of those who are still in pain and suffering because of the recent calamities and the rapidly spreading, deadly virus. This is the Filipino way—the truly Christian way.

Adelaida Lacaba-Bago, PhD, is a retired professor of De La Salle University, Manila, where she served as Director of Research and concurrently Vice Dean. She has published four books on curriculum development, supervision of instruction, and the social dimensions of Philippine education. Her latest is Thesis Writing with Confidence.

Filipino *Belen* Tradition Brings Baby Jesus to Vancouver Homes

By Eleanor R. Laquian

December 16, 2018 – When I was growing up in the Philippines, our family did not have a Christmas tree during the holidays. What we always had on our windows were homemade, brightly lit star-shaped Christmas

Christmas Belen *in a place of honour in a Vancouver home.*

lanterns called *parol* (from the Spanish word for lamp, *farol*). They represent the star of Bethlehem, which led the Magi to the infant Jesus. But the centrepiece of our Christmas decoration was the Christmas *Belen*,or crèche (nativity scene).

On a black, half-moon-shaped table at the entrance to

our house was a carefully laid out nativity scene. It was composed of papier mache figures—Mary, Joseph, and the infant Jesus, surrounded by angels, cattle, shepherds and their flock, and the adoring Three Kings—all under a makeshift cardboard stable. The stable was topped by a shining star made of white, translucent *capiz* shells.

Under the table, between its handsomely carved legs, were giftboxes of various sizes and colours, which we kids shook and rattled every time we passed by to guess what was inside them and for whom they were intended.

This manger scene or crèche, depicting the birth of Christ in a lowly manger, was a traditional Filipino Christmas symbol, called *Belen,* the Spanish name for Bethlehem, the city of David, where Christ was born.

During Christmas in the Philippines, a *Belen* could be seen everywhere – in homes, churches, schools, and even private offices and government buildings. Some *Belens* for public display in shopping malls and office buildings could be extravagant, using different materials and sizes for the figures and Christmas lights for the star, with elaborate, painted background scenery. A *Belen* is also part of some stores' Christmas window display.

In all the happy Christmases of my youth in Manila, the *Belen* was our cherished family tradition. So when I started my own family, a holiday ritual we loved to observe in Canada was the setting-up of a *Belen* on the first Sunday of Advent, often the last Sunday of November.

Prod and I had collected many nativity sets from our travels. We have carved olive-wood figures from Jerusalem, colourful painted *tablas* from Mexico, handcrafted figures of bread dough from the studio of sculptor Guayasamin in Ecuador, and a delicate porcelain set from Vienna.

In Bogota, Colombia we got a handcrafted leather nativity set. But our treasured crèche from the Philippines is a clay set of the Holy Family and angels in a manger scene, complete with a menagerie of carabaos, goats, pigs, dogs, roosters, chickens, and ducks.

Our granddaughter Maya has always been fascinated by our Christmas *Belen*, which she helps decorate. Prod has made a makeshift stable, where the Holy Family, Three Kings, shepherds, and animals are grouped in a tableau. Outside the stable sits a basket of straw. An empty manger is in front of Mary and Joseph.

We told Maya that starting on the first day of Advent and every day before Christmas, every time each of us did a good deed, we could put a straw in the manger, to make it soft and warm for Baby Jesus on Christmas day.

Maya took this tradition seriously. She always had the honour of placing the Baby Jesus on the straw-filled manger on Christmas Eve. At story time, before she goes to bed, she always asks us to read her the story of the first Christmas in a manger in Bethlehem.

When Maya was old enough, she loved to put a straw in the manger for every good thing that she did. A piece of straw went onto the crib when she brushed her teeth, put away her toys, or ate all the dollar pancakes on her plate. Once, a handful of straw landed on the manger after she helped me shell a bowl of peas.

One Christmas, Maya decided to redecorate the nativity scene. She thought the straws were not soft and warm enough, so she cut up pieces of white flannel from her old pajamas and used them instead. We had a unique *Belen* that year.

Maya and her soft and warm manger for Baby Jesus.

At a Christmas party at her preschool, her teacher was telling the children that Christmas was the birthday of Baby Jesus. Maya raised her hand and proudly announced to one and all that she knew this because "Baby Jesus lives in my Grandma's house."

When we came to get Maya after school that day, her teacher asked me about Maya's Baby Jesus. She was delighted when I explained our Christmas *Belen* tradition, and asked if she could introduce the practice to her family and friends too.

Thanks to Maya, Baby Jesus may now live in other Vancouver homes.

Sambayanang Pilipino Introduces All-Tagalog *Simbang Gabi*

By Staff

December 16, 2017- December 16 officially starts the religious celebration of Christmas in the Philippines. It begins with a nine-day novena of Masses in honour of the Blessed Virgin Mary called *Simbang Gabi* or *Misade Gallo* in Spanish, meaning "Roosters' Mass," because church bells start ringing with the crowing of the roosters, to awaken parishioners to attend the predawn Masses. It culminates on Christmas eve. This tradition started as far back as the 1500s, when Spanish colonizers celebrated Christmas in the Philippines. It was held in early morn, so farmers and fisherfolk could attend before starting work in the fields or on the seas.

In Greater Vancouver, Catholic Filipinos were introduced to a Canadian Filipino version of *Simbang Gabi* through the efforts of Sambayanang Pilipino. Filipinos in other cities of Canada and the world with large Filipino populations also start Christmas with this nine-day series of Masses.

Songs in Pilipino and the re-enactment of Joseph and Mary's trip to Jerusalem, known as *Panunuluyan* or seeking shelter, is the central theme of the celebration. The Masses heighten the anticipation of the birth of Christ and honour the Virgin Mary.

The *Simbang Gabi in* Vancouver starts nightly at 7, December 15–23, using Pilipino liturgy. But unlike in the Philippines, it does not end on Christmas Eve. The Midnight Mass in Canada on December 24 is either in English or French, for all Canadians, while *Simbang Gabi* is only in Tagalog or Pilipino.

The first Vancouver *Simbang Gabi* in 2017 was celebrated by Archbishop Michael Miller of the Archdiocese of Vancouver on December 15 at the Holy Rosary Cathedral. Filipino priests and other priests in the cathedral concelebrated the Mass. The encouragement and support of the Archdiocese of Vancouver for this Filipino Christmas tradition is evident with the active participation of the Archbishop as celebrant.

*The first Mass in Pilipino, sponsored by members of the
Sambayanang Pilipino (above with Archbishop Miller).*

The founding of Sambayanang Pilipino

The first *Simbang Gabi*, celebrated at Corpus Christi Church in Vancouver
in December 2001, was a momentous event for Filipinos, as it brought
back memories of the traditional Christmas

Masses in the Philippines. It inspired a group of friends and families to
continue this tradition in the coming years, and encourage churches with
large Filipino congregations to do the same. They got together one night
in December and reflected on the need to continue the celebration of the
Eucharist inTagalog. Thus began Sambayanang Pilipino.

Sambayanang Pilipino, the Filipino Christian Community in BC, is a
Catholic, lay, non-profit organization headed by volunteer directors under
the guidance of Filipino Catholic priests. Its main purpose is to make the
Roman Catholic Church of BC and the Roman Catholic Church in the
Philippines aware of the pastoral needs of immigrant Filipinos in BC.
It also aims to serve as a facilitating body, in communion with Church
authorities, for the celebration of a unique, culturally based worship using
liturgy in the native Filipino language—Pilipino, also known as Tagalog.

The first Mass in Pilipino sponsored by Sambayanang Pilipino was celebrated at St. Jude's Parish in Vancouver on March 19, 2002. It was officiated
by Fathers Amador Abundo, Justin Trinidad, and Vicente Borre. (Priests
are addressed as Father by Filipinos.)

Since then, the society has evolved—and it was registered on January 28, 2005 under the *Non-Profit Society Act* of BC. In March 2009, the Sambayanang Pilipino leaders had an audience with Archbishop Michael Miller, to introduce the society and explain how it is implementing the propositions of the synod and its other services to the Filipinos in the Archdiocese. 🖐

The Essence of Christmas

By Jo Leuterio Flach

December 16, 2016 – When I was growing up in Quezon City, I could hear Christmas carols on the radio by early November. Outside our front door would be a big *parol*.

Our Christmas tree, a pine tree from Baguio, was up and decorated with multicoloured electric lights by the second week of December. Gaily wrapped presents would appear under the tree a week before Christmas. By this time, neighbourhood children singing Christmas carols would be ringing our doorbell, sometimes showing up twice in the same evening.

Midnight Mass was awaited with great anticipation, never to be missed. Our *Media Noche* at home, soon after, was just for immediate family, as more sumptuous feasts were to follow in the afternoon in our house and at our relatives' on the day after. We opened our gifts in the morning. Presents for the children from Santa would have miraculously appeared under the tree. The rest of the day would be spent welcoming relatives and grazing (the dining table was laden with *kakanin* and hors d'oeuvres) until dinner, when the *lechon* (a whole roasted piglet) was brought to the table. The best part would be seeing all our relatives and catching up, and doing the same all over again the next day, at another cousin's or auntie's house.

My first Christmas in Toronto was white—everything was covered with snow. Peter brought a small fir tree to my room in a boarding house. His mother had sent him candle holders (and small, white wax candles); we attached them to the branches of the tree.

On Christmas Eve, he carefully lit each candle with a match. I had never seen real live candles on a Christmas tree before. It was ethereal. Of course, we had a bucket of water close by, and prayed the landlord would not find out.

After our first child arrived, we substituted electric lights for candles. Every year, we would go to a farm and choose our tree. Every year, it got taller as the children grew older and, every year, we would say, "This is our best Christmas tree ever."

We have our Christmas dinner on Christmas Eve (what was once a goose is now a huge turkey; the *lechon* is just a distant memory). Our Latvian daughter-in-law makes her signature mashed potatoes.

Now that we have a Swedish son-in-law, the dinners are punctuated with several rounds of a special schnapps, preceded by a rousing drinking song to put everyone in a very festive mood.

For the Flachs, home for Christmas is the best gift of all.

Even the little ones raise their glasses of juice in joyful cheer. As dessert comes to a finish, the children search the sky for any sign of reindeer. Someone turns on the TV to see if there's news about Santa's whereabouts. Carols fill the air, the children start singing.

The dining table is cleared, the kitchen hums with cleaning-up, and we all start to relax, when suddenly, the doorbell rings. Somebody answers it and, lo and behold, Santa is standing there, a heavy sack on his shoulders and a big smile on his face. The children jump up and down and run to meet him and lead him inside. They sit on his lap, he talks to them and hands them their presents. The younger ones are a little shy—maybe even scared. The older boy exclaims, "Santa, your watch is the same as Opa's!"

Last year, we spent Christmas in a tiny island resort in the Maldives. After dinner, everyone gathered at the beach and listened to Christmas carols sung by a choir of resort employees. The Maldivians are Muslim, but they sang, with great reverence, "Joy to the World," "O Come All Ye Faithful," and other traditional Christian hymns. It was very touching. Not too long after, a very glittery and noisy motorboat came close to shore. There was jolly old Santa, quite tanned, with a big sack on his shoulder. With much fanfare and many *Ho-Ho-Hos*, he waded ashore, to the cheers of children and adults alike.

A few years ago, we were in an old fishing town on the west coast of Sweden for the Yuletide season (they say "*God jul*" for "Merry Christmas"). Here, it was "Tomte" (a gnome) who brought gifts, wearing not a bright-red suit but modest, brown garb. At midnight, as we walked to the Lutheran church on a hill, tall, white candles glowed softly in the windows of houses along the way. Welcoming lamps and big candles shone brightly beside their doors, age-old safe havens in the long, dark, cold winter nights.

This year, our children and grandchildren will be home again, in Toronto (from Hong Kong, Vancouver, and Stockholm)—and that is always the best Christmas gift of all. In addition, my brother and his wife, and my sister and her husband from Virginia who have no children will join us. It will be almost like a Filipino Christmas. There will be nineteen of us—needless to say, I am having our turkey dinner catered.

When our grandchildren are a little older, we will go to the Philippines for Christmas. By then, they will be so thrilled to be overwhelmed by the hundreds of relatives and friends with whom we will spend our holidays (as my only-child husband experienced on his first visit to Manila).

How we celebrate Christmas has evolved through the years. We have also experienced it in culturally diverse ways. But, always, as everywhere, we celebrate Christmas in the spirit of giving, sharing, and family. Our *Simbang Gabi* is now a noon Mass on Christmas Day, and never fails to remind us that it all began with an act of selflessness and generosity in Bethlehem. Let's continue to spread this goodwill!

The Role of Food in Filipino Culture

By Kaye Banez of The Kusineras

March 16, 2017 – There is no Filipino gathering, big or small, where food does not play a starring role. Whether it is held in a restaurant or at home, the host makes sure that the guests are warmly welcomed, well entertained, and generously served with carefully selected dishes to suit the occasion.

Image by dreamstime.com.
Fruit salad, queso de bola (cheese). ham from Echague, and hot bibingka (rice cake) are typical Christmas Noche Buena fare.

Often, Filipinos go out of their way to make their visitor comfortable. It is a trait not only of the rich and educated, but also of the masses as well. This Filipino hospitality is not only observed in the Philippines, but found wherever Filipinos live in communities around the world.

If the gathering is held in a restaurant, the atmosphere is such that the guests feel as if they are being welcomed in the host's own home. When we cook for our family, we make sure we feed them food made with love and fresh ingredients. If we can recreate this homey ambiance in the restaurant, people will appreciate not just our food, but our culture of hospitality as well.

Hospitality is a Filipino trait that is best express through food served graciously and generously. And it's usual for the host to give a take-home package of the best dishes for the guests to continue to enjoy at home with their family.

Kape Tayo, or Connecting Cultures Through Coffee

By Iona Santos-Fresnoza

July 1, 2017 – Vancouver is a coffee-crazed city. With the cool breeze and almost-always rainy weather, it makes so much sense for Vancouverites to need a cup of joe first thing in the morning, and throughout the day.

I moved to Canada more than a year ago, not really expecting I would live away from my beloved homeland for a long time. Among the things that helped me with the transition was the presence of small, independent cafes, micro-roasters, and people who love coffee.

Being in Canada meant growth in my coffee education, and the wonderful opportunity to connect with like-minded folks about the simple joy of having a great brew.

It was in a cafe where I met a fellow immigrant who would be instrumental in getting me started with my first job in the city, it was over cups of coffee I learned from a mentor about navigating the complex Canadian workplace, and it was in our cafe back home where I met my husband-to-be.

Coffee in the Philippines

In the Philippines, coffee culture did not catch on until the beginning of the millennium, when cafes started sprouting like mushrooms in cities. There was a sudden trend of people hanging out in coffee shops. Pinoys started getting their caffeine fixes in big coffee shops, foregoing their usual instant coffee at home.

However, little did Filipinos know that in the Philippine highlands, there had been a coffee-growing industry all along. In fact, our country used to export coffee. But with lack of funding and support, coffee production declined and up to now, we have had to rely on private initiatives to spur the development of coffee farming, harvesting, and processing in backyard farms. Learning about this need has converted me from being merely a coffee consumer to being a coffee advocate.

Passion for Coffee

I can perhaps attribute this passion for coffee to my many blessed years getting to know a remarkable community of coffee farmers in the Cordilleras, the region where I was born. The farmers of the Cordilleras are hardworking growers who have inherited this livelihood from their ancestors and who no doubt will pass it on to their children now.

Arabica coffee beans in the Codilleras ready for harvest.

Since 2005, I have been happily volunteering and organizing programs for Coffee AID (Assistance for Indigenous Development), a non-profit collective bringing coffee farmers and coffee enthusiasts together.

Many hands make light work, and twice a year, Coffee AID takes volunteers to work in the farms to plant, harvest, and process coffee—letting young professionals, coffee enthusiasts and coffee newbies alike become part of the inspiring coffee story.

I have left my heart in the coffee mountains for I have always pined for those trips to the farm. I just knew I needed to do something to bring it closer to my life. What followed was this dream of a social venture that would bring the story of Philippine coffee to Vancouver.

Sharing Cultures through Coffee

Last year, Coffee AID started to introduce directly sourced, fair-trade, organically grown Philippine coffee from Coffee AID farmers to the city of Vancouver. Our mission is to elevate Philippine coffee to specialty level

EDITED BY ELEANOR R. LAQUIAN

and expand Philippine coffee market for sustainably sourced coffee among coffee shops.

Through pop-up coffee booths and partnering with local roasters, Coffee AID offers single-origin coffee beans—and by holding coffee appreciation workshops, we hope to share the story of our indigenous farmers.

By doing this, we hope that it will translate to a better livelihood for Philippine coffee farmers.

Every cup has a story, and through each coffee shared, we aim to tell the story of Filipino perseverance, patience, and hospitality, in a transformative and lasting way.

Join us in connecting cultures through coffee. *Tara, kape tayo!*Come, let's coffee. To learn more about Coffee AID and to get your trial supply of Philippine coffee for tasting, email Iona@CoffeeAid.net. Special sampler packs and coffee appreciation workshops will be offered at the Groundswell Community Marketplace in Granville Island on Tuesdays 11 am to 4 pm this summer.

CanadianFilipino.Net's social media and newsletter coordinator Iona Santos-Fresnoza has worked in government, IT, academe, and the non-profit sector. She believes in diversity and inclusion. A relentless learner, she is also a fair-trade coffee advocate.

Chapter 4:
WHEN SUCCESS MEETS FILIPINOS

Chapter four focuses on raising the profile of Filipinos in Canada by celebrating Filipinos who have succeeded in various field of academia, arts, business, community-building, education, government, healthcare, law, politics, public service, sciences, sports, and technology. Many of them have attained international recognition in some fields as well.

Their success depends on who they are, what professional expertise, technical skills, political awareness, entrepreneurship, community spirit, and Filipino values they bring to Canada, and what they do with the opportunities they find in their adopted country. The Canadian government has recognized their contributions to Canada by proclaiming June as Filipino Heritage Month.

CanadianFilipino.Net honours them with its annual presentation of Outstanding Filipinos in Canada, to showcase their success, despite systemic barriers that confront immigrants, and inspire younger generations of Filipinos to dare and dream.

Although Filipinos seemed to have come in "under the radar," and have long remained there, they have now come out from the shadows—as shown by the many outstanding Filipinos featured in this book. This chapter also heralds the achievements of Filipinos in small towns, where they are making a difference.

An inspiring story of young Filipinos turning hardships into opportunities is the worldwide success of Marvi Yap and Anna Maramba. They are the two young women—co-founder-owner-directors—behind the AV Communications in Toronto,which is a successful niche advertising agency that links mainstream brands to the ethnic consumer

They have been named "the multicultural moguls" by no less than the *Financial Post*. Theirs is the typical journey of Canadian Filipinos who pursue their dreams and contribute to Canada's development and standing in the world. 🍁

Canada Proclaims Filipino Heritage Month

By Dr. Rey D. Pagtakhan and Rachel Ramos-Reid

Salma Zahid, Liberal MP for Scarborough Centre in Ontario, filed the motion designating June as Filipino Heritage Month.

November 19, 2018 – Filipino Heritage Month, a brainchild of Canadian Filipina Paulina Corpuz, is a story of inspiration and perseverance. As president of the Philippine Advancement Through Arts and Culture—a network for advancing issues of concern to people of Filipino origin— Corpuz felt a need to make the traditional celebration of Philippine Independence more meaningful for the younger and future generations to reflect upon. She thought a monthlong celebration of Philippine culture might be a good start to arouse their interest about their Filipino roots.

When she was told that fifty public endorsements were needed for a Filipino Heritage Month declaration by the government, she worked to get the required signatures.

On November 8, 2017, exactly a year after Corpuz' brainchild was conceived, the City of Toronto gave its unanimous nod, and a request to the federal government "to declare June as Filipino Heritage Month in 2018, and for future years," making Toronto the first and only city in Canada to celebrate Filipino Heritage Month.

Other cities followed.

The birth of FHM

In January 2018, Liberal MP for Scarborough Centre in Ontario Salma Zahid sponsored Motion 155. The motion asked the government to "recognize the contributions that Filipino-Canadians have made to Canadian society, the richness of the Filipino language and culture, and the importance of reflecting upon Filipino heritage for future generations by declaring June, every year, Filipino Heritage Month."

Canada's House of Commons unanimously passed Zahid's Motion 155 on October 30, 2018. Thus, Filipino Heritage Month in Canada saw its birth after nearly a two-year gestation period. Filipino Heritage Month had its inaugural celebration in June 2019. June is an important month for Filipinos because it is when they celebrate Philippine independence Day on June 12. The first FHM was celebrated in Filipino communities across Canada.

CanadianFilipino.Net swelled with enormous pride when this online biweekly was among those mentioned during deliberations at the House of Commons about the declaration of June as Filipino Heritage Month nationwide.

Specifically, Chandra Arya, Liberal MP for the Ontario riding of Nepean, rose on the floor of the House on October 25, 2018 to support the declaration.

"There are many organizations in Canada working hard to keep the Filipino culture alive," Arya said. "One is *CanadianFilipino.Net,* a group of Canadian Filipinos who are passionate about raising the profile of Filipinos in Canada by providing news and views of Canadian Filipino communities across the country," Arya continued.

Five days later, on October 30, 2018, the House unanimously approved Motion 155, which declared June of every year as Filipino Heritage Month in Canada. It was not until the following June 2019 when the actual celebration by Filipino communities across Canada began.

Reasons for Proclaiming FHM

The 2016 Census established that immigrants from the Philippines comprised the biggest group of new arrivals who came to Canada from 2011 to 2016.

According to Statistics Canada, a total of 1.2 million new arrivals entered Canada within that five-year period, with Filipinos representing the biggest fraction at 15.6 percent. All in all, some 188,805 immigrants from the Philippines arrived in Canada from 2011 to 2016. Based on this Census, Filipinos comprise the fourth-largest visible group in Canada, and the fastest-growing then.

On June 1, 2018 Alberta Premier Rachel Notley and Lieutenant Governor Lois Mitchell signed a provincial proclamation designating June every year as Philippine Heritage Month, making it the first Canadian province to do so.

"Alberta is the proud home to the second-largest Filipino population in the country," Premier Notley said in a news release issued June 3. "For decades, Filipinos have enriched our province with their culture, their languages, and their skills."

Criteria for CFNet's Selection of Outstanding Filipinos in Canada

July 1, 2021 – As Filipino Heritage Month 2021 comes to a close, the editorial board of *CanadianFilipino.Net* is pleased to present its first list of notable Filipinos, who have excelled in various fields, helped Filipinos and Canadians alike and contributed to Canada's multicultural image in the world. This will be an annual feature of CFNet, to highlight outstanding Filipinos in Canada as they straddle Eastern and Western cultures while playing a significant role in Canada's development and progress as a multicultural country.

The CFNet selection is based on merit, because being notable is not a matter of opinion, but merit makes it empirically obvious when one is outstanding.

The editorial board uses the following CFNet criteria for selecting its Annual List of Outstanding Filipinos in Canada:

- They should have achieved their potential (in education and/or work experience) and
- Have helped or influenced Filipinos and Canadians alike with lasting effect, not just as "one-day wonders"
- While contributing to the multicultural nature of Canadian society and/or
- Whose achievements helped to promote Canada's progress and prosperity at home and stature in the world.

The CFNet's Outstanding Filipinos in Canada 2021 list includes Professor Leonora Angeles, Steve Coroza, Leonardo B. Cunanan, Phil de Luna, Eleanor Del Rio-Laquian, Dr. Eileen de Villa, Ma-Anne Dionisio, Michelle Elliot, Mable Elmore, Delia Laglagaron, Professor Aprodicio A. Laquian, Dr. Rey D. Pagtakhan, and Fely Villasin.

CFNet's Outstanding Filipinos in Canada, 2021

Professor Leonora C. Angeles of UBC, Filipino community leader and organizer, was among pioneering professors who developed women's, gender and feminist studies in the Philippines in the late 1980s, first at the St. Scholastica's College Institute of Women's Studies, then at De La Salle, and then the University of the Philippines (Diliman) Department of Political Science, where she developed the first women and gender studies courses on women and politics in 1986 and 1987.

She finished her BA (1984) and MA (1989) in political science at the University of the Philippines, her diploma in women and development policies (1986) at the University of Nottingham, and her PhD in political studies (1995) at Queen's University in Ontario.

Since resettling in Canada in 1993, she has taught at four universities: Queen's University, University of Regina, University of Saskatchewan, and the University of British Columbia, where she is currently an associate professor at the School of Community and Regional Planning and the Institute for Gender, Race, Sexuality and Social Justice, teaching courses on gender, global issues, social justice and development, qualitative research methods, field-based participatory planning, and action research.

She helped develop the UBC Asian-Canadian and Asian Migration minor program, and mentored undergraduate and graduate students in the UBC Philippine Studies Series and Philippine International Planning Studio course at SCARP. She has been president of the National Pilipino Canadian Cultural Centre since 2020 and the Canadian Council on Southeast Asian Studies since 2019.

She is a prolific writer, lecturer, and researcher. Her path-breaking MA thesis, "Getting the Right Mix of Feminism and Nationalism: The Discourse on the Woman Question and Politics of the Women's Movement" is a must-read for researchers of the history and political sociology of women's movements in the Philippines.

Since 1987, she has been principal investigator of several research projects funded by Social Science and Humanities Research Council of Canada, and other funding agencies, beginning with her Ford Foundation grant under the auspices of the UP Centre for Integrative and Development Studies. She has served as expert witness for human rights and civil cases involving Filipinos in Canadian courts. She writes regular columns for online and print newspapers and is a sought-after commentator for the Canadian Broadcasting Corporation Radio and TV, The Filipino Channel, CityNews Vancouver, and Omni TV.

She has received numerous awards: Gawad Dangal ng Plaridel (Pride of Plaridel Award), Category: Expatriate Filipinos (2009); Bright Lights Award of Pacific Immigrant Resources Society (2010); Filipino Who's Who in British Columbia, Dahong Pilipino Award (2011); Most Outstanding Alumna (Education) of St. JamesAcademy in PlaridelBulacan (2012); Queen Elizabeth Diamond Jubilee Award (2013); University of British Columbia Service (2016); and Civic Merit Award of City of Vancouver (2018).

 **Steve Coroza** is the first and only Canadian Filipino to be appointed to the Court of Appeal for Ontario, and before this, to the Superior Court of Justice in Ontario and the Ontario Court of Justice. The federal Department of Justice announced his appointment as Justice of the Court of Appeals for Ontario in April 2020.

David Lametti, Minister of Justice and Attorney General of Canada, said in his announcement that Coroza was appointed to the Ontario Court of Justice (St. Catharines) in 2009 and to the Superior Court of Justice (Brampton) in 2013.

Coroza was born in Belleville, Ontario, and raised in Toronto. His parents are Lota Banate Coroza of Roxas City in Capiz and Romy Mabilangan Coroza of Santo Tomas town in Batangas.

He received his Bachelor of Laws degree from the University of Windsor and was admitted to the Bar of Ontario in 1997. He also received a Master of Laws degree from Osgoode Hall Law School in 2003.

He was a staff duty counsel for Ontario Legal Aid in Toronto from 1997 to 1998. From 1998 to 2009, he was senior counsel with the Department of Justice and the Public Prosecution Service of Canada, with criminal law being his main area of practice.

He was a member of the Federation of Asian Canadian Lawyers. He is a past adjunct instructor of the trial advocacy course at Osgoode Hall Law School and a guest instructor with the University of Notre Dame Law School.

Coroza frequently participates as a panelist in continuing education programs for lawyers and judges. He is also a co-author of the publication *Sentencing Drug Offenders.*

Leonardo B. Cunanan, founding editor of *Dahong Pilipino* is a pillar of the Filipino community. *Dahong Pilipino* is to Filipino businesses and consumers in British Columbia what the yellow pages are to telephone users. It is the only Canadian Filipino community and business directory in BC that has published continuously for almost thirty years. Cunanan started it in 1991 as a business directory serving as a reliable guide for the local Filipino community and other residents of BC.

The directory provides the names, addresses and phone numbers of Filipino businesses, professionals, and community leaders and organizations. It also features successful Filipinos in their respective professions and businesses, to serve as role models and inspiration to younger Filipinos. Its goals are to project a positive image of Canadian Filipinos and to highlight their contributions to Canadian society in general.

In 2011, Cunanan transformed it from a print publication to a modern online directory at *DahongPilipino.ca.* Now, it is not only a business directory, but a community and business directory. Its website gets over four thousand hits per month. Now on its thirtieth year of publication, it continues to improve its contents for Filipinos, and to keep track of developments in the home country as well as current events in Filipino communities in BC. Cunanan arrived in Vancouver in 1971. In addition to his fulltime job at the YMCA, he published the first Filipino community paper, *The Philippine Chronicle*, in 1981—but sold it to devote more time to *Dahong Pilipino*. His son Leo. Jr. took over when he became a member of the Immigration and Refugee Board (1997–2005).

Phil de Luna, at twenty-nine, is a rising young star in climate change focused on getting ahead of the rapidly changing world by way of clean, renewable energy.

Of his many hats, the most recent and current is as program director of National Research Council Canada's Energy Materials Challenge Program, a seven-year, fifty-seven-million-dollar, multidisciplinary, collaborative research program aimed at developing made-in-Canada material solutions to decarbonize the country to transition to net-zero emissions by year 2050—a goal legislated by the Canadian government in late 2020. His appointment in 2019 makes De Luna the youngest ever to hold such an executive level position at NRC.

De Luna also sits as vice chair of the Carbon Management Canada Research Institute's board of directors, is a member of Canada's Organisation for Economic Co-operation and Development's Advanced Materials Steering Committee and the founding mentor of Creative Destruction Lab, a non-profit helping science-based start-ups bring technology to market.

The many awards to his name include *Forbes's* 2019 Top Thirty Under Thirty, the 2020–21 Action Canada Fellowship, and a Governor General's Gold Medal.

De Luna was only five when his family left the Philippines for Canada, where he grew up without much money in suburban Windsor, Ontario—but his parents made sure he got a good education. He plunged headfirst into academe, earning degrees in quick succession: a bachelor's in chemistry from the University of Windsor in 2013, and a master's in chemistry in 2015 and postgraduate degree in materials science and engineering in 2018—both from the University of Toronto.

Explaining NRC's mission, De Luna said that the program portfolio currently consists of twenty collaborative research projects across four countries, including Canada, the UK, Germany, and the US. "The areas we cover include new materials to convert carbon dioxide into renewable fuels and chemicals, new materials to produce low-carbon hydrogen, and robotic self-driving labs to help accelerate the pace of discovery." He explains that typically, the process from idea or hypothesis to actual commercial rollout takes about twenty years, but they try to make it faster by using artificial intelligence and robotics to help automate some of their experiments. The impact will be technologies that help meet Canada's net-zero emissions goals by 2050, resulting in a healthier and more sustainable Canada for everyone.

 **Eleanor Del Rio-Laquian** did her BA in journalism and literature at Maryknoll College in Manila, her MA in public administration at the University of the Philippines, and postgraduate studies at the School of Public Communications, Boston University in the US. She has a career as an international civil servant, journalist, editor, author, researcher, and activist community organizer. Before she immigrated to Canada in 1969, she worked as an information writer for the UN Food and Agriculture Organization Regional Office for Asia, based in Bangkok, Thailand, the UN Information Centre in Manila, and the World Health Organization regional office for Asia and the Western Pacific.

In Canada, she worked at IDRC (International Development Research Centre) in Ottawa, which sent her to the IDRC Regional Office for Africa based in Kenya as project coordinator from 1977 to 1979, to help train African graduate students in social science research. She became fluent in Swahili. From 1984 to 1990, she was bureau manager and researcher for *TheNew York Times* in Beijing, China, where she became fluent in Mandarin Chinese.

Back in Canada in 1991, she was researcher and manager for administration and programs at the Institute of Asian Research, University of British Columbia (1991–2000). As primary researcher and coordinator of the Institute's Asian Immigration project, she organized an international conference on Asian immigration and racism in Canada in 1998. It resulted in a book, *Asian Immigration and Racism in Canada*, which she edited with professors Aprodicio Laquian and Terry McGee.

She also edited a coffee table book about the first environmentally sensitive building on the UBC campus—*Design for the Next Millennium: The C. K. Choi Building for the Institute of Asian Research*—published by UBC in 1995. In addition, with her husband, Aprodicio Laquian, she co-authored *Seeking a Better life Abroad (A Study of Filipinos in Canada, 1957–2007)*, published by Anvil Publishing in Manila in 2008.

She is the first and only researcher who has conducted a nationwide questionnaire-plus-personal-interview survey of Filipinos in Canada—which she did by driving cross-country from Ottawa to Vancouver in 1972, interviewing Filipinos along the way for her University of the Philippines master's thesis on administrative and policy aspects of Filipino immigration to Canada. It was published by the United Council of Filipino Associations in Canada (UCFAC) in Ottawa in 1973 as *A Study of Filipino Immigrants in Canada, 1952–1972*.

After retiring from UBC in 2000, she volunteered with the Vancouver Committee for Domestic Workers and Caregivers Rights, teaching English to caregivers, writing funding proposals for their activities, and organizing the "Singing Nannies" as a CDWCR fundraiser, with herself as guitarist.

In 2016, she helped set up the Maple Bamboo Network Society, a non-profit that publishes *CanadianFilipino.Net*, a nationwide online newsmagazine for and about Filipinos in Canada. She has been the editor of this biweekly publication since 2016 to date.

Dr. Eileen de Villa, a Boston-born and Toronto-raised Canadian Filipino, is at the forefront of Toronto's fight against COVID-19. As Medical Health Officer for Toronto, a post she has held since March 2017, she heads the biggest local public health agency in Canada. The Toronto Public Health Agency provides public health programs and services to 2.9 million residents.

In March 2019, she led a number of municipal groups, health coalitions, and advocacy organizations in protesting Ontario Premier Doug

Ford's cuts to provincial public health funding. In a statement to reporters in April, she warned that the cuts would have "significant negative impacts on the health of Toronto residents." Toronto estimates a loss of provincial funding of about one billion dollars over the next ten years, thereby doing without services like free injection sites.

De Villa may have inherited her "champion of the people" genes from her parents, cardiologist Dr. Maria Antonina de Villa and the late Dr. Guillermo de Villa, an obstetrician-gynecologist. She was born in Boston, where her parents did their residencies. In 1972, the family returned to the Philippines, but political unrest during the Marcos regime soon made them immigrate to Canada.

Hesitating at first to follow in her parents' footsteps, de Villa finished a science degree with majors in psychology and women's health at McGill University. An internship with the United Nations supporting developing countries led her to become interested in "community health," as it was called at that time. It was then that she realized she could help even more within public health if she became a doctor. She went on to complete her Doctor of Medicine and Master of Health Sciences degrees from the University of Toronto, and a Master of Business Administration from the Schulich School of Business.

After serving as Peel Region's medical officer of health, de Villa was appointed to Toronto Public Health's top position in 2017. She quickly came to realize that the city faces a formidable enemy: the opioid crisis. Though very controversial, de Villa advocates for the decriminalization of all drugs for personal use. She released a report on the issue last year, adding that "Our belief, based on the evidence, is that the criminalization of people who take drugs is actually contributing to this opioid overdose emergency . . . because it forces people into unsafe drug practices and presents a barrier to those who might be seeking help."

Ma-Anne Dionisiois an award winning singer-actress with a bright future. After taking the Toronto Broadway by storm and getting nods from the Dora Mavor Moore Award for her role as Kim in the Toronto production of *Miss Saigon*, she became the second Asian to play Eponine, after Filipino singer-actress Lea Salonga, in the international and US productions of *Les Misérables*.

Before moving to Canada with her parents and siblings in 1989 and settling in Winnipeg, Dionisio started dabbling in musical performance by joining singing contests on television back in the Philippines when she was fourteen years old.

In Canada, she indulged her love of music by joining the church choir at St. Edward's Parish in Winnipeg, Manitoba. Dionisio started her professional singing career after winning the lead role in "Experience Canada: Spirit of a Nation," a musical tour that celebrated Canada's 125th anniversary. Her love for performance art didn't stop at acting and singing; she is also one of the founding artists of Theatre 20, a musical theatre company formed by Toronto artists in 2009.

Dionisio has performed as Maria in *West Side Story* at Ontario's Stratford Festival and appeared on Broadway as "Little Girl" in the 2002 revival of *Flower Drum Song*. In February 2016, she was cast in the Broadway musical *Closer than Ever* staged at the Gateway Theatre in Richmond, BC. She also starred in *The Secret Garden*, directed by Theatre Calgary's artistic director Stafford Arima. The musical was Dionisio's debut with Theatre Calgary.

The Toronto-based singer and actress keeps busy with film and TV. She played the role of Patricia in *The Waiting Room*, a Canadian drama film released in 2015, and has a recurring role in *Schitt's Creek*, a TV comedy series.

 **Michelle Elliot** was only twelve when her family moved to Canada from Manila. It was at CBC that Eliot started her career, first as an intern eighteen years ago, after graduating from BC Institute of Technology's broadcast journalism diploma program. Eliot worked as an associate producer, reporter, and guest host on local and national CBC programs: *The Early Edition, On the Coast,* and *The180.*

She now hosts *BCToday,* a daily noon-hour call-in show on CBC. It airs Monday to Friday. The provincewide radio show engages callers in sharing their opinions about current issues, as well as provides an open platform for virtually any topic callers may wish to discuss.

Her work has been recognized by the Radio Television Digital News Association and the Jack Webster Foundation, garnering awards for stories she either produced or wrote. She has worked as a journalist at CBC for over twenty years.

 **MLA Mable Elmore,** holds the record for being the first politician of Filipino heritage to get elected as B.C. Member of Legislative Assembly in 2009. She was re-elected in 2013 and 2017 and cruised to victory on election night in 2020 for a fourth term as MLA representative of Vancouver-Kensington in the October 24 provincial election.. She serves as Parliamentary Secretary for Poverty Reduction for NDP.

Elmore is passionate about building community engagement and connecting people around issues that matter to them. She is dedicated to doing whatever she can to make the lives of people in her community— and across BC—better, and has worked tirelessly on a wide range of immigrant, social justice, and workers' rights issues.

Elmore wouldn't offer any hints on her possible Cabinet position. "If I'm called, [in] whatever capacity, I'm willing to serve." If given a choice, though, she'd like to work in areas she has been involved in—namely, immigration, temporary foreign workers, multiculturalism, and finance.

"My heart is really to be of service to the community and to work on behalf of the community. My view is that government should work for the people," she said.

A known advocate of immigrant rights, Elmore considers affordability the top issue that needs to be addressed. Working with immigrant communities, Elmore said their individual stories impressed her, citing a meeting with a twenty-two-year-old newcomer from the Philippines who can barely afford to pay 550 dollars per course to upgrade her skills. Elmore considers it an important issue to provide affordable post-secondary education.

She lamented the fact that British Columbians have the highest student debt. "The government receives a higher collection from student debt than from corporate taxes." She said there is "chronic underfunding" of schools, while the dropout rate for immigrant youth is "critical."

Meanwhile, Elmore noted that Filipinos come to Canada with higher levels of education than others, but end up receiving the lowest wages. "We have to make sure our foreign credentials are recognized in the province."

As a second-generation Canadian Filipino, Elmore is only one among very few elected officials in Canada who are of Filipino heritage. A staunch advocate for caregivers and immigrants' rights, social justice, and women, gay, lesbian, and transgender issues, Elmore is likewise passionate about concerns regarding affordable housing and childcare, accessible education, and the need for mental health support for youth and children.

Prior to her election as MLA, Mable worked as a transit operator for ten years for the Coast Mountain Bus Company, and became an advocate for workers' rights. Over that time, she played an active role within her union—Canadian Auto Workers Local 111—and led successful campaigns as a transit advocate in Vancouver's Canadian Filipino community.

Elmore's mother immigrated to Canada from the Philippines as a nurse in 1965, and met Elmore's father, of Irish descent and a manager at a pulp and paper mill in Prince Rupert, BC. Two years later, Elmore was born in Langley—but she spent her youth in Winnipeg, Manitoba. After high school, she studied physical education at the University of British Columbia. Elmore has resided in Vancouver for over twenty years.

Delia D. Laglagaron was the deputy commissioner and deputy administrative officer of the Greater Vancouver Regional District, now called "Metro Vancouver." GVRD was the primary planning body for the Lower Mainland of BC.

She has an architecture degree from the University of Santo Tomas in Manila, and topped the national architectural board in 1975.

She also has a master's degree in urban and regional planning from the University of the Philippines. She immigrated to Canada in 1976.

In 1994–95, she went on study leave from GVRD to get a master's degree in public administration from the Kennedy School of Government at Harvard University in the US.

On her return to GVRD, she was promoted in rapid succession until she got the second highest executive position at GVRD. She retired in 2015.

 **Professor Aprodicio Arcilla Laquian** obtained a Bachelor degree in public administration, *cum laude,*from the University of the Philippines in 1959 and a PhD in political science and urban studies from MIT in the US in 1965.

Due to political turmoil in the Philippines, he immigrated his family to Canada in 1969 and worked as director of research at the International Association of Metropolitan Research in Toronto (1969–70), as associate director of social sciences at the International Development and Research in Ottawa (1971–77) and as project director at the IDRC Regional Office for Africa, based in Nairobi, Kenya (1977–79).

In 1981, he joined the United Nations Population Fund as country director for the South Pacific (1982–84) and as country director for China, Outer Mongolia, and North Korea (1984–90). After six and a half years in China, he was credited by China's Family Planning Commission for averting about twenty-four million births by funding modern contraceptive factories with his fourteen-million-dollar annual UNPF budget and improving family planning programs to minimize abortions during China's one-child family campaign.

In 1991, he returned to UNPF-HQ in New York as head of its Evaluation Division.

His academic career included jobs as professor at the University of the Philippines (1965–68); visiting professor at the University of Hawaii (1969–70), University of Nairobi (1977–79), and De La Salle University in Manila (1979–81); honorary professor at Peking University (1984–90); and professor and acting director of MIT's Special Program in Urban and Regional Studies (2001–02). He is now a professor emeritus of community and regional planning at UBC, after having retired in 2000 as a tenured professor and director of the UBC Centre for Human Settlements (1991–2000).

After UBC, Laquian served briefly as Chief of Staff to Philippine President Joseph Estrada in 2000, a year as resident scholar at the Woodrow Wilson Center for International Scholars in Washington, DC in 2001, as a consultant for Asian Development Bank, and as a coordinator for a study of basic urban services in seven hundred cities and towns in sixteen Asia-Pacific countries funded by United Cities and Local Governments in Barcelona, Spain and the UN HABITAT in Nairobi.

He has international recognition, and a reputation as one of the world's top researcher-practitioners in the integrated fields of comprehensive city and regional planning, local government, and reforms. He has authored twenty books and numerous articles on urban planning, governance, and delivery of urban infrastructure and services to the poor.

He is president and CEO of Maple Bamboo Network Society, the non-profit publisher of CFNet, the online nationwide news magazine for Canadian Filipinos.

The Honorable Dr. Rey D. Pagtakhan, PC, OM, LLD, ScD, MD, MSc, made history as the only MP of Filipino heritage in Canadian history when he was elected to the House of Commons—the highest elective body in Canada—on November 21, 1988, almost twenty-one years after he immigrated to Canada on January 6, 1968. Up until his election, he was a professor of pediatrics and child health at the University of Manitoba Faculty of Medicine and director of the Manitoba Cystic Fibrosis Center at the Winnipeg Children's Hospital.

He had written several book chapters and articles for textbooks and journals, and had lectured widely, in Canada and abroad.

A 1961 graduate of the University of the Philippines (UP), Dr. Pagtakhan did his initial postgraduate training at the UP–Philippine General Hospital as a research assistant (1961–63); his first research paper won the 1962 Manila Medical Society First Prize Award. Then, he went to

St. Louis Children's Hospital of Washington University School of Medicine as a resident and fellow in cardiology (1963–67), where he held a two-year Missouri and St. Louis Heart Association Joint Research Fellowship Award. Later, he came to the WCH and UM Faculty of Graduate Studies and Research as a fellow in respirology and postgrad student in perinatal physiology on a fellowship grant (1968–71).

Four months after Dr. Pagtakhan took his oath of office as MP, Canadian historian Charlotte Gray wrote in the *Canadian Medical Association Journal*, "Pagtakhan is the sole MD in the Liberal ranks . . . also, the first Canadian MP to have been born in the Philippines. His history is that of every successful Canadian immigrant: a combination of hard work and community values, combined with humour and enthusiasm for his adopted country."

Reflected award-winning writer/broadcaster Lesley Hughes in her 2005 book, *We Chose Canada: Eleven Profiles from Manitoba's Mosaic*, "There is no shortage of tangible results to which Rey Pagtakhan can point as his legacy, but the intangible effects of his life in this country may be even more crucial to its development.

"Of the man who was educated as a boy by the generosity of his community, then Prime Minister Jean Chrétien may have made the best observation. 'Rey,' he said, "represents what this country is all about.'"

He takes pride in having persuaded two ministers of immigration to permit two Filipina deportees back into Canada and obtaining cabinet support to compensate aboriginal veterans and former prisoners of war who were late in filing their claims for benefits. Presently, he volunteers on the Advisory Council of Immigration Partnership Winnipeg and the Board of the St. Paul's College Foundation at the University of Manitoba.

Dr. Pagtakhan contributes regularly to Winnipeg-based *Pilipino Express* and the - *CanadianFilipino.Net* newsmagazine with his semi-monthly column *Medisina at Politika*, devoted almost exclusively to the COVID-19 pandemic since February 2020.

A biographee in *Canadian Who's Who* and former parliamentary secretary to Prime Minister Jean Chrétien, Canadian Filipino Dr. Pagtakhan is the recipient of many honours, medals, and awards, including lifelong membership in the Privy Council for Canada (since 2001), Silver (1977),

Gold (2002), and Diamond (2012) Jubilee Medals from Queen Elizabeth II, the Philippine Jaycees's Most Outstanding Filipino Overseas for Medicine (1981), the Canadian Society for Clinical Investigations's Travelling Fellowship Award (held while on sabbatical leave as Visiting Professor of Pediatrics at the University of Arizona College of Medicine, 1982–83), recognition as the UP Medical Alumni Society's Most Distinguished Alumnus (1992), the Philippine Presidential Citation (1997), honorary doctor's of laws (2002) and doctor's of science (2010) degrees, the UP College of Medicine Centennial Award for Community Service (2005), and the Order of Manitoba (2017). The City of Winnipeg has designated a Dr. Rey Pagtakhan Park in St. Vital, where his family resided while he served as Winnipeg police commissioner and chair of the finance and personnel committees of its School Division No. 6.

Fely Villasin graduated with a BSc in foreign service from the University of the Philippines at age fifteen because she was accelerated in elementary and high school. She received a four-year scholarship to study at the Sorbonne in Paris, and on her return to Manila, worked at the French Embassy in the Philippines before she immigrated to Canada in 1974.

She was one of the early Filipino activists in Toronto advocating for social justice, which she had started doing in the Philippines—where she was a vocal critic of the Marcos dictatorship. She and her husband, Ruben Cusipag, had to leave the Philippines to avoid persecution by Marcos's supporters. They continued their activism in Toronto until the popular uprising, called "EDSA," the people revolution, with the support of the United States, ended the Marcos dictatorship in 1986. Cory Aquino became president through the strength of people power.

In Toronto, Villasin set up INTERCEDE in 1979 to champion the rights of domestic workers and caregivers. She organized other Filipino activists to fight for landed immigrant status for domestic workers and caregivers—a fight yet to be won. They advocated full coverage for domestic workers in the Ontario Employment Standards Act and, in the Ontario Human

Rights Code, the granting of full coverage for domestic workers under the Workers' Compensation Act and upholding of the right of domestic workers to organize under Ontario's Labour Relations Act. As founder and coordinator of INTERCEDE, she devoted herself to the rights of domestic workers and caregivers in Canada—mostly Filipinos—until she succumbed to cancer in 2006 at age sixty-five. She was survived by her daughter Nadine.

She was also one of the founders of the Kababayan Community Centre, the Kapisanan Philippine Centre, and, in 1982, the Carlos Bolosan Theatre, the only longstanding professional Filipino-Canadian theatre company in Toronto, for which she wrote plays and acted for many years as a pastime.

CFNet's Outstanding Filipinos in Canada, 2022

January 1, 2022 – There are almost a million Canadians of Filipino ancestry all over Canada today. They are found not only in big cities, but also in small towns, where they are beginning to make a difference. The current Canadian Filipino community includes a growing number of 1.5 and second generation Filipinos raised and/or born in Canada by first-wave Filipino immigrants who arrived in the 1960s. They are now ready to take their rightful place in Canadian society.

This year's list of outstanding Filipinos in Canada includes names that can rival any name in the Ministry of Diversity and Inclusion's current list of notables. They are: **Marichu Antonio**, Calgary's 2020 Citizen of the Year; **Paulina Corpuz**, initiator of Filipino Heritage Month; sixteen-year-old **Leylah Annie Fernandez,** the number-one junior tennis champion in the world in 2019; **Eleanor Guerrero-Campbell,** cofounder of Multicultural Helping House; **Emmie Joaquin,** multimedia pioneer; **Ann Makosinski,** Under-30 scientist and inventor; **Flor Marcelino,** politician and glass-ceiling-breaker in Manitoba; **SYM Mendoza**, Legendary artist and maestro; **Tony** and **Marissa Peña,** philanthropists; **Mayrose Salvador,** cofounder and director of Pueblo

Science; **Mel Tobias,** maven of the arts; **Marvi Yap**and **Anna Maramba,** advertising "multicultural moguls," **Stephanie Valenzuela,** first Canadian Filipino elected to Montreal City Council and **Rechie Valdez**, first female Canadian Filipino elected MP in 2021.

Marichu Antoniomade history as the City of Calgary's Citizen of the Year in 2020, when on June 1, 2021, the City of Calgary unveiled recipients of its 2020 Calgary Awards.

A champion of multiculturalism and diversity, Antonio thus became the first woman of colour and Canadian Filipino to receive such an honour.

The city established the Calgary Awards in 1994 to celebrate the achievements and contributions of its residents. Individuals, corporations, community groups, and organizations receive awards in five major categories, and Antonio was one of those honoured for community achievement.

Online, City Councillor Antonio was recognized as a "pioneering leader with fifty years of experience in community development and advocacy." And as executive director of ActionDignity, formerly the Ethno-Cultural Council of Calgary, for twelve years, the Canadian Filipino raised the "collective voice of culturally diverse communities" in the city.

"ActionDignity serves as a platform for over a hundred ethnocultural organizations that promote collaboration toward more equitable policies and accessible and culturally relevant services," the city announced. Antonio grew ActionDignity to become an "important advocate for racial equity and social change."

Passionate about communities, Marichu meets crisis head on, instigating innovative approaches to community-led action. During the pandemic, she quickly shifted ActionDignity's focus to emergency support to Calgarians, including essential workers in the Cargill and JBS meat plants.

She co-founded the Multilingual Hotline in response to COVID-19, and sits as a key player in the Calgary East Zone Newcomers Collaborative. Offering support in 24 languages, CENC served 12,400 COVID-impacted

Calgarians with food and financial and mental health support as they healed with dignity. Marichu's leadership is felt in many city initiatives, including Calgary's Cultural Plan, the Calgary Local Immigration Partnership, Calgary Arts Development's Initiative, and Advocacy for Workers' Rights. She retired from ActionDignity in June 2021.

Paulina Corpuz is the initiator of the effort to celebrate June nationwide as Filipino Heritage Month. She worked hard to make it come true until on October 30, 2018, when June was officially declared Filipino Heritage Month every year nationwide.

June 2019 was busy and memorable for Corpuz as she celebrated the first FHM in Canada. She organized *Larawan* (Tagalog for photograph) an exhibit featuring inspiring images of Canadian Filipinos. It's a project of Philippine Advancement Through Arts and Culture, an organization for which Corpuz was founding president.

Corpuz also chaired a community get-together for the Philippine Independence Day Council to celebrate Filipino heritage. In addition, she participated in the June 12 flag-raising event of the PIDC, held at Toronto City Hall. During that occasion, she was recognized for her role in initiating the declaration of Filipino Heritage Month in the city, an initiative that led to similar declarations in other provinces across the country. Corpuz's brainchild culminated in the 2018 declaration by the House of Commons of June as Filipino Heritage Month throughout Canada.

"The work is not done," Corpuz told *CanadianFilipino.Net*. "The declaration is just a step toward the goal to make us visible." According to Corpuz, the Canadian Filipino community's biggest challenge is invisibility. "Yes, we are one of the largest diverse communities. Yet we are not visible in important places, such as in the three levels of government—we do not see our faces around the governing table."

She believes that much education is needed. "We have to inspire our community and our younger generations to engage in civic and political affairs," she stated. "We have to be courageous in raising our voices and to step up." She urges Filipinos to be active in supporting young Canadian Filipinos, particularly artists. "Right now, it is active in the Greater Toronto Area," she said about PATAC. "It would be great if other Filipino organizations become part of PATAC as allies, and work towards a strategic goal to engage and promote our community's agenda."

Corpuz was born in the Philippine. She studied psychology at the University of the Philippines in Diliman, Quezon City. She was active in the student movement during the time of President Ferdinand Marcos. She came to Canada in 1993 with her daughter to join her husband, Ben. Scarborough Southwest has been her family's home for years. She is an entrepreneur-CEO of an accounting and bookkeeping company, as well as writer, producer, and host of the Filipino TV program, *Workers' Agenda*. She also cohosts TV Migrante.

Corpuz was the past president of the Filipino-Canadian Parents Association in Catholic Education. She's an organizer of the Filipino Workers Network. She is on the PIDC board. She was also recognized as Pinoy of the Year by the Golden Balangay in 2018. She has been recognized by the Canadian Multicultural Council–Asians in Ontario and the University of the Philippines Alumni Association in Toronto for her more than thirty years of community service and her work toward declaring June Filipino Heritage Month. Toronto was the first jurisdiction in Canada to declare June Filipino Heritage Month in 2017.

Sixteen-year-old **Leylah Annie Fernandez of Québec** as the number-one junior tennis player in the world in 2019—gave Canada cause to celebrate in the international tennis scene on June 8, 2019. She became the first Canadian to win the French Open junior singles title at the Roland-Garros clay courts in Paris. Aside from being the first Canadian to ever win the French Open juniors championship, Fernandez holds the distinction of winning a junior Grand Slam singles title since Felix Auger-Aliassime won the 2016 junior U.S. Open in 2016. She is also the first Canadian female to win a title since Eugenie Bouchard won junior Wimbledon in 2012.

The left-handed Fernandez, from Laval, Québec, is the daughter of a Canadian Filipino mother and an Ecuadorian father, who coaches Leylah and her sister Bianca Jolie full time. Her younger sister, Bianca Jolie, recently made her professional tournament debut in Ecuador.

Fernandez beat number-eight seed Emma Navarro of the US in a 6-2, 6-3 victory to claim the number-one spot. The win over Navarro was built on sheer perseverance. Her journey to the finals was marked with cold, wet, and muddy conditions on the difficult clay courts, a number of earlier losses, and exhaustion—even playing a total of three matches in one day on June 6.

In an interview with Sportsnet Canada, Fernandez recalled the day's event: "I thought, 'OK, I'm a little tired, but I'm sure my opponent is tired, too.'" She adds, "I just thought of the physical work, the hours [I had] put in with my father, the hours I cried because I didn't want to run anymore. I used all that experience . . . so I could get the momentum back."

This teenager tennis champion is bound for more victories. Hardworking and determined, she not only excels at but truly enjoys the sport that she does so well.

Eleanor Guerrero-Campbell is a city planner, community champion, and writer. She came to Canada in 1977 with a degree in English and comparative literature and a master's degree in urban and regional planning, both from the University of the Philippines.

In Canada, she went on to work as a planner-manager in Edmonton in Alberta, and Surrey, Richmond, and Vancouver in British Columbia.

Guerrero-Campbell co-founded the Multicultural Helping House Society in Vancouver, which opened its doors in 2003 with a budget of sixty thousand dollars, serving twenty-five hundred clients per year. As cofounder and executive director of MHH, she was responsible for fundraising and establishing programs to assist newcomers succeed in Canada. Sadly, MHHS started to lose momentum after she left it to become the chief executive of the Minerva Foundation for BC Women, where she managed leadership programs for women in various stages of their careers.

She currently co-convenes the City of Vancouver's Immigrant Partnership Program Committee on Access to Services.

Her first novel, *Stumbling Through Paradise: A Feast of Mercy for Manuel del Mundo*, depicts the struggles of a Filipino family's immigrant journey in Canada through three generations.

She is one of the founding members of the Maple Bamboo Network Society (MBNS), a non-profit that publishes *CanadianFilipino.Net*, a nationwide twice monthly online newsmagazine for, about, and by Filipinos in Canada.

Eleanor has been a recipient of many awards, including the Vancouver Civic Merit Award (she is the only Canadian Filipino to receive this award thus far) and the Queen Elizabeth II Diamond Jubilee Medal for community service. She is currently working on her second novel. More details about Eleanor and her first novel can be seen at *EleanorGuerreroCampbell.com*. She also wrote several articles for *CanadianFilipino.Net*, available on CFNet's website.

Her husband, Clay Campbell, was CFNet's first legal counsel until his retirement in 2019.

Emmie Joaquin and colleagues Rey-ar Reyes and Paul Morrow established The Pilipino Express, Inc. and began publishing the *Pilipino Express News Magazine* in Winnipeg. Joaquin is currently the company's president and the news magazine's editor-in-chief.

Joaquin was a recipient of the Queen Elizabeth II Golden Jubilee Medal in 2002, and the Queen Elizabeth II Diamond Jubilee Medal in 2012, for media and community service. She earned her degree in broadcast communication from the University of the Philippines. She worked in media and public relations before immigrating to Canada in 1988.

In Winnipeg, Joaquin produced and co-hosted the daily morning drive-time show, *Good Morning Philippines*, on CKJS Radio 810 AM. She also produced and hosted a daily afternoon show, *Manila Sound*, and the Saturday show, *Tunog Pinoy Pang Sabado*.

After almost fifteen years in radio broadcasting, Joaquin left CKJS in December 2003 to serve as special assistant for communications for then federal minister of Western economic diversification, Dr. Rey Pagtakhan. She also had a brief stint as executive assistant to then deputy mayor and councillor Mike Pagtakhan on the City Council of Winnipeg in 2005. She continues as editor-in-chief of *Pilipino Express News Magazine* to date.

 **Ann Makosinski** is not just the girl next door but a young scientist, who, for the last five years, has not only come up with two energy-saving inventions, but also started a company called Makotronics Enterprises with her father. On top of all that, she made it to Forbes's "Thirty Under Thirty" list, and, in 2013, when she came out with her first invention at age fifteen, made it to *Time* magazine's "Thirty Under Thirty" list for that year.

Makosinski got her inspiration for her first invention, the hollow flashlight, when she visited the Philippines, where her mother, Sandra, was born. The inspiration came out of a desire to help a friend there, because constant power outages prevented her from finishing her homework. Makosinski recalls, "She had no light to study with at night."

The hollow flashlight is made of Peltier tiles that produce energy when one side is heated by a hand holding it, while the other side within the hollow inside part is cooled, to power the flashlight's LED bulb. Makosinski won in her 15–16 age category at the 2013 Google Science Fair. In 2013, the flashlight could hold power for twenty minutes. Today, she promises a much better version of the flashlight, designed with a brighter light and longer-lasting power.

Winning the popular international science fair brought Makosinski to the forefront of international recognition. Aside from being named in the two prestigious magazines' "Thirty Under Thirty" lists, she went on a series of TV guest spots, TEDx talks, and speaking engagements. On the *Tonight Show with Jimmy Fallon*, Makosinski demonstrated the use of the hollow flashlight, as well as another invention, the eDrink Mug, which acts as a charger using heat from the drink to keep it hot.

Makosinski recently joined Canada 150 C3 (Coast-to-Coast-to-Coast), a shipping research expedition that went from the East Coast of Canada in Toronto, up through the Northwest Passage, and down the West Coast through the Inside Passage, finally ending in Victoria. In August, Makosinski joined leg nine of the fifteen legs, hopping onto the ship in Pond Inlet, and off in Cambridge Bay in Nunavut. Makosinski recalls, "It was life-changing. It was an amazing experience that can't be topped by anything else I do. For now. " She sees a brighter future for inventions.

Makosinski is now taking an English literature degree program at the University of British Columbia, a surprising choice of studies given her penchant for the sciences. "I want to have a balance of both the arts and sciences in my life, as I believe that the arts and sciences complement one another very well," she explains. "I learn about art and writing while at school and manage my business and work with technology outside of school."

Her father, Art, is recently retired, and now helps her with the patents on her two inventions through their company Makotronics Enterprises—which also manages licensing deals for and releases other inventions.

In a short video she made with *Vice.com* in November, Makosinski expounded on what an inventor is. She points out, "It is not always someone who's really good in science and gets straight As. For me, I really struggled in my chemistry and physics classes. It's really about loving to tinker and finding solutions to problems." In summary, she says, "It's really about taking that crazy, creative idea you have and not [being] afraid to follow through." Asked what her next project would be after the hollow flashlight and the eDrink Mug, Makosinski said, "A surprise!" For someone who started so young, it could mean not just one, but many more surprises.

Flor Marcelino'strack record has had many break-throughs, in her storied career in politics and as MLA of Manitoba. In over a decade as politician, she has elevated the status of visible minorities and women of colour in Canada.

In 2007, she became the first ethnic minority woman to be elected as a Member of the Legislative Assembly of Manitoba.

For Canadian Filipinos, her victory in the electoral district of Wellington that year was significant. She was the first immigrant woman from the Philippines to be elected as MLA in Canada. Marcelino went on to win a second term in the new electoral division of Logan in 2011.

By the 2016 provincial election, the Manitoba NDP had been weakened by internal dissension, and suffered a collapse in the polls in April of that year. Even though Marcelino secured a third term as MLA for Logan, her party lost the election to the Progressive Conservative Party of Manitoba, prompting then defeated Premier Greg Selinger to step down as provincial NDP leader.

On May 7, 2016, Marcelino was chosen as interim head of the Manitoba NDP, becoming the first woman leader of the party. Faced with the task of helping rebuild the NDP in the province, Marcelino declared in a CBC report, "This is a party that will keep on fighting for what we believe is right, for our values, for our social justice goals, for everyone."

After heading the New Democratic Party of Manitoba for more than a year, Flor Marcelino passed on the baton to a new leader. It marked the culmination of yet another chapter in the career of the Philippine-born politician, who came to Winnipeg with her family in 1982.

Before joining Manitoba politics, Marcelino owned a small business. She was also editor of a local community paper, *The Philippine Times*. She also worked as a support staff member for the Red River College.

According to her official NDP profile, Marcelino served as minister for culture, heritage, and tourism, and minister for multiculturalism and literacy between 2009 and 2016. Her appointment to the Cabinet in 2009 was also another first. She was the first woman of colour in the province to be named to the Cabinet.

On September 16, 2017, the New Democrats in Manitoba elected Wab Kinew, a rookie MLA and an Indigenous rights advocate. This also signalled a fresh episode in the political career of Marcelino, who was appointed by the new leader as the Manitoba NDP's opposition critic for immigration and multiculturalism.

Sofronio Ylanan Mendoza, better known by his initials, SYM, was an internationally renowned artist—also called "maestro" or "master"—for mentoring and nurturing young, aspiring artists in the Philippines and

in Canada. He had two such groups of artists in the Philippines, called Dimasalang I and Dimasalang II.

When he immigrated to Vancouver in 1981 with his family, he formed Dimasalang III. Dimasalang was a street in Manila where SYM began his career in a modest studio/workshop.

As an arts teacher, SYM imparted a wide spectrum of knowledge to his students—from the basic, fundamental principles of drawing and painting to art history and outside-the-box nuances and approaches to art not generally taught in art schools. He shared everything he knew with his students and other artists, to uplift and inspire them.

In Vancouver, he continued to nurture and share his knowledge and techniques in art with devoted young artists, as well as artist who have already distinguished themselves in their own right, like Maria Apelo Cruz, Leo Cunanan Jr., Simeon Dee, Jess Hipolito, Edgardo Lantin, Andy Naval, Rod Pedralba, and Noel Trinidad.

He hoped that his Dimasalang groups will continue to prosper in the international scene and pass on his legacy to new generations of artists, who will, in turn, nurture and inspire younger artists to improve how they see beauty, translate it onto the canvas, and share it with the rest of the world. He passed away in 2021.

Extraordinary among almost a million Filipinos in Canada are philanthropists **Antonio "Tony"** and **Marissa Peña.** They know how to share their good fortune where it will do the most good. A popular room in the Irving K. Barber Learning Centre of the University of British Columbia has been remade, transformed, and upgraded thanks to a generous gift from this Canadian couple, Filipino philanthropists Tony and Marissa Peña of Vancouver.

The Lillooet Room, part of the Chapman Learning Commons of UBC, has been renamed the Antonio and Marissa Peña Learning and Events Room. The space is used for workshops by UBC faculty, staff, and students.

The Peñas' gift funded upgrades to the room and improved student support, making it a more effective space for learning. More than a study space, the room will host unique learning opportunities open to all students.

Marissa and Tony Peña have a strong history of support for UBC, having established an endowed entrance award for undergraduate students in 2014. The award is given to students involved in the Filipino community, on the basis of both academic excellence and financial need.

"With many Filipino parents coming to Canada for work, their kids back home often struggle in their absence," Marissa explains. "When families are eventually reunited in Canada, it can be hard for the students to integrate into a new culture while they are still getting to know their parents again at the same time. They often suffer academically because of pressure to achieve and the stress of trying to fit in."

Tony adds, "Students who have received our award have been in touch to say how helpful it is to have our financial support. Their stories really inspire us."

After arriving in Canada from the Philippines in 1978, Tony and Marissa operated a successful money remittance services and shipping business for many years, serving the Filipino community in Vancouver.

In 2005, Tony, together with five other friends, established Societe Lifeline Society to support cancer research and raise awareness of non-related stem cell transplants. In 2014, with permission from the society's board of directors, they renamed it the "Peña Family Foundation" and turned their focus to support of secondary and post-secondary students with scholarships.

The Peñas' charitable gift is inspired by their firsthand experience with English language learners in Vancouver high schools—notably John Oliver Secondary and Sir Charles Tupper Secondary.

"We met with the Vancouver School Board multicultural liaison officer to find out where the needs were greatest," Marissa says. "We got involved in the ACE-IT program that helps students with technical training, and then we found out about the Kababayan Academic Mentorship Program."

KAMP is a collaboration between the Filipino Students Association at UBC and the Vancouver School Board. It delivers tutoring and mentorship to newly arrived Filipino high school students. Every summer, KAMP brings students to the beautiful Loon Lake Lodge and Retreat Centre in UBC's Malcolm Knapp Research Forest to connect with nature in their adopted province of BC. This gives the students an opportunity to know each other better and help each other adjust to their new environment.

"We went to Loon Lake, and we were really impressed by the programs that these Filipino university student mentors had created for their mentees," Tony says. "So, we started giving to the Loon Lake Redevelopment Fund in the UBC Faculty of Forestry."

The Peñas have always supported education and leadership, having sponsored university scholars since 1988. In 2013, Tony and Marissa established an endowment fund in Tony's alma mater, Ateneo de Manila University, a Jesuit-run university in the Philippines. They continue to support university students in the Philippines with donations through the UP-Ateneo alumni association in BC and in Vancouver through the Peña Family Foundation Scholarship Program.

In addition to official gifts to schools and universities to support education and enhance learning opportunities for poor but deserving students, the Peña are also engaged in a personal mission of sharing their good fortune.

Quietly and unceremoniously, they often share their meals with homebound senior Filipinos in need, personally delivering packaged complete meals to them.

Known to friends and neighbours for their humility, kindness, and generosity, they are among the highly respected and admired leaders of the Filipino community. They are always the first in line to contribute to a worthy cause—whether it is for typhoon victims in the Philippines or a family devastated by COVID-19.

Mayrose Salvador is co-founder and director of Pueblo Science, which brings science to small, rural communities around the world.

Science brought Dr. Mayrose Salvador out of poverty in rural Philippines. Now, she's paying it forward, by making science education accessible, hands-on, and—most importantly—fun, through Pueblo Science.

Salvador and her fellow scientist-mentor Goh founded Pueblo Science in 2010. It is a non-profit organization based in Toronto that delivers programs designed to make science interesting to children through active, hands-on learning experiences, discovery, experimentation, and problem-solving opportunities, thereby advancing science literacy.

The poor villages (pueblos) in the Philippines were top of mind when coming up with a name, thus "Pueblo Science" was born. Co-founder and executive director Salvador relates, "We wanted the children in these communities to get the same opportunities to access quality science education as the students in the cities."

Growing up poor in northern Philippines, Salvador remembers, "My parents only finished elementary school, but worked really hard for me and my siblings to get educated." She went on to finish a degree in chemistry at the University of the Philippines (UP) and, through a series of scholarships, completed her doctorate at the University of Toronto. It was at UP that she met Goh, who, at that time, was her thesis adviser. It was Goh who persuaded her to pursue a doctorate degree in Toronto.

"During visits to my town after doing my PhD, I realized that very little had changed in how children were taught science since my grade school days," Salvador recalled. "Science education was too theoretical, which made it too abstract and seem difficult."

The hopes and dreams of Pueblo Science were hers and Goh's: to inspire children, particularly in low-resource communities, to love and learn science, technology, engineering, and math, and become the next generation of scientists and engineers.

To achieve its aims, Pueblo Science invests not only in delivering science classes, but also in teacher training programs—and developing hands-on teaching kits using inexpensive and locally available materials.

One Pueblo Science program called RISE (Rural Initiative for Science Education) sends volunteers from Canada to join local counterparts in conducting professional development training for science teachers in rural schools. RISE has been implemented in rural areas in the Philippines, Thailand, Guyana, and Bolivia.

Salvador firmly believes that a career in STEM would help youth break free from the cycle of poverty. Salvador explains, "Having a good foundation in science and math will help children develop critical thinking, allowing them to understand the world around them and make better decisions."

In less than ten years of Pueblo Science, Salvador is already seeing results. Among its alumni who are interested to continue studying, she helps them receive scholarships to further their education, while others prefer to use what they have learned to generate income, such as starting an ice cream making business, and she helps them too. "Through surveys with teachers, we are also seeing an increase in the number of students pursuing degrees in STEM after a Pueblo Science training."

Salvador's personal goal is to become a "social millionaire"—someone who positively impacts the lives of a million others. "I would like to share my story, to inspire as many children as possible; if they dream big and work hard, they can achieve anything they set their minds on."

Pueblo Science is close to the halfway mark of a million beneficiaries. Since its establishment in 2010, its programs have impacted over four hundred thousand students in Canada and abroad, trained over thirty-five hundred teachers, and engaged over eight hundred volunteers in Canada, Thailand, Jamaica, Guyana, Bolivia, India, and the Philippines.

Salvador looks to the future of science. "There is so much to be done. But there is no better reward than seeing the look of students and teachers changing from fear and disinterest to excitement and enthusiasm."

 **Mel Tobias** (1939–2017) was a man of many parts, and a connoisseur of life. A quintessential Vancouverite, Tobias was adored and esteemed in and outside the Filipino community for his joyous celebration of life. He was a world traveller, but in all that he did, he always sought to highlight the positive contributions of what he described as "global Canadian Filipinos." He was always looking for "a place where his spirit could run free." He found "his corner of the sky" in Vancouver, British Columbia. He became the quintessential Vancouverite—learning, earning, yearning, and living for life.

Tobias immigrated to Vancouver after twenty-five years of having a lucrative, multilayered career in Hong Kong, where he managed the PR group of San Miguel Corporation in the eighties, hosted the radio program *Off the Beaten Track* at BBC Radio Television Hong Kong, and wrote for the *Hong Kong Standard* as a film critic. For seventeen years, his love for cinema brought him annually to Cannes International Film Festival as a film critic and foreign correspondent representing Hong Kong and the Philippines. His writings had been published in *Variety Magazine* and the *Hollywood Reporter* in the US.

Although he left behind a rewarding profession in Manila and Hong Kong, he firmly believed that when one door closes, another door opens—an inspiring adage that kept him grounded as he tackled his new life's adventure in Canada.

Tobias moved to Canada on November 16, 1993 and settled in Vancouver, where he practised his many moving parts as movie critic, lifestyle and entertainment editor, author, foreign correspondent, amateur actor, broadcaster, festivalier, impresario for the arts, proprietor of a vintage collectibles boutique, frustrated saloon singer, gourmet who knew where all the good eating places were, avid collector of esoteric and nostalgia recordings and books, and avid fundraiser for charitable causes.

He was also busy with Anyone Can Act Theatre as its co-founder and artistic director. Under his direction, ACAT's first production was a dramatic stage reading of Nick Joaquin's *Portrait of the Filipino Artist* at the Gateway Theater in Richmond.

He also organized two musical productions. The first featured Dorothy Uytengsu and Victoria Francisco in Piano Duo on Fazioli, while the second event featured an evening of classic torch songs performed by jazz vocalist Armi Grano.

ACAT also supported the book launch of Eleanor Guerrero-Campbell's *Stumbling Through Paradise: A Feast of Mercy for Manuel del Mundo.* Another production was a fashion show presenting the Barong Mindanao collection designed by Davaoeno Michaelangelo Dacudao.

The city that Mel Tobias so dearly cherished has honoured the late Canadian Filipino writer and arts lover. The City of Vancouver has named a plaza after Tobias, whose passing in 2017 brought great sorrow to the community.

On September 19, 2018, the city council designated the southwest corner of Kingsway and Joyce Street as Mel Tobias Plaza. Currently called the Collingwood Clock Tower Garden, the Mel Tobias Plaza is the first plaza in BC—if not in Canada—to be named after a Canadian Filipino.

The city's announcement: about the plaza said, "Mel Tobias (1939–2017) was born in the Philippines, spent many years in Hong Kong, and in 1993 settled in Vancouver.

"As a writer and radio host, Mr. Tobias chronicled the challenges and achievements of his community in Canada and inspired countless Filipino-Canadians to celebrate their unique and multi-faceted culture. He also championed causes that sought to uplift newcomers, live-in caregivers, immigrant youth, and women leaders."

The Mel Tobias Plaza is at the southwest corner of Kingsway and Joyce Avenue in Vancouver.

Marvi Yap and Anna Maramba are co-founder-owners, and co-directors of AVCommunications. They have been named by no less than the *Financial Post* as "the multicultural moguls." They are the two young Filipino women behind a successful niche advertising agency that links mainstream brands to the ethnic consumer.

AVCommunications is a full-service, mega-million dollar super company, and winner of many top awards in marketing and advertising. Their secret is a more personal approach in their advertising and marketing to multicultural groups, says Anna, "by creating advertising that elicits an emotional response to the brand, beyond just simply putting an ethnic face." Marvi adds, "We go deeper and ensure the nuances of the culture are reflected in the ad. There is an effort to understand in terms of grassroots." They build emotional connections between the mainstream brand and the ethnic customer.

Not quite strangers in a strange land in terms of language and culture, Marvi and Anna came to Toronto in the early 2000s, brimming with optimism, secure in the success of their early careers in the Philippines (Marvi owned an advertising boutique, Anna was in interior design). Both were graduates of exclusive private girls' schools. Marvi was at Maryknoll College before going to Michigan for her senior high school year as an exchange student, Anna studied at Assumption College. Marvi then obtained a degree in mass communications at the University of the Philippines, while Anna specialized in behavioural sciences at De La Salle University, and then went on to pursue her special interests at the Philippine School of Interior Design.

They were children of privilege in the Philippines, and were not quite prepared for their new life in Canada, where they had to settle for part-time work, often menial, in order to support themselves, because they had "no Canadian experience."

One morning at the subway, Marvi noticed an ad across from her and nudged Anna. "Do you understand that?" "No," was the reply. They "knew" English, and were brought up immersed in American culture, and yet were puzzled by the expression, "Why break the bank?"

"That's when it hit us," Anna says to CFNet's Jo Leuterio-Flach who interviewed them for this article, of this serendipitous moment. "We thought, let's start a multicultural agency to cater to people just like us!"

To start their business, they borrowed money from family and friends, because no banks would lend them money, since they had no assets or steady jobs. They got the break they needed when they put together a brochure for Western Union in Tagalog, with komiks-style cartoons. Since 2006, the Philippines has been Western Union's No. 1 destination country.

Today, Western Union is just one of AVCommunications' mainstream clients. Its roster includes BMW, Cineplex, Scotiabank, Elizabeth Arden, World Vision, and the Bank of Montréal, among others. Because of its unique, multicultural approach, it is often hired to collaborate with agencies of record, which do not have the same core competencies. For example, Marvi explains, "we have worked with Saatchi on the Toyota account." The agency has also worked on an integrated advertising platform with the agency for Western Union to promote its holiday campaign, winning a prestigious CASSIES award for creative and marketing effectiveness.

Since its beginning in early 2000s, AVCommunications has garnered many awards. They have been recognized as one of *Strategy Magazine*'s Top Creative Agencies for 2018 in its "Creative Report Card." They are repeat awardees of the coveted Marketing Magazine Awards, the "Golden M," which recognizes the most creative and effective work in the marketing industry. They have received Summit Awards and the NAMIC Emmas for their marketing campaigns directed at multicultural markets around the world. An award-winning campaign for World Vision, *"Pinoy para sa Pinoy,"* appealed to Filipinos' *"malasakit"* (empathy, concern for others) to raise funds for their needy fellow Filipinos, and was an unprecedented success.

They credit much of their success to their "team." They employ skilled, new immigrants and give them the opportunity to gain Canadian experience because they knew how discouraging it was to be turned down for lack of it—and how unreasonable it was for companies to expect a newly arrived immigrant to have "Canadian experience."

In addition to their business activities, they are involved in projects that benefit Filipino communities across Canada. They do volunteer work with the *Kababayan* Community Center in Toronto. They do pro bono work for Filipinos who need help. They prioritize and try to help those who most need it. All of their volunteer work for the Filipino community is done as quietly and invisibly as possible.

"The more we gave back, the more fortunate we became. Every time we are presented with the opportunity to give, we take it, because we know that this is what we need to do in exchange for all the blessings we have received."

There are certain uniquely Filipino traits and values that have helped them as they built their company. To what do they attribute their success? Here, Anna and Marvi speak as one: "Tenacity, hard work. *Malasakit*. And a *do more, talk less* mindset." To new immigrants to Canada looking for jobs, and to would-be entrepreneurs, they would also add: "Focus on your goals and go for the finish line, no matter what obstacles you face. Always find solutions, be resourceful, and just keep on. Keep learning, be adaptable, welcome change—because this is the way you will attain success."

And to those who have "made it," this is what they have to say: "Don't take advantage of anyone. People will take advantage of you, that's a reality—but keep helping others anyway. Be fair, be honest, and keep your values, no matter what. Remember that integrity and values are more important than money and success."

Stephanie Valenzuela, a daughter of Filipino immigrants, has been elected to the city council of Montréal. She won the November 7, 2021 election, becoming the first Canadian Filipino to earn a seat in Montréal City Council. Valenzuela ran with the Ensemble Montréal party. She won in the district of Darlington in the borough of Côte des-Neiges–Notre-Dame-de-Grâce. She is fluent in French and English. Born and raised in Côte-des-Neiges, Stephanie is a second generation Filipino-Canadian. She speaks fluent Tagalog. She began her involvement in her community at an early age. With only a few members of her family in Canada, her parents turned to the Filipino community and volunteered to build a tight-knit network.

From joining services—such as the yearly flower distribution in the borough of Côte-des-Neiges–Notre-Dame-de-Grâce—to offering meals at shelters, Valenzuela developed a strong belief in giving back to the community and to those in vulnerable situations.

A graduate of McGill University who majored in political sciences and international development, Stephanie has focused her efforts on non-profit organizations and community initiatives. In 2014, post-graduation, she volunteered and worked in Monterrey, Mexico for an NGO called La

Paz Comienza Con Los Niños ("Peace Begins with Children"). Through her work, she learned and acquired skills in project management, public relations, and fundraising.

Her experience in Mexico also led her to return to Montréal with a desire to work on local issues and give back to her community. Today, she is part of the Strengthening Families Program team led by the Côte-des-Neiges Black Community Association. She is also the director of communications for the Filipino Heritage Society of Montréal.

After seventeen years without a FilipinoCanadian representative in the House of Commons, the snap federal election in 2021 saw the election of **Rechie Valdez** as Member of Parliament for the riding of Mississauga–Streetsville, the first-ever female Canadian Filipino to hold such an office. For her acceptance speech, Valdez wore a red terno-style top, paying homage to her Filipino heritage and thanking her immigrant parents Norma and Zosimo Salazar.

A wife and young mother of two, Valdez declared, "This is a 'we' moment. We did this together . . . . Today, we made history and herstory, as you helped elect the first #Filipina in parliament."

In an interview with Global News Toronto, Valdez pledged to "listen and learn" in order to take the concerns of not just her constituents in the Mississauga-Streetsville riding but the larger Canadian Filipino community so that "their voices can be heard in Parliament." Issues she identified as unique to the Filipino-Canadian community included care of seniors, affordable and accessible housing and healthcare workers.

Valdez was born in Zambia, in Central Africa, to Filipino parents, and raised in the Mississauga–Streetsville riding. The many hats she has worn over the years, Valdez said, would help her understand the needs of the Filipino community. She feels privileged to represent both her riding and the community.

Prior to her election, Valdez had no political experience. She was an entrepreneur and a professional baker specializing in cakes and dessert tables. She co-founded a Filipino fusion line of pastries that supplied two national Asian grocery chains in Mississauga. She competed in *The Big Bake*, a Food Network Canada baking show, and produces/hosts her own TV show called *Fearlessly Creative* where she challenges cultural norms and pushes the boundaries of creativity by sharing the artistic creators' success stories. 🐾

Filipinos in Small Towns Making a Difference

June 1, 2021 – Early Filipino immigrants chose to go to big cities like Montréal, Vancouver, and Winnipeg. Recent Filipino immigrants, however, have been going to smaller towns and remote provinces and territories for better opportunities.

Canada is made up of ten provinces and three territories, one of which is the Yukon. The territory is on the westernmost point of the country, bordering Alaska.

A small number of Filipinos have moved to the Yukon and are making their presence felt there. Others are making a difference in small towns of Ontario, BC, Saskatchewan, and New Brunswick.

Yvonne Clark, First Filipino MLA of Porter Creek, Yukon

May 16, 2021 – On May 6, 2021, Currie Dixon, leader of the Yukon Party, announced critic roles for the official opposition party in the Canadian territory. The critics will serve as Dixon's shadow cabinet. One of these critics is Canadian Filipino **Yvonne Clark.**

Clark was elected member of the legislative assembly—or MLA—for the constituency of Porter Creek Centre on April 12, 2021. With her election, Clark made history as the first Canadian Filipino to win a seat in the Yukon Legislative Assembly. She was named critic for the Yukon Housing Corporation, Women's Directorate, and French Language Services Directorate.

On February 4, 2021, the *White Horse Star* described Clarke as a multi-lingual mother of three adult children. "Now that my children have left the nest, I feel I have the time to focus on what I am most passionate about," Clarke said in the report.

Online, the Yukon Party provides a profile of the territory's first Canadian Filipino MLA: Yvonne Clark is a proud parent, entrepreneur, and dedicated member of the Yukon-Filipina community, and was elected in the 2021 Territorial Election to represent the growing riding of Porter Creek Centre.

Having moved to the Yukon nearly three decades ago, her wide-ranging professional background spans from public service to small business ownership—and to extensive volunteer roles. She wants to use her experience in areas relating to poverty, education, health, human rights, the economy, and violence against women to give back to the territory.

Her experience includes serving over twelve years as a board member of the Yukon Learn Society, helping adults improve their literacy, numeracy, and computer skills, and as a former board member of the Yukon Public Legal Education Association, co-authoring the third edition of "Splitting Up," a resource for women involved in family breakdowns.

Clarke also currently serves as the chair of the Yukon Advisory Council on Women's Issues, advancing the legal, social and gender equality in employment Yukon women. She sits as a Yukon representative on the RCMP commissioner's Diversity Advisory Committee.

Of all her many roles in the community, she is perhaps best recognized for her leadership in the Canadian-Filipino Society of the Yukon, serving many years as its president and providing advice and guidance on integrating immigrants into mainstream Canadian culture.

Edwin Empinado on Safeguards for North Gateway Pipeline

November 1, 2018 – Kitimat Town Councillor **Edwin Empinado** wants to have environmental safeguards for the Northern Gateway Project. In 2011, Empinado became the first Canadian Filipino to be elected as municipal councillor in BC. He went on to win a second term in 2014, and a third one in the 2018 campaign.

Empinado was a nurse at the Kitimat General Hospital. In 2004, he and his wife, Doris, also a nurse, arrived in Vancouver from Dublin. In December of the same year, they moved to Kitimat.

As a councillor in Kitimat, a town on the northwest coast of British Columbia, Edwin Empinado knows a lot about the Northern Gateway project. The $6.5 billion project by Calgary-based Enbridge, Inc. involves two pipelines. One will carry bitumen from the oil sands of Alberta to the port of Kitimat. The second will transport condensate, a substance to dilute bitumen, from Kitimat back to Alberta.

In June 2014, the Conservative government at that time approved the controversial project, with 209 conditions.

Justin Trudeau of the Liberal Party pledged that if he were to become prime minister, Northern Gateway would not push through.

Empinado emphasized: "The residents' concerns are safety, protection of our environment, value-added taxation, quick emergency response, consultation, [and] jobs."

Restaurateur Estela Aguilar Chow Helps the Poor in Ontario and the Philippines

August 1, 2019 – Timmins is home to a small community of Canadian Filipinos. In the 2016 Census, Statistics Canada counted 135 people of Filipino descent in the northeastern Ontario city, which has a total population of less than 42,000. The Canadian Filipino community may be small, but one member of the community has been noted by the online only *Timmins Today* publication for having a big heart. Her name is Estela Aguilar Chow, owner of Lady Luck Restaurant and Buffet in downtown Timmins.

"Estela Chow is hoping to have Lady Luck on her side as she ventures into Timmins's restaurant scene," the publication reported. "She is definitely generating good karma by always looking to help others less fortunate."

Lady Luck Restaurant and Buffet offers Filipino and Canadian dishes, and by the end of the day, Chow donates whatever is left to two organizations helping the homeless in Timmins.

Chow explained. "Why waste food if you can donate it to people who need it? And in our community, there's a lot. If only all the restaurants followed what I'm doing, maybe they can help these people rather than throwing their food in the garbage."

According to *Timmins Today*, Chow also helps others back in the Philippinesto get new clothes. "Since I came to Canada, every time I go home, we do a feeding program there and give clothing to people in need," Chow said. "I have Giant Tiger (on Riverside Drive) is helping me out. Summer clothes, I ship back home. Winter clothes, they stay here, and we give them to people in need." Chow came to the city in 1991.

Rowena Santos, Lisa Abarquez Bower Elected to Municipal Councils in Ontario

November 19, 2018 – They're the first Canadians of Filipino ancestry in Ontario to be elected to council in their respective municipalities. On October 22, 2018, Rowena Santos and Lisa Abarquez Bower made political history for their election as councillors of Brampton and Ajax, respectively.

Santos is a community leader, known for her grassroots organizing. She has volunteered as board member for several non-profits, like Neighbourhood Watch Brampton. Before entering politics, she worked in business, including a stint as a financial analyst with a major bank. She was educated at Ontario's Schulich School of Business and the London School of Economics in the UK. She is a proud mother to a young boy.

Her parents moved from the Philippines to Canada in the 1970s. Her mother is from Pangasinan, her father from Manila. They settled in Brampton in 1984, when Santos was only six. Her platform calls for "getting the basics right" for residents of Brampton, a suburban city in the Greater Toronto Area. These include the upkeep of parks and neighbourhoods, better road infrastructure, hiring more police officers, and support for arts in the downtown core. She was elected as Brampton city councillor for Wards 1 and 5, with a term of four years.

Lisa Abarquez-Bower was elected as Ajax local councillor for Ward 3. Before politics, Bower worked in insurance and financial services. As a cancer survivor, the proud mother of two has also raised funds for cancer research. During the campaign, Bower pledged to work in finding supplementary sources of municipal revenue to relieve residents from the current full cost of property taxes. According to Bower, attracting new businesses to open shop in Ajax will increase the commercial tax base and lessen the bill for residential property taxpayers.

Bower was born in Ajax to Filipino parents and grew up in Toronto. She moved back to Ajax in 1999 to raise a family. She cherishes her family's Filipino heritageby supporting the Fiesta Filipina Dance Troupe, to honour her late mother, who worked closely with the cultural group for over thirty years. She serves a four-year term in Ajax, east of Toronto, by Lake Ontario.

First Filipino in City Council of Whitehorse

November 1, 2018In 2012, **Jocelyn Curteanu**became the first Canadian Filipino to win a seat on the city council of Whitehorse, the capital of Yukon. The mother of four, who is a longstanding federal employee, won a second term in 2015, garnering the most votes among the candidates for council.

Curteanu, who came to Canada from the Philippines with her family when she was six, wants to do more for her community. "My community means everything to me," Curteanu wrote on her website. "In my role as a Whitehorse city councillor, it has been my privilege to meet Yukoners of all ages—thousands of inspirational northerners who have important stories to tell about their families, their careers, their ambitions, and their challenges."

Upon winning a third term in 2021, Jocelyn Curteanu thanked voters of Whitehorse for giving her another term in city council. She promised to continue to help build an inclusive, affordable, and sustainable community. She is active in the community as a member of Yukon Cultures Connect, the Whitehorse Regional Women's Committee, the Racially Visible Committee, the Canadian Filipino Association of the Yukon, and the Yukon Area Council. She has served in the council since 2012. She is proud of having contributed to a better relationship between the city and First Nations.

When Curteanu's family arrived in Canada, they first settled in Vancouver. Curteanu lived in Whitehorse from 2003 to 2006, managing the local Canada Revenue Agency office. She moved to Alberta later, and returned to the Yukon in 2011.

Curteanu thinks visible minorities are underrepresented in Yukon politics. "They're still trying to build their lives. They're still trying to adjust, adapt to our community," she said in a *Yukon News* report. Curteanu noted as an example that Filipino immigrants often work multiple jobs, and don't have time for politics.

"As a city councillor, I learned very quickly how important it is to work with other departments of government, community partners, and stakeholders to deliver services to our citizens efficiently, effectively, and economically," Curteanu said in a report by the *Whitehorse Daily Star.*

Curteanu is now the regional coordinator of the Canadian Northern Economic Development Agency.

On being elected in public office, she said: "Well into my fourth year of politics, I've grown to really understand and appreciate the weight of responsibility and extent of influence our government leaders have. Personally, the ability to affect positive change and the opportunity to raise awareness and assist others are my greatest satisfaction.

"Canada has provided foreign-born citizens like us, Canadian Filipinos, with a better life and a chance to reach our full potential. Committing to a life in politics is not for everyone, but it is one of the best ways to give back to a country that has given us so much. Politicians help connect us with resources, [and] inspire us to do more and try harder to serve our community. I hope that as a Canadian politician of Filipino origin, a wife, a mother of four, and a full-time public service employee, I have demonstrated that there are *no* glass ceilings. If you can see it, you can break it!"

Cardeno's Grill Brings Pandesal to Small Town in Ontario

By Rachel Ramos-Reid

September 16, 2019 – In the town of Minto, Ontario (which has a population of under nine thousand) lies an unassuming restaurant that offers *pandesal* specials: pandesal bruschetta, pulled pork sliders, pandesal garlic toast, and a pandesalBLT. Among its breakfast and lunch staples is a Filipino dish—a crispy adobo rice bowl.

Cardeno's Grill sits on the Harriston junction in Minto, which lies between Toronto and Lake Huron, one of the five Great Lakes of North America. Harriston is a town travellers usually pass by, not one considered as a destination. But owner **Gardian Cardeno** and his family hope that the Grill will make visitors stay longer.

" Our pandesal bruschetta is a bestseller, closely followed by the pulled pork pandesal," Gardian proudlytold *CanadianFilipino.Net*. His Grill opened in July, but is slowly gaining popularity among locals and travellers. The restaurant initially served seven hours a day, six days a week. However, due to popular demand, the restaurant is now open from 8 a.m. to 4 p.m. Mondays to Saturdays, with plans to offer a dinner menu.

Gardian, his mother Nancy, and his sister Fenny hail from another small town in Davao del Norte called Barangay Patrocenio, in the City of New Corella, almost an hour away from the city proper by *habal-habal* (motorcycle). Mom Nancy always knew Gardian would be good at business because, at age nineteen, he opened his first business in Tagum, selling packaged food for travellers. The family immigrated to Canada in 2015, first settling in Mississauga.

In an interview with *SouthwesternOntario.ca*, Gardian recalled: "Mississauga was too much for us; too much stress, work . . . and we didn't have a life." When a friend introduced them to the town of Minto, the family began packing. Gardian describes himself as "not a chef, but an ordinary Filipino who loves food."

Grill's pulled pork pandesal and a lunch special of shrimp fritters.

Gardian tells CFNet of Minto, "This town kind of reminds me of where I came from: it's quiet, peaceful, and away from the bustle of the city." A year of research and planning led to the opening of Cardeno's Grill in July. He adds, "I am now focusing on how to introduce Filipino cuisine to other Canadians, so I've started playing with our ingredients; fusing them with different cuisines might develop interesting fusion dishes."

Newcomer Junifer Torralba Launches Online Grocery in Fredericton

On March 11, 2019, the Fredericton Chamber of Commerce in New Brunswick shared a story on Twitter about a new immigrant to the Maritime province. "Great article," the business association said about the online *Huddle Today*'s piece regarding Junifer Torralba, who hails from the Philippines.

Torralba, his wife Myra Lynn, and four others have launched an online grocery to serve the growing Canadian Filipino community in Fredericton. As an Internet-based business, the enterprise provides customers with the convenience of ordering online, with their groceries delivered to their doorsteps.

Called Ang Kapitbahay (*AngKapitbahay.ca*), the store offers a wide array of Filipino groceries, from canned goods to condiments, noodles, *pandesal* or buns, and dried fish. *Kapitbahay* is a Tagalog word that means "neighbour."

"Selling Filipino goods to Filipinos here is quite fulfilling, because . . . you bring to people a taste of their own home," Torralba said in the *Huddle Today* article. According to the online publication, the Torralbas came up with the idea for an online store after they moved to Fredericton in May 2018 and found it difficult to find Filipino goods. "Instead, they'd have to wait for a vendor from Saint John to make weekly deliveries," reported the publication.

In February 2019, Torralba and other newcomers graduated from BIMP (Business Improvement Program). Global News reported that the province's minister of post-secondary education, training, and labour attended the ceremony and said that BIMP will attract more newcomers to open businesses and job opportunities. "These are amazing opportunities to grow the workforce, to grow business that we desperately need here in New Brunswick."

According to Global News, the BIMP program has been running for a decade. It is a five-month course meant to integrate immigrants into the local business community. Torralba delivered a speech at the graduation ceremony, saying the program showed him the ropes of doing business in Canada. "If you work with the right people—with the same motivation, with the same passion as you—collectively— you build something very tangible and useful for the community," Torralba said.

Torralba and his wife are trained professionals in the Philippines. According to *Huddle Today*, Torralba worked as a certified public accountant for two global accounting firms for seven years before moving to Shell for thirteen years. There, he helped the multinational oil firm set up their shared service centres in Manila, and supported teams in Poland and Malaysia. Myra Lynn was formerly an operations manager at global testing company SGS, which stationed her in Nigeria for some time.

Torralba visited Canada often when he worked with Shell. "My work required me to travel a lot, long hours in the office—the same with my wife's job. So, we asked ourselves – is there something more to life than this? We've been married for 12 years and decided, why not take some time off and maybe start a family somewhere," said Torralba. They found that place in Canada. 🔥

De Leon's Grill Caters to NWT Legislature

March 8, 2016 – Filipino food has gone mainstream in the Northwest Territories, thanks to the De Leons' Epic Grill and its *Silog* specialties and other Filipino signature dishes like sinigang na hipon and pork adobo.

Joselito de Leon and wife Dorothy are the official caterers at the legislature of the Northwest Territories, where Filipino food has become mainstream, and is served to top politicians in the territory.

"Other offerings include soups, sandwiches, salads, desserts, and specials- of- the-day. Ask about the *Silog*—a breakfast speciality, the website notes. The *Silog* is a popular Filipino food of *sinangag* (fried rice)and *itlog*

(fried egg), which goes well with *tapa* (beef jerky), *longanisa* (sausage), *tocino* (sweet pork), or any meat or fish dish.

Owned by couple Joselito and Dorothy De Leon, Epic Grill moved to its twenty-eight-seat space in the government building in the capital city of Yellowknife in April 2015, after winning a two-year contract. "We're not doing this just for the two of us," De Leon told *Northern News Services*. "It's for all the Filipino community."

Dorothy added: "It's an honour and a pleasure to serve the Government of the Northwest Territories. We have a commitment to them to do our best."

Epic Grill first opened in Yellowknife in 2014 at the Arnica Inn. It sought to bring a taste of Filipino cuisine to the city with its *Silog* offerings—including one with fried *bangus* (marinated milkfish).

De Leon used to be a cook at the Shangri-La Hotel in Makati, Philippines. Dorothy was pastry chef. According to *MyYellowknifeNow.com*, the De Leons came to Vancouver in the 1990s. They moved to Yellowknife in 2012.

Chef Audie Banania Gives Back to Community

By Rachel Ramos-Reid

May 1, 2020 – **Chef Audie Louie Banania** first caught the attention of local newspapers in early March when *Alaska Highway News* featured Banania, his Audielicious Restaurant, and its promise to support charitable causes in Fort St. John, BC—something he started as soon as the business opened in 2019.

Banania and wife Jenny moved to Fort St. John in 2013 with a dream to open a restaurant—a dream they realized in 2019. Soon, they were giving back to the community that had helped them by holding a burger fundraiser by donating half the price of every burger they sold to help a couple of young cancer patients with medical expenses, the Fort St. John Women's Resource Society, the Salvation Army, and the North Peace Seniors Care Foundation.

Banania has never forgotten his homeland. He fundraised and initiated donation drives for victims of Typhoon Tisoy in the Philippines in December, and of the Taal Volcano eruption in January 2020. He helped another small business owner fighting to survive by giving Audielicious Restaurant patrons between a 10 and 15 percent discount upon proof of purchase from the other business in trouble. Things rapidly changed since March with the closure of most businesses throughout Canada after cases of COVID-19 started to rise. Soon, Banania was forced to lay off most of his restaurant staff—but, like most immigrant Filipinos, he is no stranger to hardships.

In his interview with the *Alaska Highway News*, Banania shared what it was like growing up in the Philippines. "I had a tough childhood," he recalled. "We could not afford to buy rice or bread or coffee; we were really starving." He said that his motivation to help those in need stems from his childhood. "I give back because I know that feeling, when you have nothing."

Banania grew up in Albay, Bicol, while wife Jenny (Gayo) is from La Union. The pair met while both were working as OFWs in Singapore. It was there that Banania built his career as a chef. It was Jenny who found a job in Fort St. John, and Banania did not hesitate to leave his career in Singapore to start over in Canada.

On March 20, Banania set up a mini food bank inside the restaurant, with a note that says, "Please take what you need. We are all in this pandemic together." The food bank consists of cereal, canned goods, toiletries, and cooked meals. He keeps the "food bank" regularly stocked for community members in need.

Encouraged by Banania's initiative, several Fort St. John residents started donating to his cause—so much so that by early April, he was able to deliver food to health workers at the Fort St. John Hospital and Peace Villa Care Home using his own money and funds donated by locals. On Easter weekend, it was grocery workers that got fed *pansit* and *lumpiang shanghai*. "I just want them to feel appreciated," says Banania.

In a feature on Dawson Creek's CTV News, Banania confirmed the community's participation and support for his initiatives. "Some customers would give us cash when they go [to the restaurant] to pick up their food orders, or they'd say, 'add this to your fund.' I thank this community I call home, for without their support, we wouldn't be successful here at all."

Filipinos Reelected in Municipal Elections

November 1, 2018 – A number of Canadian Filipinos emerged as winners in municipal elections held across the country in October 2018. All of them are incumbent officials. They have secured fresh mandates. One is **Rommel Silverio,** Councillor, City of Yellowknife, Northwest Territories. After the counting was over, Rommel Silverio posted on Facebook: "It was a long night of waiting. Finally, the results are in. I sincerely thank you, Yellowknife, for giving me a second chance to serve you."

Silverio was first elected city councillor of Yellowknife in 2015. He arrived in the city during the 1990s and worked several jobs, including as a cleaner at Stanton Territorial Hospital. While working, he took up nursing. He currently works as a nurse.

November 1, 2018 – First elected in 2006, Luz del Rosario secured a fresh term as trustee of the Dufferin–Peel Catholic District School Board. Del Rosario represents Wards 6 and 11 of the City of Mississauga. She graduated with a commerce degree in the Philippines. After arriving in Canada, she found she needed to upgrade her credentials so she studied human resources management at the University of Guelph.

November 1, 2018 – **Garry Tanuan**, Trustee, Toronto Catholic District School Board, Ontario, won another term as a trustee of the Toronto Catholic District School Board, representing Ward 8. Tanuan was first elected to the TCDSB in 2012.

Tanuan was born in Dumaguete City, Philippines. He has a degree in electrical engineering from Silliman University. He worked for many years as a consultant and project manager in the financial, biotech, clinical research, energy, and education industries. 🐚

Tony Flores Advocates for Persons with Disabilities

January 16, 2021 – In late 2018, Alberta appointed **Tony Flores** as its first advocate for persons with disabilities. Flores, a Canadian-Filipino and an international para-athlete, was given the task to raise awareness of the rights of Albertans with disabilities and the services available to them.

"We have a long road ahead to become fully equal citizens in our communities, and I believe we can make this happen," Flores said at the announcement on October 30, 2018. "We can make this happen by making voices of Albertans with disabilities central to all that we do, by doing nothing about us without us," he explained at the 2018 announcement of his appointment by the Alberta provincial government.

Flores lost the use of his right leg to polio. He moved to Canada from the Philippines with his parents when he was eighteen years old. As a para-athlete, he competed as a wheelchair-racer. He also competed in para-nordic skiing.

An elite athlete, Flores was a member of Canada's national para-canoe team from 2009 to 2013. He holds a Bachelor of Arts degree in economics and political science from the University of Alberta.

On his office's website, Flores is described as a "self-advocate who believes strongly in empowering people with disabilities to reach their full potential." He is an "accomplished athlete, has extensive experience working with non-profit organizations, and has volunteered—both locally and internationally—to mentor and coach athletes with disabilities.

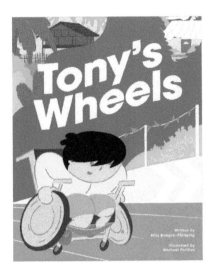

His story has inspired a picture book titled *Tony's Wheels*. Written in both English and Tagalog, the book was authored by Mila Bongco-Philipzig, who was born and raised in Manila and now lives in Edmonton.

The book was illustrated by Michael Parillas, a graphic designer raised in Canada in a Filipino household. It was published by Anak Publishing and supported by the Edmonton Arts Council.

Boxer to Entrepreneur: Rey Fortaleza's Game Plan

By Emmy Buccat

May 1, 2017 – Former Philippine Olympic boxer turned businessman Rey Fortaleza rose from humble beginnings in Manila to become a prominent entrepreneur and community builder in British Columbia.

Rey came from a family of boxers. Three of his brothers also boxed for the Philippine national team. They may not have been heavyweight champions, and the financial reward was far from promising, but their father insisted that boxing was their best route to get an education.

"We were trained as pugilists, but then, our goal really was to get a scholarship and get a proper education," Rey shared with CFNet. Fortaleza

ended up winning six golds, one silver, and two bronze medals in eleven international amateur boxing competitions. Representing the Philippines in the 1976 Montréal Olympics was the highlight of his boxing career.

After completing his Bachelor of Science in accounting at the Far Eastern University in Manila, he gave up his gloves for a new career in the banking industry.

Rey Fortaleza and wife Araceli.

Over the next decade, he worked with *Gintong Alay* and the Amateur Boxing Association of the Philippines as a technical consultant to develop and enhance the grassroots level of amateur boxing in the country. This work included coaching then up-and-coming boxer Onyok Velasco, 1992 Olympic silver medalist, and Roberto Jalnaiz, lone Filipino gold medalist in the Asian Games in 1990 in Beijing, China.

Rey's entrepreneurial prowess was tapped when he opened a sports equipment trading business in Manila, but this was cut short when his parents sponsored him to immigrate to Canada.

"Life was not all glitz and glamour when we immigrated to Canada—and just like boxing, you don't always come out a winner. We have to learn how to roll with the punches," said Rey.

Fortaleza attempted to open a boxing gym in Richmond, BC, but he had to close it down after a year.

"Education is a formidable force to reckon with so I went back to school and trained to become a licensed life insurance broker," said Rey.

The moment Fortaleza took his gloves off and started getting his hands dirty establishing an independent insurance brokerage in Surrey, his business began to flourish and took off in different directions.

"I've learned a lot about the Filipino community in BC, and learned to readjust along the way," said Rey.

The scale of his business expanded from publishing a newspaper and a glossy magazine to producing TV shows for airing on cable news, promoting concerts, and bringing famous entertainers and celebrities from Manila to entertain Filipinos in Canada.

"I am happy to keep right on fighting, not with boxing gloves but with business. The fight is not over until you have tried to turn failures into gains," Rey vowed.

The *Philippine Asian News Today* is the flagship publication of the ReyFort Media Group. It then published *Living Today*, a Filipino-Canadian glossy magazine, and subsequently produced *Philippine News Canada— Balitang Vancouver*, a TV news production capturing the day-to-day life of the third-largest ethnic community in BC.

Aside from providing diverse media opportunities for the Filipino community, Fortaleza also heads the Filipino Canadian Cultural Heritage Society, a non-profit organization dedicated to celebrating Filipino culture, heritage, values, and traditions. The society gives out the Maharlika Awards, recognizing individuals' and organizations' outstanding achievements and contributions to the Filipino community.

Fortaleza encourages everyone—especially those who feel stuck in a listless job—to follow their hearts and turn their passion into a career or a business.

"Just like in a boxing match, analyze what went wrong and readjust. Pick yourself up and do what you have to do to be better. Make sure to come back stronger in the next round," concluded Rey.

*MBNS director and social media manager **Emmy Buccat** is a donor relations professional at the University of British Columbia's Development and Alumni Engagement office. She supports communications, stewardship, and events team in keeping donors informed, involved, and engaged. She moved to Canada in 2008, with 10 years of experience in marketing communications, public relations, and event management for brand FujiXerox and Speedo. She has a degree in journalism from the University of Santo Tomas, Asia's oldest university, a certificate in integrated marketing strategy from UBC's Sauder School of Business and an associate certificate in fundraising management from BCIT. She is a MBNS board member in charge of fundraising through grant applications.* 🐾

Gemma Dalayoan: 2019 University of Manitoba Distinguished Alumni for Community Service

By Rachel Ramos-Reid

April 16, 2019 – Over the last sixty years, the University of Manitoba has recognized its distinguished alumni for their outstanding accomplishments. As the university notes, they are "trailblazers, innovators, and visionaries", whose achievements have "inspired people at home and around the world." On May 9, 2019, they were each officially honoured with a Distinguished Alumni Award.

One of the recipients was **Gemma Dalayoan**, an educator, who was recognized for community service. According to the university, Dalayoan, who holds bachelor's and master's degrees in education, made community service her mission in life since immigrating from the Philippines to Winnipeg more than forty years ago. She taught students to believe in themselves.

In giving her the award, the university stated: "As a founding member and three-time president of the Manitoba Association of Filipino Teachers, Inc., she played an instrumental part in the preservation, promotion, and sharing of Filipino cultural heritage through a variety of programs and student scholarships." The university recalled in its announcement: "She also spent decades as a teacher and vice principal whose guidance has helped shape students into future community leaders."

Quiambao, Laxamana Honoured for Global Cooperation Work

By Rachel Ramos-Reid

February 16, 2020 – Every year, the Alberta Council for Global Cooperation recognizes young people for their contributions to making the world a better place. It presents the award to thirty people under the age of thirty, to honour their work in achieving the United Nations' "17 Global Goals for Sustainable Development."

On February 4 this year, the "Top 30 Under 30" award was handed out to recipients at the Calgary Central Library—and two of the award-ees are Canadian Filipinos. They are Krisha Quiambao, a public health professional, and Kevin Laxamana, an anthropologist—both residents of Edmonton, Alberta.

"Coming from a small village in the Philippines where the nearest health centre is over two hours away, Krisha understands firsthand the reality of global health disparities," the Alberta Council for Global Cooperation says of Quiambao, twenty-six, on the organization's awards website.

"Now a global health professional, she works toward improving access to healthcare and strengthening health systems to protect against emerging global challenges," says the organization.

Quiambao was recognized for her contributions to the SAM Project, a Canadian undertaking in the dry lands of Zambia.

"In 2019, I collaborated with the SAM Project and two of my peers to propose strategies to respond to and mitigate the health effects of climate change in rural Zambia," said Quiambao.

SAM stands for "Sustainability through Agriculture and Microenterprises," and the project aims to help Zambians achieve digni-fied livelihoods.

Quiambao says on her personal online account that she is working toward a master's degree in public health. She is currently working with the Alberta Council of Women's Shelters.

Kevin Laxamana and Krisha Quimbao

Kevin Laxamana is described by the Alberta Council for Global Cooperation as an "anthropologist, teacher, mentor, community builder, and a first-generation immigrant with roots [in] Pampanga, Philippines."

"More than anything, he considers himself a storyteller who is privileged to lend his voice to the trans community by telling their stories through his research," says the organization about the twenty-seven-year-old awardee.

A graduate student in sociocultural anthropology, he was recognized for his research on the transgender community in Asia.

"Through my past involvement as president (2015–16) of the University of Alberta Philippine Students' Association, I have mentored Filipino student leaders and worked on projects that have impacted not only Filipinos in Edmonton but also those who live in indigent communities in the Philippines," said Laxamana.

"Through my research, I am advocating for the fair and equal treatment of transwomen sex workers in Singapore and Bali, Indonesia, by bringing forward their stories of transitioning and survival," added Laxamana.

Toronto Filmmaker Patrick Alcedo Wins Recognition for Works

By Rachel Ramos-Reid

August 1, 2021 – By any measure, Patrick Alcedo has accomplished much since he left the Philippines in 1996 to pursue higher education in North America. The Canadian academic was born and raised in Aklan. He moved to the US for his graduate studies after completing a Bachelor of Arts degree at the Universityof the Philippines. From the US, **Alcedo** came to Canada in 2007 to teach at York University, where he is currently an associate professor at the School of Arts, Media, Performance, and Design. He has also produced films, which have received international recognition.

On July 14 this year, the Philippine Consulate General in Toronto congratulated Alcedo for winning the Best Short Documentary prize at the Cannes Indies Cinema Awards for his film *They Call Me Dax*, a documentary about a fifteen-year-old student in the Philippines trying to survive as a ballet dancer.

TheyCall Me Dax and two of his new documentary films—*A Will to Dream* and *Am I Being Selfish*—were funded by Canada's Social Sciences and Humanities Research Council Grant and the Canada Council for the Arts. Moreover, Alcedo has written and directed other award-winning films. These include *A Piece of Paradise, Dancing Manilenyos,*and *Ati-atihan Lives.*

Lawyers Ho and Gatchalian Named to Highest Courts of Nova Scotia and Alberta in 2021

By Eleanor R. Laquian

April 16, 2022 – Canada's Minister of Justice and Attorney General David Lametti announced in April 2021 that Lawyer **Gail L. Gatchalian**, QC has been appointed as a justice of the Supreme Court of Nova Scotia. In August, he announced the appointment of **L. Bernette Ho** to the Court of Appeal of Alberta, the highest court in the province.

Lawyer Gail Gatchalian, daughter of Dr. Celso Gatchalian, who immigrated from the Philippines, is the first female Canadian Filipino to be appointed to a provincial supreme court. She graduated from Dalhousie University with a Bachelor of Science degree, with honours, in 1993, and a Bachelor of Laws from the University of Toronto in 1996. In 2018, she received her Queen's Counsel (QC) desig-nation for her exceptional contribution to the legal profession. She was a former president and equity chair of the Canadian Bar Association's Nova Scotia branch, former chair of the CBA National Labour and Employment Law Section, and former chair of the Nova Scotia Human Rights Board. She recently chaired the CBANS Sexual Harassment Work Group, leading the development and delivery of an Empowering Bystanders training to address sexual harassment in workplaces.

Justice L. Bernette Ho was named to the Court of Appeal, the highest court of Alberta, was first appointed in 2018 to the Court of Queen's Bench, the trial court of Alberta; the first Philippine-born judge in Alberta. She came to Canada when she was only six months old with her parents, both born of Chinese descent in the Philippines. She completed her early education in Cochrane, Alberta, got a BA (with honours) in communication studies from the University of Calgary in 1992 and an LLB from the University of Alberta in 1995. She was called to the Bar of Alberta in 1996.She is the youngest of five children and credits her parents for teaching her the value of education.

Filipino Hospitality at Baldwin Village Inn, Toronto's Urban Oasis

By Jo Leuterio-Flach

March 16, 2017 – In the early 1980s, **Rogie and Tess Concepcion** were living in the Toronto suburb of Mississauga with their young family. Rogie, an investment and corporate banker with the Royal Bank of Canada, and Tess, a portfolio investment manager with BCE (Bell Canada Enterprises), put their thinking caps on together and started buying small properties in the downtown core of Toronto populated by Jewish and Chinese shops.

Innkeepers Tess and Rogie Concepion (left) at breakfast with guests.

In September 2006, they opened their first bed and breakfast at 9 Baldwin Street, already known for its small, quaint restaurants serving international cuisine. They had had no prior business experience in the hospitality industry, but, according to Tess, it was simply an extension of what they were doing, renting out houses—except that "instead of long-term rentals, we have shorter stays." Also, she adds, their Mississauga home had been "house central" to many visiting relatives and friends they had hosted over the years. The only difference, Rogie added with a smile, is that "today, we charge people to stay—and even accept credit cards."

Baldwin Village Inn is a six-room B&B within walking distance of the University of Toronto campus, Queen's Park Legislature, Toronto General Hospital, Wellesley Hospital, the towering Toronto Hydro building, and other corporate offices.

A pale-yellow-bricked Victorian two-storey house, it has become a retreat for academics, scientists, and creative types on overnight or short-term stays—perhaps participating in seminars, giving lectures, or attending business or professional meetings. Pleasure travellers love it for its proximity to the tony shops of Bloor Street and Yorkville, the Royal Ontario Museum, Roy Thomson Hall, and the Art Gallery of Ontario.

Not surprisingly, Baldwin Village Inn has become an urban oasis for travellers from all over the world. These have included scientists, professors, and doctors, as well as writers, artists, musicians, and curators—many of whom are at the top of their fields. Indeed, one of their guests was a Nobel Prize winner in mathematics.

Their day starts with breakfast at a communal table. A physicist can be chatting with an artist, a doctor with a writer of fiction. Indeed, it is a veritable salon, à la Gertrude Stein. "The intellectual stimulation is priceless, and that is hard to duplicate. Sometimes, it makes my head spin," Rogie says of their many gifted guests.

Over twelve thousand visitors have stayed in these modestly priced Urban North Inns (*UrbanNorthInns.com*). They are recommended in over twenty travel guides, including *Lonely Planet*, *Michelin* and *Time Out*. The *Guardian* (UK) has included Baldwin Village Inn in its "Top 10 Toronto Hotels."

Chapter 5:
THE BEST OF TWO WORLDS

Because first and second waves of Filipino migrants came to Canada in the prime of their lives, the Filipino community now includes a large number of young adults of the 1.5 generation—born in the Philippines but raised in Canada—and a fast-growing second generation (born and raised in Canada).

Chapter 5 is focused on these young generations of Filipinos as they try to define their identity as Filipinos growing up as Canadians. Study after study has shown that children of immigrants generally succeed in Canada. That's good news for parents, who have made tremendous sacrifices in building new lives in the country, primarily to give their children a better future.

As a whole, children of immigrants also attain higher levels of education compared to the mainstream population. A 2018 academic paper at the University of Ottawa noted that better educational attainment "plays an important role in economic outcomes, with those who have more educational attainment generally having higher incomes and better career prospects."

"In Canada, second generation immigrants tend to have higher levels of educational attainment than those with two Canadian-born parents," author Mitchell John Bryan wrote. He also noted that "having immigrant parents of any education level is correlated with a higher likelihood of obtaining a university degree."

CanadianFilipino.net has an abiding interest in chronicling the success of second generation Canadian Filipinos as they negotiate and forge their identities. Being born or raised in a country whose culture is different from their parents' presents dynamics that make for a multilayered process in arriving at conceptions of self and sense of belonging. Having the best of both Eastern and Western worlds, second generation Canadian Filipinos will define and own their rightful space in the cultural mosaic that is Canada today. They are the Filipino community's future. 🌰

For 1.5 and Second Generation Canadian Filipinos, the Best of Two Worlds

By Prod Laquian

August 1, 2016 – A study by Angela Rai of Simon Fraser University showed that at the national level, young Canadian Filipinos are doing very well in school.

When my wife, Eleanor, and I were writing our book *Seeking a Better Life Abroad* (Manila: Anvil Publishing, Inc., 2008) based on her study of Filipinos in Canada from 1957 to 2007, we were impressed by the potential of the 1.5 generation we interviewed. They were so called because they had arrived as young children and had grown up in Canada, and thus were halfway between the first and second generations.

*Members of the Filipino Students Association at the
University of Ottawa during their annual general meeting..*

The first wave of the 1.5 generation were the children of middle-class professionals who had come to Canada as landed immigrants in the 1960s and 1970s. They had gone to good schools in the Philippines and had no trouble adjusting to the Canadian system of education. They lived in a Filipino home, imbibing Philippine culture, values, and traditions, while growing up socialized in Canada's diverse society.

When asked how they saw themselves in Canada, they were unanimous in saying: "We are proud of our Filipino heritage but also appreciate what Canada has given us."

As Ellie Flagg—who arrived as a three-year old and is now married with kids of her own—explained, "I feel fortunate to have been able to choose and keep the best of two worlds—the East and the West. I like being an Asian with good, Filipino values while living in Canada, with plenty of opportunities to rise on merit. This is an extraordinary gift."

As more and more immigrants have arrived in Canada, the children of succeeding waves of Filipino migrants have not all fared as well. There were reports that some of these children were dropping out of school, though the 2015 study "Canadian Immigrant Youth and their Academic Performance," by Angela Rai of Simon Fraser University, showed that young Canadian Filipinos are doing very well in school at the national level.

From the 2011 National Household Survey data, Rai found that between 2005 and 2011, 94.9 percent of second-generation Filipinos age twenty to twenty-four have finished high school. Those who did not complete high school made up only 4.6 percent in British Columbia, 6.5 percent in Alberta, and 5 percent in Ontario. The young Filipino cohorts in Québec did not fare as well, with 22 percent of them not finishing high school— probably because of language difficulties.

Disadvantaged Few

The young Filipinos surveyed in Québec belong to a small, disadvantaged group found in other provinces of Canada as well. They were mostly children of caregivers and temporary foreign workers with low-income and low-status jobs. They did not have a good Philippine education before coming to Canada. They suffered from years of familial separation before they could join their parents as immigrants. They endured adjustment difficulties in school and were bullied by gangs because they were timid—or their heavy accent was made fun of. Their parents, though skilled, were minimum-wage earners, so the children had to work part time to contribute to the family income.

Despite positive findings about the more recent 1.5 generation in a nationwide survey, some studies claim that the 1.5 youngsters have lower educational attainments than their parents. These conclusions are counterintuitive because, in general, the children of immigrants do better than their parents. Could there be problems with these studies themselves?

First, it might be a problem of small sample size in the studies. A 2012 study by Geraldine Pratt and May Farrales, for example, was based on interviews with forty-five Filipino high school students who were doing well in their studies and forty-six who were facing problems. This was out of 12,238 total ESL or English as a Second Language high school students in Vancouver. Moreover, the students were drawn from only two high schools in East Vancouver, where many low-income Filipinos live. Thus, these findings should apply only to this small sample of forty-six, not to all 1.5 generation Filipinos in Canada.

Second, it might be a question of the explanatory variables chosen. A 2008 study by Pratt and the Philippine Women's Centre found that Filipino high school students who spoke Tagalog at home had lower grade averages than other ethnic groups. Again, by choosing students who spoke Tagalog at home, the study mainly reached recent migrants still dealing with adjustment problems, including difficulties with Canadian system of education.

Finally, it might be a problem of purposive sampling. The 2012 Pratt and Farrales study targeted schools where the Vancouver School Board had set up a program to assist Filipino students facing difficulties. This approach, of course, may have biased the research findings.

Despite the methodological problems of these studies, it is important for Canadian Filipinos to recognize that a small number of young Filipinos are facing problems because of four factors.

First, when young Filipinos arrive in Canada, they are humiliated when set back two grade levels, because the Philippines requires only ten years to finish high school, while it takes twelve in Canada.

Second, although most Filipinos understand spoken English, their grammar is imperfect, and their heavy accent makes communication difficult.

Third, high school mathematics in Canada is different from math taught in the Philippines. Filipinos who are already in college when they arrive in Canada find they have forgotten high school math.

Finally, for a number of Filipino children who had been separated from their parents for about eight years or so, the adjustments to a life in a foreign country could be traumatic.

While limited to a small, disadvantaged group, these problems of recent 1.5 Filipinos and their parents need to be recognized and rectified if this group of next-generation Canadian Filipinos are going to be upwardly mobile. If not, there is a danger that these Filipinos, who came to Canada seeking a better future, may not realize their dreams. For many of these youngsters, the best is yet to be.

Living Hyphen: Untangling the Knots of Our Identity

By Justine Abigail Yu

March 30, 2019 – Where are you from? It's a question that I've always struggled to answer because, well, it's complicated.

I was born in Manila, Philippines, but moved to Toronto, Canada when I was just four years old.

Growing up, I never felt particularly Filipino. My family never really adhered to cultural traditions. We didn't subscribe to the Filipino Channel to watch the latest teleseryes. I didn't have a debut or a cotillion for my eighteenth birthday, and my family rarely, if ever, went to church. The truth is, I always felt like a watered-down version of what a Filipino is sup-posed to be.

And yet, there's something about our giant, extended family, the fact that any and every Filipino I come in contact with instantly becomes my *tita/tito/ate/kuya*, my love for and commitment to karaoke and *lumpia*, the gratitude and obligation I feel toward my parents, and the spirit of resis-tance that runs through my veins—all that has always made me feel so fiercely Filipino.

But of course, I'm also proudly Canadian! My progressive values, my welcoming and empathetic nature, my "eh" and my "oh, I'm so sooorry!", my embrace of multiculturalism and diversity—these make me want to shout out like the beer commercials of the nineties that "I. Am. Canadian!!!"

And yet, there are many times when I don't really feel like a Canadian, either. Mostly because I don't even know what it means to be one. When you grow up in one of the most ethnically diverse coun-tries, and yet only see white Canadian faces and voices represented in the media, well then, what's "Canadian"? When ethnic "minorities" are the majority in your school, but you learn in your textbook that the "first Canadians" were European, and everyone else who came after is an "immigrant"? And never mind the various Indigenous nations who were here long before the "first Canadians." Well, again, what or who, exactly, is a Canadian?

I've spent the majority of my life in the true North, strong and free, but somehow, despite spending such little time there, I still feel a deep and powerful connection to my ancestral land of *Mabuhay!* Philippines. My life has been this constant tug of war, an ongoing push and pull of these two places, two cultures, two identities. In short, it has been a life of living in between, of living in the hyphen.

As I've opened up about these feelings to people within the Filipino diaspora and other ethnic communities, I realized that my experience is not unique. I've learned that I'm not alone in navigating this ambiguous in-between place. That flash of recognition and connection whenever I describe my entanglement of contradictions is like a surge of electricity that fuels me each and every time. And that's why I brought life to *Living Hyphen.*

Published in October 2018, *Living Hyphen* is a magazine that explores the experiences of hyphenated Canadians—that is, individuals who call Canada home but who have roots in different, often faraway places. Through stories, photography, poetry, and illustration, we examine what it means to be a part of a diaspora.

From the Haitian-Québecois commuting along the Montréal Métro to the South Asian trans man applying for permanent residency, from the young Filipino-Canadian woman texting her immigrant mother to the Plains Cree and Métis man meeting a traditional healer, this magazine reveals the rich inner lives of Canada's diverse communities. Our inaugural issue, titled "Entrances and Exits," boasts of contributions from artists and writers who hail from over thirty ethnicities, religions, and Indigenous nations.

Within one month of our launch, we sold out our first run of five hundred copies. We've since reprinted, and secured distribution in bookstores all across Ontario, including select Indigo Chapters locations, with our sights set on national distribution.

We're just getting started, but already, we are growing rapidly. And it is abundantly clear that Canadians are hungry for these stories, which better reflect their own experiences. In a country that boasts of multiculturalism, where millions of people claim over 250 distinct ethnic origins, and where "diversity is our strength," it is no wonder that this magazine has been hitting a nerve.

The contradictory knots of our identity may never untangle themselves. And maybe they aren't meant to. But hopefully together, through *Living*

Hyphen, we can come to intimately know all their shapes, curves, and intersections. You can purchase *Living Hyphen*'s inaugural issue online at *LivingHyphen.ca.*

Justine Abigail Yu *is a fierce advocate for diversity and representation in Canada's arts and literature scene. Her mission is to stir the conscience and spur social change. In a parallel life, she is also a marketing and communications strategist for the social impact space.*

Learning (to be) Beyond the Book

By Dominique Bautista

February 16, 2017 – Last year, I had an opportunity to facilitate classes to supplement students' social studies curriculum at a Vancouver school. It hasn't been that long since I was a curious high school student myself!

I entered the classroom and was greeted by faces who looked a lot like mine. I read out last names from the class list that sounded a lot like mine. We had conversations and shared personal experiences that were a lot like mine.

But I also immediately observed some notable differences. Students seem to experience strength in numbers. They see their family's stories reflected in each other: such joy in reminiscing about Lola's *arroz caldo* or *lumpia,* or the way *Nanay* exclaims *"ay sus!"* when she hears an excuse for a poor test mark.

It is possible to speak Tagalog about your home at school without being told, "This is Canada. We speak English here," as if honoring your mother's mother tongue is a shameful cuss word to be soaped out of your mouth.

To my surprise, students seem comfortable sharing experiences about growing up here or speaking about culture and identity more than I would or could have done at their age. And truthfully, I'm a little jealous.

A few years after my parents migrated in 1990, I was the first in my family born outside of the Philippines on the other side of the Pacific Ocean. .I grew up in Richmond, hearing an unabashed medley of languages and dialects—including Tagalog—spoken so quickly they blend into one.

In high school, I was part of the growing Asian demographic in the Lower Mainland. Yet I found myself struggling to make sense of where I fit within the Asian imaginary.

At fourteen, this was sometimes hard to stomach. I floated between friend groups, fitting totally in with neither the four Filipino girls in my grade nor with those who called Vancouver home. Still, I knew the must-know Filipino telenovelas. I could hum popular K-pop songs. I learned cuss words in Cantonese. I could order my favourite Taiwanese dishes. I was almost enough, and yet not quite.

To some, I was Filipino. To others, some kind of Asian. A Canadian. A mish-mash. So, which was it? All? Something else?

I know that my grappling with identity as a hyphenated Asian-Canadian would have been less of a struggle and more of a discovery had there been spaces for me to sample, digest, and explore parts of my cultural upbringing beyond the static, white box of school—a core institution responsible for our socialization.

High school students in this province use the same social studies textbooks published in 1997, the same textbook I used as a student and as a teacher. It's as if this proud country's history and people have stayed stagnant and unchanged for twenty years.

When we read textbooks, we're required to learn them as truths. But that often doesn't leave room for the histories our parents have lived to tell or come to know.

This was my experience, at least: Pa interrupting me as I was studying my Social Studies 9 textbook, which claims explorers like Magellan "discovered" an Indigenous Canada. He recounted *Labanan sa Mactan*: how Lapu-Lapu resisted Magellan and his colonizing conquest for land. It was the same individual, the same act, but two totally different histories and values competing for a memory in my head. Stuck in between worlds, it's no wonder others couldn't identify me—I couldn't do it myself.

So long as old systems and narratives continuously produce the same traditions of defining "Canadian" based on dated historical knowledge and language, without room for other diverse voices, so many of us are caught in-between. So many of us are still struggling to identify as second-generation Filipinos, and/or Canadians. "*Ako ay Pilipino: sa puso, sa isip, sa salita, at sa gawa.*" To be is more than just a label, it involves heart, thoughts, words, and actions.

Teetering on the hyphenated unbalance of being connected to different worlds, these are opportunities for difficult conversations that explore experiences of (un)belonging and (dis)connections, to support spaces for voices of colour to be heard, and for multifaceted identities to exist beyond the prescriptive constraints of what society dictates. We don't have to identify with being just Filipino or just Canadian. There is room for both and more, because who to be and how to be is decided by us, for us—and certainly not by an aged twenty-year- old textbook.

Dominique Bautista is a community-based humanities educator who is comfortable with multiple hyphens connecting her identity. She is happiest when listening to elders tell their version of histories and when hunting for mango shaved ice desserts. For her musings on education, community, and identity politics, see twitter.com/DBAUTISTA.

Young Filipinos Create Individual Identities

By Prod and Eleanor Laquian

February 16, 2017 – Among Filipinos in Canada today, there are two distinct groups that will eventually become the face of Canadian Filipinos of the future: Filipinos who arrived young in Canada with their immigrant parents and grew up here (the 1.5 generation), and those who were born and raised in Canada to Filipino parents (the second generation).

These young Filipinos are different from each other in the ways they shape their lives as they grow from youth to adults, finish their education, find employment, pursue careers, and start families of their own. This demographic, because of its size, will define the roles of Filipinos in Canada's diverse society of today.

Of Rice and Roots event at the University of British Columbia Student Nest. Photo by Abby Oira.

From our ongoing study of Filipinos in Canada, started in 1969, we find that most 1.5 generation Filipinos agonize about their racial identity and their ignorance of their Philippine culture and mother tongue. They suffer difficulties with their sense of belonging and feelings of anxiety about their future in a place they cannot truly call their own. Some of them may suffer from insecurity, isolation, and rootlessness due to their loss of ethnic identity and culture. Some may even encounter their parents' initial difficulties with racism. However, despite the fact that they do not blindly cling to indigenous Philippine cultural traits and find no problems integrating into a new and different culture, they are able to create an identity of their own, based on their own particular experiences.

Second generation Canadian Filipinos, however, have the advantage of having been born in Canada and grown up in a multicultural society. Most of them are equipped with better social and communication skills, which provide them with more educational opportunities. They do not worry much about their cultural identity, because they create their own identity with a combination of the Philippine culture they inherited from their parents, the Canadian culture they are growing up in, and the influence of peers they are growing up with. Their identity comes from their own personal skills, traits, and values, rather than from the collective traits of Filipinos back home, or the particularistic Filipino community abroad to which they may belong.

An upbringing in a multicultural society has many advantages for second generation Canadian Filipinos: proficiency in multiple languages and the ability to communicate across cultures, based on intercultural sensitivity, open-mindedness, cross-cultural understanding, empathy, and tolerance. Their appreciation of other cultures starts early in life.

This group of second generation Filipinos tend to be highly educated (with at least a bachelor's degree), live in big cities, and have an interest in international affairs. They have strong organizational and leadership skills. They may pursue careers in the arts, education, health services, human service fields, international relations, law, media and technology, or self-employment.

Their sense of adventure makes an international career attractive. They may live as expatriates in foreign postings and add a third culture to their upbringing. They tend to be bilingual and have many friends across cultures, because they are sociable and develop strong bonds based on personal relationships and not on countries of origin. In fact, they socialize more with people outside their ethnic group at work and at play.

According to a Statistics Canada study in 2006, about one third (33 percent) of couples involving a Filipino were married to or living common-law with someone outside their ethnic group. Both 1.5 and second generations Filipinos tend to intermarry and produce beautiful, multiracial children.

In the Philippines and in Filipino communities abroad, their children would be called *mestizos* or mixed-race, and regarded as beautiful because they are fair-skinned, taller than the average Filipino, and have somewhat non-Filipino features. They have physical characteristics that most Filipinos aspire to and admire in celebrities, like movie stars and beauty queens. Some may consider this a sad commentary on Filipino values, but it is simply the result of the influence of other cultures on them, just as they influence other cultures themselves.

Even in Canada, these children of mixed marriages stand out because they look naturally tanned and have thick, wavy hair, dark brown eyes, and full lips that are quick to smile.

In today's multicultural Canada, where there is no one dominant culture to dictate social norms for minorities to follow, the ability of second generation Filipinos to blend in and adapt makes it easy for them to succeed in their chosen careers. Their lives are enriched by meaningful relationships with others and a wider worldview that goes beyond Canada and the Philippines.

They are at home wherever in the world they may be, as long as they are able to pursue their dreams, treasure their memories, and live their values and beliefs as free and independent individuals. They are the true global citizens of the future.

My Filipino Identity

By Phebe Ferrer

March 1, 2017 – In an event organized by the Asian Canadian and Asian Migration studies Dialogues at UBC, one speaker's words resonated with me deeply. Paraphrased, what was said was that moving away from home to another place makes home seem and feel more important. The act of leaving home etches it more deeply into your thoughts and being.

This simple but bittersweet statement pretty much sums up my feelings about my Filipino identity. Being away from home, the Philippines, and living for an extended time in other countries has made me seriously consider what it means to be Filipino. The absence of home, and the insecurity I feel now, as a young adult, in identifying as Filipino, having grown up elsewhere, has made me question my identity.

My experience may be a little bit unique compared to others. As the daughter of a diplomat, I have indirectly been given the opportunity to experience different settings and cultures throughout my childhood and young adult years. I have called different places home at different points in time, but as a child, I never questioned what I thought was the fact that I was Filipino. My Tagalog may not have been the best (even today, it is still a bit off), but the sound of my language never failed to make my head turn and my heart quicken a bit—the sound of home in each foreign place.

Now, as a young adult in my third year at UBC, the simple acceptance in my childhood of my being Filipino has turned into a complicated jumble of insecurity, academic concepts I try to use to explain myself, bitter feelings of unbelonging, and lessening certainty that I can call myself Filipino.

Probably, this is because things have changed, and the things on my list I saw as qualifying me to be Filipino have been dwindling every day. Am I religious? Not so much anymore. How's my Tagalog? I understand it and can speak it, but with an obvious accent that shows that I did not grow up in the Philippines. Do I say "*po*" and respect my elders? Yes, I try to. Do I feel like you belong to the Filipino community? At times, not really.

All this uncertainty—culminating in the summer of 2016, when I realized that I could not, and would not, follow Christianity any longer—all of it gave me an identity crisis. I felt broken from the fact that I felt like an outsider to the community I thought I belonged to. My list of things that qualified me as Filipino was almost empty, and at this point, I decided I needed to know more about what I called my Filipino identity. I wanted to know if I still belonged. So, I decided to turn to research.

Currently, I am doing research toward what I hope will be a course at UBC that will engage students, both of Filipino and non-Filipino heritage, towards the topic of identity and the Philippines. As part of my research, I am interviewing members of Filipino communities in Vancouver and looking at academic and non-academic texts from Filipinos who navigate this question of Filipino identity.

My research is helping me to personally orient myself as well as realize that instead of being a definitive list of characteristics like I previously thought, my Filipino identity is how I relate to it in terms of historical connections, the diaspora, and my family. I would argue that this is my Filipino identity—not a definitive thing that I must try to fit in, but a definition I have for myself.

More broadly, I hope that this research can engage more Filipinos with the topic of identity and, more importantly, contribute to the discussion and creation of community-based solutions for issues that face Filipino communities in the diaspora. I hope that my research, as much as it is born out of my own identity crisis, can help the wider Filipino community as a result.

That is not to say my research has solved my identity crisis. It is something I still face every day, and grapple with as I go about my life. However, if nothing else, I find comfort in the fact that my love for Filipino food has never once faded away. Despite my insecurities with language, religion, and culture, I always find comfort in my mom's *lutong bahay*—her adobo, Lola's *kare kare*, lolo's *paksiw,* and the sweetness of *taho,sans rival,leche flan.* The absence of home has etched it more deeply into my being. So, as much as it makes me miss it and question myself, home is also within me, and will ground me, even as it makes me stumble.

Phebe Ferrer is a third-year International Relations student at UBC. Her father was consul general at the Philippine Consulate in Vancouver at the time, but was moved to a new posting the following year, leaving her at UBC to finish her studies.

Reflections of a Second Generation Canadian Filipino on "Filipino Identity"

By Joseph Planta

February 1, 2017 – It is important to reflect on one's heritage. But what if, upon reflection, you realize you don't think about it that much?

I was born in Canada to Filipino parents. My experience as a Filipino in Canada is probably very different from someone who was born in the Philippines. One of the benefits of growing up in an urban city like Vancouver is that you don't have to think about your racial identity, because racial diversity is the norm rather than the exception. Sure, it comes up. I've run into well-meaning but exceedingly patronizing people who, in an effort to initiate a conversation, will resort to speaking some foreign lingo they assume I know because I happen to look like someone they think speaks that language.

When I ride the bus home late at night, I'll often overhear people's conversations, either with other passengers or with someone on a cellphone. The Filipinos on the bus I frequently see are going home from shift work. I sometimes wonder what it would be like to ask some of them about their identity. I'm assuming they're probably a lot more concerned with making ends meet, paying the bills, getting more hours at their job, or getting a better job. I'd ask them about their lot in life, whether it's as expected, whether they think it's as good as it gets, if they wonder how they're perceived, what their dream are.

I have made a concerted effort on the interview program I host to find guests that illuminate the Filipino experience a little bit better, because it is so underrepresented in the wider media.

I have realized that for a lot of people, their racial identity can be a barrier more than a benefit at times. It's up to those who feel they need to speak up to do so. Forums like this are a marvelous opportunity for people to enlighten themselves and others. And it's up to us all to take the time to listen to those voices.

And we should listen more, ask more questions, and perhaps take the time to highlight the challenges that arise because of identity. Perhaps it might do something to address the inequities and inequalities that exist not only in the Canadian Filipino community, but in the wider Canadian context as well.

Forging a New Canadian Filipino Identity

My parents, who came in the 1970s, were too busy getting here and too tired after work to do anything more than read the paper and vote, let alone write, or run for office. I suppose it is the luxury of the second or third generation to ponder what it means to be a Canadian Filipino today. But it is also the responsibility of those of us in the second and third generations to expand what it means to be a Canadian Filipino.

Most people think about their identity when they're young, thinking about their place in this world and what that space might encompass. The search for identity might concern people at the end of their life, when considering the totality of their years and just what their legacy might be. But I suspect as I get older, I might think about my own background more. I suppose as one approaches midlife, as people from one's past and present fall away, it's no longer self-indulgent, but urgent. Maybe, given the chance, going boldly to the past, uncovering whatever might need to be unsheathed, might present some idea about what the future might hold.

Joseph Planta has hosted a podcast at TheCommentary.ca *for over thirteen years.*

On What It Means to Be a Filipino

By RJ Aquino

December 16, 2017 – When I asked my children what they wanted for dinner one evening, they said, "We want Filipino food." That gave me pause, because at their age, it never occurred to me to qualify what I eat. Everything I ate was Filipino food.

It feels that my family's exposure to Filipino culture has revolved around many informal rituals integrated in our daily lives, but what struck me that evening was that in my children's eyes, their choice for dinner was compartmentalized as being Filipino.

What makes us Filipino? I feel like I'm perpetually preparing an answer that may never be satisfactorily articulated, if and when my children ask me that question.

I immediately think about my upbringing in the Philippines, but my mind also wanders to the different Filipino communities around the world that I've been fortunate enough to have encountered. It's also wonderful to see how these communities have adopted local customs and quirks. Our shared mannerisms and numerous cultural cues immediately breed familiarity among us and a sense of belonging.

Immigration trends in recent years saw the Filipino community growing fast. Over the course of this population growth, it's no coincidence that the number of Filipino restaurants has increased across Metro Vancouver.

I also hear our languages spoken more frequently when I'm out and about in the city, and it's no longer a surprise to locate Filipino goods and publications at a local corner store. We are slowly making our presence felt.

Unfortunately, there are gaps in our community's expression of our traditions. There's a preposterous fetishization of celebrity culture and all its accoutrements. There's a lack of widespread appreciation of our history and associated critical assessments on its effects on present situations.

It's increasingly apparent that we need more substantive cultural institutions on the forefront of raising the profile of the Filipino community, like Kathara Society in Vancouver and Kapisanan in Toronto, along with the involvement of academics like those at the UBC Philippine Studies Series.

Many of us will make a conscious effort to have mindful discussions with the younger generations about what it means to be Filipino. However, as time and generations pass, so, too, will the distance between those of us who grew up in our parents' and grandparents' adopted home country and those of us whose idea of what it means to be Filipino has been informed by a shared existence in the Philippines.

We need to recognize that building these bridges across generations requires traditions that are reinforced beyond our immediate tribes. As our community continues to grow, so does the opportunity to create meaningful links that highlight and advance the evolving Filipino experience.

Rafael Joseph "RJ" Aquino is a young parent and community activist. He works in the Vancouver high-tech sector. Aquino co- founded the Tulayan Filipino Diaspora Society, and OneCity, a Vancouver electoral organization.

Making the Next Day Better in Vancouver

By Sammie Jo Rumbaua

February 15, 2017 – I am actively involved with Next Day Better, a platform for multicultural speakers. It helps us to understand our language, culture, and traditions. So, yes, we eat rice every day with a spoon and fork, we bless our elders and answer with "*opo*," and we take off our shoes when we enter a house.

I love how Canada is so multicultural, and I have many friends from different countries. I'm so proud to represent the Philippines! There is so much to talk about—the good, the bad, and the ugly, from the delicious food and amazing beaches to the colonization of our people and government corruption. When I meet newly arrived Filipinos, they would be so surprised at how much I know about our country and culture. I tell them that it is important to keep our Filipino culture and customs alive in Canada so we would not lose our Filipino identity.

In the mainstream media, people of color barely get recognized. I always wanted to see and hear more about multicultural people on the radio, the big screen, board of directors, and around decision-making tables. I would always ask, "How can we inspire the next generations to reach their potential to create a movement within our community?"

When I was approached to be part of the Next Day Better Vancouver Team, I knew it could be the vehicle to answer my question. Next Day Better is a storytelling platform for multicultural creative speakers to discuss important and difficult local and global issues in a safe and positive space. We want to build bridges between communities and facilitate joint efforts to fight injustice and spark action. We also include a food element in the program, featuring local Filipino chefs, since food is such a huge part of our culture and gatherings.

By having this kind of event, people will acquire knowledge and awareness. Next Day Better connects a large network of peers and like-minded change-makers. We provide opportunities by sharing resources and collaborative efforts for social change to build more inclusive communities. This will also promote respect for diversity. We want to fuel people with inspiration they can apply in their everyday life, so they can take the steps to make the next day better in their own way. See *NextDayBetter.com.*

Sammie Jo is a single mom, businesswoman, and community organizer. She owns and operates an event-planning company with her sisters, Power of Three. She also works at the Mount Pleasant Neighbourhood House. See more at SammieJo. ca.

Second Generation Filipinos in Trudeau's Post-National Canada

By Mary Ann Mandap

February 2017 – As Canadians gear up to celebrate their nation's 150th anniversary, Prime Minister Justin Trudeau has outlined a new governing principle for Canada: the principle of postnationalism. He boldly asserted this philosophy in a recent interview with the *New York Times,* where he described Canada as the first post-national state. "There is no core identity, no mainstream in Canada," Trudeau claimed. "There are shared values— openness, respect, compassion, willingness to work hard, to be there for each other, to search for equality and justice."

To the international community, Canada is a land synonymous with multiculturalism and diversity. It has been highly praised for its audacious example of keeping its doors open. Multiculturalism, however, is achieved at the price of national identity. It is evident nowadays that many have trouble pinpointing exactly what it means to be Canadian.

Filipino Canadian youth on Parliament Hill.

What exactly does an "international" Canada mean for second-generation Canadian Filipinos—those born here, of immigrant parents? How does the second generation cope with dual identity?

Second-generation Canadians make up more than 5.7 million people, according to the latest National Household Survey in 2011. That's 17.4 percent of the total population—millennials who are youthful, urbanized, and well-educated. They have wide-reaching roots that span across 200 two hundred or more countries.

In British Columbia, second-generation individuals account for over 23 percent of the population, the highest proportion among the provinces and territories. Two other provinces were above the national average of 17.4 per cent: Ontario, where the second generation represented 22.5 percent of the population, and Alberta, where it represented 19 percent.

Among the second generation Canadians of Filipino descent, we see a growing number of young adults who grapple with their ethnicity or dual identities. They often find themselves having a different set of values or ideals from that of their immigrant parents. But their physical attributes—like having black hair, brown skin, or a small stature—set them apart from the rest of the population. Or, perhaps because they have been raised in a Filipino household, they need to confront and understand what being Filipino in Canada means. Some embrace their part in the Canadian mosaic and accept life's complexities.

A survey conducted by Filipino Youth Transitions in Canada reveals that the overwhelming majority of second-generation Filipino Canadians think of themselves as both Filipino and Canadian. Of this group, a higher number lean toward Canadian.

Second generation identities are often multiple and overlapping. But instead of treating their mixed identity as a liability, people with this dilemma can take pleasure in being in Canada these days, as this country styles itself "postnational," welcoming immigrants, promoting tolerance, and embracing diversity even more.

Spoken word poet and arts educator Patrick de Belen summed this up beautifully in a recent Toronto Forum on Filipino Canadians: "I am a Filipino seed, yeah, but I am planted in Western soil— which means my branches may bear plenty of fruit, but my roots are subconsciously digging for oil."

Mary Ann Reyes-Mandap has over three decades of experience in journalism, public relations and corporate communications work, and was a staff member and writer for Mr. and Ms. *magazine,* Malaya, *and the* PhilippinesFree Press *in the Philippines. While living in San Francisco from 2003 to 2007, she worked as associate editor of* Philippine News, *the oldest and most widely circulated Filipino newspaper in the United States, and as editor of* Filipino Insider *magazine. In Vancouver, she worked as community news editor of* Philippine Canadian Inquirer, *and was associate editor of* Dahong Pilipino. *She has also authored a book, the soon-to-be published* Lakbay: Immigrant Seniors Find Their True North. *She completed a Bachelor of Arts in communications (with a major in journalism) and a Master of Arts in Asian studies from the University of the Philippines (Diliman), and was granted scholarships by the Japan Foundation and the local scholarship program of the Philippine Civil Service Commission. She also earned the California Health Journalism Fellowship from the Annenberg School at the University of Southern California.*

Two Lands, One Heart

By Carissa Duenas

December 1, 2017 – I am an immigrant, but I'm careful using the word "home" these days. In fact, sometimes, I'd rather not use the word at all. It's not because I feel like I don't have one. On the contrary, it's because I have two. By saying, "This place is home," I worry that the other place, just as close to my heart, will be perceived to be of less significance.

I made the decision to move to Canada in 2005 under the government's Skilled Worker immigration program. I was in the thick of my twenties then, living in the Philippines, and at a season of life where I felt that I could touch the moon. The requirements were daunting: binders' worth of education and employee documents from years past, interviews at every turn, a physical exam, an "exploratory visit" to the country. The scrutiny was unnerving.

But the toughest requirement—as I would find out—was to have a heart that could hold both hope and grief at the same time.

My application for permanent residency was approved a year later, and the announcement of my impending move had to be made to my loved ones. No one really tells you about this chapter of the immigration story and nothing prepares you for it.

It is the same sunset, seen by the one heart from two lands.
Photo credit: Government of Canada

I told my family I was leaving during our weekly get-together. My mother's side of the family gathers in my grandmother's house every Friday. It's tradition: my aunts, uncles, and cousins take their assigned seats at the long dining table, feast on one another's stories over home-cooked dishes, and dissect the week that's transpired. You need to raise your voice to be heard, because conversations are so animated, and laughter—startling, contagious laughter—often fills the dining room.

One end of the table could be talking about politics (or the odd relative), while the other end could be discussing the plot of the latest movie. Whatever the case, there were full bellies and nourished spirits by evening's end.

I tried to be casual about making the announcement, because the last thing I wanted was to alter the emotional climate of the room.

"So, my application to Canada was approved. I'll be leaving in two months," I told Cara, my youngest cousin, in an almost hushed tone. She was seated next to me at the table.

"Wait . . . you're leaving?! What?" Her reaction caught the attention of the rest of the family. Within seconds, a silence fell. I looked at the faces around the table. These were the people who had seen me grow up, cheered me on, and nurtured me. The pillars of my life.

I studied my aunts' faces, my mother's sisters, and memories rose to the surface of their kindness, understanding, and compassion throughout my life. I looked at my uncles: the men who taught me how to ride a bike, tinker with electronics, and engage in sports.

My chest tightened. It dawned on me that by leaving, I could no longer repay them with the same gift of time. And then there were my cousins—all of whom I love and regard as siblings. I remembered all six of us in Grandma's garden, lying down on our backs, eating half-ripe mangoes while staring at the clouds—that, ultimately, brought me to tears.

The same sky, no longer the same dreams.

While there was shock, sorrow, and confusion in the days that followed, it was in my family's quiet, graceful acceptance that I understood the depth and breadth of their love.

On the eve of my flight to Canada, the entire family gathered in the dining room to send me off. When my aunt hugged me goodbye, she whispered, "Your dreams await. But remember that you'll always have a seat waiting for you at the table."

I would drink from the bittersweet cup of both hope and grief since my decision to move. It's been a little over a decade now since I arrived. I've pursued my graduate studies, nurtured relationships, embarked on a business career, and gone full throttle with my passion for writing. I'm not done yet, and it is because of this country that I still believe that the moon is within my reach.

I can't recall the exact moment when hope became bigger than my grief. But I do know this: today, my cup runneth over. And I have more of myself to give.

I left behind a life in the Philippines—a good one—but Canada has given me better lives to choose from. I have the freedom to explore and celebrate who I am, because opportunities in Canada are not constrained by race or social class or upbringing. I will spend the rest of my days thanking Canada for that.

I return to the Philippines annually for a three-week visit. It's always an interesting, joyful time: I see family that I've missed and reconnect with old friends. But returning to Manila entails leaving my home in Toronto, and it's not always easy. I have "family" here, now, as well—close friends I've chosen. They are part of the blueprint of my goals and dreams, and are the constants in my evolution and growth.

I used to wish that I could have all the people I love in one room. But, realistically, I'll never make these two worlds of mine converge—especially since I've lived two vastly different lives in each place. I don't think they were ever meant to intersect—but that doesn't mean I have to abandon one for the other.

I am profoundly lucky. I have two homes. One holds my past, the other my present. Together, they have enriched my life.

Carissa Duenas moved to Canada in 2006, leaving behind a career in the management technology consulting space. She pursued her master's in business administration at Queen's University in 2008, and has since worked in various finance and marketing positions for companies based in Toronto, Manila, and Hong Kong. Despite being rooted in the corporate world, she has always maintained a passion for writing. She writes essays that delve into everyday life experiences in her spare time. Her work has been published in the Philippine Daily Inquirer *and the* Globe and Mail. *More of her writing pieces can be found at CarissaDuenas.com. She hopes to complete her book of personal essays soon.*

Chapter 6:
THE LIFE-UPENDING COVID-19

As year 2019 wound down, a new virus sneaked in and upended the entire global community at the beginning of the new decade.

Named COVID-19, the virus struck the world with a dizzying swiftness and ferocity, mutating into variants for which health experts and scientists were caught unaware. Two years in, the world is still all totally unprepared, and the virus continues to test humanity's resilience and—at its very soul—people's kindness toward each other.

CFNet is fortunate to have Dr. Rey D. Pagtakhan, a retired lung specialist, who started the series *Medisina at Politika* in February 2020, which regularly gave CFNet readers not just information about the ever-evolving pandemic, but an expert's point of view.

Apart from keeping track of case numbers and developments during the pandemic, CFNet's volunteer writers and contributors shared commentaries, news, and features on issues around this public health dilemma, which continues to impact people's daily lives and test the human spirit. The pandemic exposed inequities—at least according to one province's report, which noted that, at one point in time, over half of those infected were people of colour.

But while the pandemic exposes inequities, Canadian Filipinos found opportunities to show gratitude to healthcare workers during this time by making a grateful noise barrage at seven at night. Like the perpetual optimists that they are, they also found opportunities for self-improvement. They made good use of time in isolation and turned isolation into opportunities to help others and push for advocacies on behalf of those at the frontline in this battle against the pandemic. A great number of Filipinos in the service and healthcare industries became frontline workers in this pandemic, providing daily essential services to keep everyone safe, fed, healthy, and secure.

On February 1, 2020, Dr. Rey Pagtakhan, a retired lung specialist, dedicated his column, *Medisina at Politika,* to the COVID-19 pandemic even before the new coronavirus respiratory disease had been given its official medical name and was officially declared a pandemic by the World Health Organization. He has since continued with his series nearly twice monthly in order to keep CFNet readers well informed about the new disease, its evolution, the scope of its clinical manifestations, its human toll, and developments in drugs and vaccines as well as on the importance of heeding public health advisories. Below is his list of articles.

List of published articles from February 1, 2020 to May 1, 2022:

1. New Coronavirus Infection: Information and Guidance
2. Epidemic in China: A Global Concern
3. Preparedness for a Potential Pandemic
4. Canada and Around the World
5. Clinical Horizons for Hope
6. Potpourri of the Latest Developments
7. Stressful Times for Kids and Youth
8. Re-starting Canada's Economy
9. Living with the Virulent Virus in Our Midst?
10. Long-Term Care Homes Cry Out for Care
11. Twin Global Public Health Concerns
12. A Ground-breaking Treatment and Other Updates
13. Wearing a Mask in Public: A Simple, Life-Saving Act of Humanity
14. Children in the Eye of the Pandemic Storm
15. Back to School: More Understanding, Less Agonizing
16. College Life in the Age of COVID: Challenges and Solutions
17. Pandemic and the Seasonal Flu: A Fearful Duo
18. Epicentre USA: Anatomy of Failure and Three Great Hopes
19. Avoidable Deaths and Circle of Tragedy
20. Follow Public Health while Waiting for the Promises
21. Vaccines in Sight, Masking Continues

22. Pfizer/BioNTech's COVID-19 Vaccine: A Triumph of Science
23. COVID-19 is a Vaccine-Preventable Disease
24. Update on Canadian COVID-19 Vaccination
25. Review of a Year's Coverage and Vaccination Update
26. Vaccination: Urgent Path to End the Pandemic, But Not Enough
27. New SARS-CoV-2?
28. Mass Vaccination and Related Issues More Crucial Than Ever
29. Third Wave Calls for Intensive Public Health Action
30. Pandemic Healthcare and Healthcare Workers in Dire Situation
31. A Pediatric COVID Vaccine: A Wonderful Milestone
32. Vaccinating the World and Canada's Pledge Doable
33. Get Fully Vaccinated: A Duty of Care to Self and to Others
34. Is a Fourth Pandemic Wave Likely, or Preventable?
35. A Critical Time for Children and A Must for Vaccine Certificate
36. Get a Vaccine—It's an Act of Humanity and Humility
37. Get Vaccinated! Get Vaccinated!! Get Vaccinated!!!
38. On the Verge of Having a New Pediatric Vaccine for Kids Five to Eleven
39. New Pediatric Vaccine Approved, Finally but Why Only Now?
40. Human Security of Foreign Farm Workers Left Vulnerable
41. Ominous Omicron: Impact, Implication, and Insight
42. Time to Enlist Untapped Foreign-Trained Nurses and Doctors
43. When Will It End?
44. The COVID-19 Pandemic: More Than a Two-Year Viral Journey—Lessons, Insights, What's Next

The COVID-19 Pandemic: More Than a Two-Year Viral Journey—Lessons, Insights, What's Next

By Dr. Rey D. Pagtakhan

May 1, 2022 – The COVID-19 virus—originally referred to simply as "2019-nCoV" (short for novel Coronavirus identified in 2019) and now officially referred to asSARS-CoV-2 (short for Severe Acute Respiratory Syndrome Coronavirus 2)—has been making its global journey for over two years since its start, and it isn't over yet. What lessons have since been learned, what insights have since been gained, and what should now be our attainable goal?

Beginnings

The initial eleven unexplained cases of pneumonia with a common history of exposure to live animals in the Huanan South China Seafood Market were seen in Wuhan, China on December 8, 2019. They were clinically suspected to be caused by an unknown virus. When the number of cases increased to fifty-nine, the patients were gathered and admitted into one hospital, where a multidisciplinary team, including public health experts, did a full investigation and reported their findings to the UN World Health Organization on December 31. The offending virus was identified on January 1, 2020, and its genome characterization was achieved a few days later and shared instantaneously with the global scientific community.

COVID-19 Spread Beyond National Borders

Soon after China ordered a lockdown of the whole province of Hubei and quarantined its population of sixty million, the first case was diagnosed in Thailand on January 13, followed promptly by reports of similar cases from eight more countries. In response to the increasing spread, on January 22, the Johns Hopkins University's Center for Systems Science and Engineering launched its online global coronavirus dashboard, to track, in real time, the reported cases coming from all countries on the daily timescale. It has since continued to provide this valuable service. By January 30, the WHO declared a "health emergency of international concern" to help "fight further spread in China and globally [and] to protect nation-states with weaker health systems."

Before February ended, Canada and the US had already seen their first cases, and the likelihood of a full-blown pandemic was becoming more evident.

"COVID-19 is a Pandemic"—March 2020 to April 2022

On 12 March 2020, the UN health agency announced the somber global moment: "COVID-19 is a pandemic"—a global public health and a socio-economic crisis that had afflicted over 100,000 patients, claimed the lives of over 4,000 citizens, and reached 114 countries in 6 continents and all regions of WHO, all in less than 100 days from its beginning.

The new viral disease received its designation "COVID-19"(short for COronaVIrus Disease first described in 2019) and the **offending virus received its official name SARSCoV-2,** short for "Severe Acute Respiratory Syndrome Coronavirus 2 (the number "2" differentiates it from the first coronavirus that caused SARS in 2002-2003).

In the beginning of the pandemic, we were filled with fear and apprehension as the viral disease rapidly caused the illness of thousands and the deaths of hundreds, with the elderly and those with underlying medical conditions most at risk. Hospitals and providers of care were overwhelmed. We seemed helpless; there was no specific drug to effect a cure, and there was no vaccine to prevent the disease. We could only rely on non-pharmacologic public health measures. They helped mitigate the situation until vaccines were developed and approved in December 2020. Mass vaccination started to make a difference, and new drugs were developed, too. The situation began to appear better —so much so that many felt the end was on sight. In fact, most public health restrictions and mandates had been lifted. But lately, resurgence has been seen. When will the pandemic really end? That was the question I asked in my last Commentary in February.

What's Attainable?

In March, I read the article "The Concept of Classical Herd Immunity May Not Apply to COVID-19"in the March 21, 2022 issue of the *Journal of Infectious Diseases*, by Drs. David Morens, Gregory Folkers, and Anthony Fauci of the US National Institute of Health. Dr. Fauci is also adviser on the COVID-19 pandemic to US President Joe Biden. Allow me to share their expert viewpoints. They provide answers to the questions I raised at the outset of my CFNet Commentary.

To refresh our understanding, a classical herd immunity threshold for COVID-19 is the proportion of the population with immunity against the COVID virus above which transmission of the virus is largely prevented. That is, if someone gets infected by the COVID virus, he/she would be "surrounded by enough people who are shielded against infection so that the virus has nowhere to go; it fails to spread."

Below are the lessons that have emerged, the insights that have been gained, and our anticipation of the future (A, B, and C). I have summarized them in itemized format for greater clarity, and have, in fact, quoted abundantly from their journal article.

A. Five Lessons Learned:

1. The COVID-19 virus mutates continually into variants that can escape from infection-induced and vaccine-induced immunity.
2. The COVID-19 virus can be transmitted from asymptomatic carriers and, thereby, hinder public health control.
3. COVID-19 does not substantially engage the systemic immune system.

4. Infection or vaccination does not induce prolonged protection against the virus in most people.
5. Public health officials have met strong opposition to vaccination, mask-wearing, and other interventions.

B. Insights Gained

1. Obstacles to achieving complete herd immunity with COVID-19 are significant.
2. Eradication or elimination of the virus is almost certainly an unattainable goal.
3. Controlling the virus and its cycles of new variants is a formidable challenge.
4. Any level of herd protection against the virus can be overcome by . . .

   a) ever-changing levels of immunity among numerous sub-populations;
   b) crowding, changes in social or prevention behaviors;
   c) demographics;
   d) vaccination levels;
   e) variations in durability of infection- or vaccine-induced immunity; and
   f) evolution of viral variants.
5. COVID-19 is likely to be with us for the foreseeable future.
6. There is now a high degree of background population immunity to the virus.

C. What's Next?

1. More broadly protective vaccines.
2. Developing "universal" Coronavirus vaccines (or at least universal SARS-CoV-2 vaccines that elicit durable and broadly

protective immunity against multiple SARS-CoV-2 variants) is an important goal for the immediate future.

3. Optimal COVID-19control will require both 1) classic, non-pharmacologic public health approaches and 2) vaccination of many more people globally with the virus-specific vaccines, with booster shots.

4. Living with COVID is best considered not as reaching a numerical threshold of immunity, but as optimizing population protection without prohibitive restrictions on our daily lives.

5. Effective tools for prevention and control of COVID-19 (vaccines, prevention measures) are available.

6. **Countermeasures** such as antiviral drugs and monoclonal antibodies to prevent progression of disease, and widely available diagnostic tests.

Indeed, COVID-19 control, not classical herd immunity, should be our goal—and that is attainable.

Lessons from the Pandemic

By Jo Leuterio-Flach

May 16, 2021 – It's been over a year since we started living in the shadows of the pandemic. Now, by following the stay-home advisories and getting vaccinated, it seems we can finally look forward to a carefree summer. We may still have to wear masks and observe social distancing, depending on where we live, but hopefully, we won't be living in fear of getting the virus anymore.

Isolation

I consider myself to be living in purgatory—not in limbo—anticipating a return to normal. When this whole idea of isolation started, I associated it with a kind of freedom—more time for myself. No obligations of any kind, for one thing. Hours curled up with a book. Binging on Netflix, and takeout.

Of course, it isn't exactly as I expected. One can have enough television—and restaurant meals are so much better when dining in the restaurant! You can only read so much before you fall asleep or ennui sets in.

 And there are obligations: to stave off infections, and almost obsession with house cleaning and sanitizing (I have never wiped doorknobs this often), lots more laundry (especially with clothes worn outside—luckily, I have a jacket I can put in the washing machine), lots of housework (even without having people over), such as more thorough washing of fruits, disinfecting shoes worn outside, etc.

For my family, the biggest deprivation is the restrictions on travel—no visits with our children who live in Vancouver, Hong Kong, and Stockholm. Our plans to get together have been postponed once again—from this summer to Christmas!! But thanks to FaceTime, emails, and Instagram, we can see each and converse almost as though we were together in the same room. In the meantime, our eldest grandson has grown several inches, to six feet, and I am no longer taller than the younger ones anymore.

The restrictions imposed on us to control the spread of the Coronavirus at first seemed to be too much of an infringement on our freedom. But after looking at how some countries have handled the pandemic, we have decided to stop complaining, and are only too glad to accept the trade-off. In Sweden, masks are not even a requirement; only recently have Swedes been asked to wear them when using public transportation. Restaurants are open till 8:30 p.m. Shops are open. However, the rate of infection is high.

On the other hand, in Hong Kong, everyone wears masks, including children. Restaurants and shops are open, with social distancing. But heaven help you if you travel over there—you will spend several days in quarantine in a designated hotel, even after you have presented proof of vaccination. However, the rate of infection is low indeed! Life in Vancouver is almost normal—restaurants and shops are open with restrictions. This is the envy of those like us who live in Toronto, with its prolonged lockdowns

Making the Most of It

But this is our purgatory, and we have to suffer in order to be safe—hoping to be rewarded when the pandemic ends. On the other hand, this isn't Hell. We all know that this is temporary. Indeed, there is much to enjoy and be grateful for. In spite of the stay-at-home orders, we can go for long walks for exercise, long drives for a change of scene, long walks for leisure, and meetings to exchange ideas on Zoom. We travel by cooking dishes from other countries that actually taste as good as they look in the pictures in recipe books. We do the best we can to make this experience productive and meaningful, learning a few lessons along the way. I am now getting ready for the long-awaited after-pandemic time and putting my house in order, literally.

In the midst of lockdown, I decided to de-clutter. I am still at it, but have made much progress. Amazing how much more spacious and neat our home is now. If you come across household items and clothing that you have too much of or that you don't need anymore, pack them in boxes and share them with charitable institutions or neighbourhood organizations. You will breathe a sigh of relief, as I did, and you will make someone smile with these small "gifts."

And have you ever tried going through your photos and souvenirs? It breaks my heart to throw these out, but now, I have a big box for each of my children, where I retire precious mementos for them to sort out. They all love looking through photo albums when they are home, so I know memories are important to them.

Stores and shopping malls are closed, and it really hasn't been fun to spend money on anything, so I have been shopping my closet! It is such a wonderful feeling to discover a much-loved outfit from "olden days" hiding somewhere in the closet. And because we don't go anywhere, I have been wearing the same clothes over and over again—no point in getting all dressed up. I have many T-shirts with holes in them, and have extended their lives by embroidering over them. My hole-y T-shirts look stylish now.

Having saved a good amount of money from not shopping and not going anywhere, I opened my own trading account through my bank. One doesn't need an exorbitant amount of money to invest. It is a learning experience, researching companies and reading quarterly and annual reports. So far, it hasn't been painful, because the market has been buoyant, and I haven't lost any money yet. And I can't wait for Monday when the stock exchange opens, so I can watch my stocks go up and down in the market.

One of the best things about this pandemic is how people reach out to each other. Even strangers will wish that you "stay safe." How many of you have called friends you haven't talked to in a long time, or regularly get in touch with friends who live alone? Let's continue to do so, even when this pandemic is over—as my mother-in-law always used to say, "It's nice to be nice."

Getting Ready for the Good Times

So far, many of us have been fortunate enough to remain free of the coronavirus. Many of us don't even know anybody who has COVID-19. And the rate of infections is going down.

But we are not resting on our laurels, so to speak. We have had our first "jab," and we hope everyone goes for it. In the meantime, let's continue to wear our masks and practice safe distancing. Let us continue to be careful, even if it means less joy and no hugs. The rewards when this pandemic is over will feel heavenly.

Jo Leuterio Flach, a graduate of the University of the Philippines, came to Canada to attend the University of Toronto Graduate School. She adores her family, which includes seven grandchildren, as well as books, food, and travel.

Bayanihan in the Time of Social Distancing

By Rachel Ramos-Reid

April 1, 2020 – You don't have to be a scientist to figure out that what has befallen the entire world in the last two years will not go away as quickly as it is spreading. COVID-19 has further upended an already topsy-turvy world. The virus knows no gender, country, age, or social standing. It doesn't choose who to infect.

No one has a crystal ball that can tell us how humanity will come out of this crisis. If and when we do, no one will come out of this the same person they were before it started, because a crisis of this magnitude reveals one's true character; it tests our character. Will we be better because of the crisis? Or will we lose our humanity?

We're all in this together, but did we follow social/physical distancing as directed by the experts and health officials? Or did we make fun of it by blatantly ignoring the signs that asked you to observe social distancing? Did we stay home when there was no need to go out, or did we think we were invincible?

Did we worry about not going on that trip of a lifetime or did we support, thank, or offer a prayer for those who have been called to fight this battle? I refer to our health workers and caregivers many of whom have come to Canada to share their gift of caring. Did we consider the young family struggling to make ends meet before we bought more than we needed? Or did we refrain from bulk-buying those critical protective face masks, so that health workers would be able to access those masks? Did we stand by and let others do the work, or did we do our bit by phoning a neighbour who lives alone, just to see how she's doing? Remember, social distancing is not social disconnecting.

This is the time to fully use modern technology. Phone, text, message, Instagram, Twitter—use any of them to let others know that we're in this together. If there is an upside to a crisis like this, it is the opportunity to be creative, resourceful, and thoughtful. In short, it's an opportunity for humanity to shine at its best.

Rachel Ramos-Reid started writing for magazines and newspapers when she was still a junior in the University of the Philippines's communications degree program, major in journalism. She continued to write in a public relations/corporate communications capacity for private and government offices until moving out of the country in 1997 to work as programme officer for the arts and culture branch of the Southeast Asian Ministers of Education Organization in Bangkok, Thailand. At the end of her term, in 2000, she immigrated to Canada, and again searched for new beginnings. She is a governance professional at a small community college on Vancouver Island.

Introducing RESPECT: Filipino Workers in Pandemic

By Leonora C. Angeles

June 1, 2020 – Welcome to this column's first entry. RESPECT stands for Responsive Engagement, Service, and Possibilities for Empowerment and Collective Transformation. Contributing to our collective empowerment and transformative change is the end. Our responsive engagement, service, and imagining of new possibilities are the means to this end.

Filipino health care workers with other nursing staff at a hospital in Victoria. Photo Credit: Rose Doller.

This column serves as an exchange of ideas and resources for transformative change within Filipino communities in Canada through the cultivation of critical thinking and life-long learning skills.

Educators, academics, and community activists promote critical thinking among citizens and learners of all ages, so that we can engage in civic discourse and informed conversations about our economy, politics, health, education, culture, and overall life and well-being.

We need critical thinking and life-long learning skills now more than ever in the age of information technology, social media, knowledge economy, and unimaginable crises and catastrophes, such as climate change and COVID-19. It is only fitting to start this column with a piece that honours Filipinos who are frontline service workers, considered essential in the current pandemic.

Recognizing Filipino Service Workers in Pandemic

Chances are seven out of ten Filipinos you know or have met in Canada work in the six Cs—caring, clinical, cleaning, cooking, cutting, and cashiering—service sector components. Beyond revealing the structural vulnerabilities of our food production, health, and senior care systems, the pandemic has also unveiled the class, racial, and ethno-national origins of those doing "dirty, difficult, dangerous," and now, distanced work.

The pandemic exposed racialized immigrants of colour, including Filipinos, doing frontline essential services needed to keep us clean, well fed, safe, and healthy. It revealed previously invisible Filipinos working in meat-packing plants from High-River, Alberta to Brandon, Manitoba. Laid bare are seniors care homes from Vancouver Island to Nova Scotia that Filipino nurses, health care aides, and personal support workers run.

Filipino service workers encounter the stealthy virus, causing disproportionate illness and deaths among their ranks. Some have suffered racialized misidentification, class discrimination, verbal abuse, and physical attacks amidst increasing anti-Asian racism.

How do we explain Filipinos' over-representation in the caregiving professions and other service sectors in Canada and other countries with Filipino overseas contract workers? To answer this adequately, we need to avoid cultural explanations. Often, we hear Filipinos and non-Filipinos say, sometimes with pride, that "it is in our culture," "it is in our personality genes." We buy into these racial and cultural stereotypes without thinking about their empirical bases, historical origins, and social implications.

There is nothing "cultural" that makes Filipinos "genetically fit," "naturally fit," or "better-matched" for care-giving and domestic work. We share our love for family, respect for parents, care for children, and compassion for the elderly with many cultures around the world. Why is it immigrants from the Philippines, not Pakistan, India, or Indonesia—countries with surplus labour for migration—who end up disproportionately working in the six Cs?

Instead, we need to understand colonial history, immigration policies, and post-war Philippine and Canadian national interests. Under US occupation, American colonizers constructed Filipinos as "subservient," "docile," and "industrious" workers essential to its imperial ambitions. The empire also promoted public healthcare, nutrition, and hygiene in the country, producing many Filipino healthcare professionals trained in local and foreign universities and hospitals, who became early immigrants to the United States. Some of them moved to Canada in the 1950s through the 1970s.

As the Canadian economy expanded in the 1980s and women entered the labour force in droves, Canada needed other source of domestic workers to join West Indian and Caribbean immigrant women caregivers, who earlier replaced late-nineteenth-century British nannies. During this period, the Philippines had already been sending contract workers to the Middle East since the 1970s, and was looking to other countries in need of foreign labour to generate dollar revenues.

Canada and the East Asian economic tigers – Taiwan, Singapore, Hong Kong and South Korea – where housewives and mothers also started working outside their homes – imported Filipino domestic workers. The Canadian government introduced the Foreign Domestic Movement (FDM) policy, replaced by the Live-In Caregiver Program in the 1990s.

Canadian policymakers view domestic work as the natural pool for low-wage service sector jobs in schools, hospitals, restaurants, airports, and commercial establishments. Facing barriers to entry in regulated health professions, Philippine-trained professionals who migrated as caregivers retrained to become licensed practical nurses or healthcare aides. A majority went into low-wage service jobs. However, almost half of those who finished the LCP program still do caregiving and domestic-like work, even with open work visas. Government data also shows that live-in caregivers receive comparable income levels fifteen years after finishing the program.

The burden of maintaining senior care homes that remain underfunded and under-staffed fall on undervalued and under-compensated Filipino service workers.

We need to respect, recognize, and take pride in Filipinos working in essential services. They deserve nothing less from Canadians. As we pay tribute, provide redress, and show gratitude to Filipino frontline workers in this pandemic, we need to consider the implications of this over-representation. Over-representation in underpaid, undervalued service sector work has serious social, economic, and educational outcomes, especially for youth and future generations.

Chapter 7:
AGEING IN CANADA

Advances in the health sciences have allowed us to live much longer than our parents and those before them. And so, the significant shift in demographics not just in Canada but around the world shows an ageing population in need of long-term care.

This chapter discusses myriad issues affecting those in their golden years: from long-term care needs to retirement plans (whether in Canada or the Philippines), wills and estates, funeral costs, and medically assisted death and its place in Catholic Church rules and beliefs. It also includes perspectives from younger generations, whose lives continue to be molded by their elders.

Respect for the elders sits high on the Filipino totem pole of values—so much so that discussions around ageing and death are extremely uncomfortable among Filipinos. But those discussions add value to the rest of one's life, and ultimately give peace of mind to those who will be left behind to carry on.

Writing a will, planning for your funeral, and other such end-of-life topics are considered morbid and taboo subjects, right up there with religion, sex, and politics.

Filipinos do not generally give too much thought to the end of life, but looking ahead and planning, as these articles share, allows those left behind to breathe a little easier, and makes the pain of loss a little more bearable.

What occupies the minds of many Filipino seniors in Canada today is whether quality of life is possible in old age, and where and how it can be achieved as they get older.

This chapter tries to answer some of their questions, to help them make an important decision on what to do with the rest of their lives, and to help the family face and accept the inevitable. 🐦

Is There Life after Sixty-Five for Filipinos in Canada?

By Prod Laquian

December 16, 2016 – The first wave of Filipino immigrants, young professionals who arrived in the 1960s and 1970s, are now reaching retirement age. They were at the prime of their lives when they came, full of hope for a new life in a new country. They are the ones who are likely to stay in Canada for good. These early immigrants have their reasons for staying.

According to some of these pioneers, they easily found jobs suitable to their qualifications back then. Vancouver was also affordable. Rent for a house on King Edward Avenue was fifty dollars a month, a Mustang was two thousand dollars, bus fare was twenty-five cents (or five tokens for a dollar), a pound of chicken was nineteen cents, and domestic postage was five cents.

For a family of four, their bill for a cartful of groceries was twenty dollars a week. The salary of a registered nurse at Vancouver General Hospital was $149 every two weeks, and she was able to work as a registered nurse straight away. The Filipino community in Vancouver at the time was about 250 people, and they were all friendly and helpful to each other.

Fast-forward to 2016, when these early immigrants are now reaping the fruits of their labour. After working for fifty years or so, many of them are retired grandparents, enjoying their well-deserved rest with family and friends. Now, their conversation tends to focus on various aches and pains, surgeries and medication, and the high cost of housing in Vancouver.

In 2005, in the one and only nationwide survey of Filipinos in Canada for the purpose of finding out their plans after retirement, conducted by Eleanor Laquian for a book she was writing, of the 514 respondents, 28.4 percent planned to stay in Canada, 39.7 percent planned to stay in Canada with frequent visits to the Philippines, 5.6 percent planned to return to the Philippines for good, and 4.5 percent planned to move to other places, where their children are staying or taxes were lower. As these early immigrants grow older and their family expands to include interracial marriages, it is likely that a high proportion of them will stay in Canada for good.

This may be explained by a number of factors. First, in the last fifty years, many have spent more years in Canada than anywhere else. Second, a significant number have sponsored their close relatives, so they have their family and friends in Canada. Third, they like their quality of life in Canada, and might find it difficult to adjust to conditions in the Philippines.

When asked what they like best about Canada, the majority cited medical services, a clean environment, and a diverse population living in peace and order, with freedom, tolerance, and equal opportunities for all. Plus, life expectancy for both men and women is higher in Canada than in the Philippines, so there are more years for enjoying a happy life. Still, even for some long-time Canadian Filipinos, there is no home like where one was born.

Why I Prefer to Grow Old in the Philippines

By Paz Antonio

October 16, 2016 – Beautiful British Columbia—to anyone who has ever visited BC—is a place synonymous with breathtaking scenery.

The TV ads promoting tourism in BC show off the grandeur of its majestic mountains, lush valleys, and sparkling waters. Its West Coast, with its mild climate and easy accessibility to various social, cultural, and recreational venues, would be a wonderful place for a satisfying retirement.

But having spent a few months of every year in the Philippines since my early retirement from teaching in the late 1990s, I find myself leaning more and more toward spending the rest of my life there, because retirement cannot be all leisure. One must have some purpose in life other than a comfortable existence.

I think the Philippines is an ideal place for me to lead a purposeful life. While Canada has made provisions for its needy citizens, the Philippines has no such widespread safety net. Many of the disadvantaged are left to their own resources. Some lucky ones have their needs met by charitable groups and foreign and local medical missions. These organizations can always use volunteers to help with their work. I could be one.

Although the controversy is still unresolved, some public schools in the Philippines have opted to use English as the medium of instruction. My neighbourhood schools are in need of English resource persons to help with teacher training. I could offer some assistance in this area. In addition, I could also organize classes for teaching conversational English to those students interested in improving their English speaking skills.

With the exchange rate favourable to the Canadian currency, my Canadian pension can afford me a comfortable life in the Philippines, with enough left over to provide post-secondary education for one or two deserving students. There are many capable and gifted young people whose talents are wasted because they have no means to attend institutions of higher learning.

Steeped in Catholic culture and ritual, the Philippine environment fosters the devout practice of religion. Sincerely devoted Catholics abound in the Philippines. One can't help but follow suit in their zealous practice of hearing daily Mass and attending other Catholic devotions. Catholic holy days are still strictly observed throughout the country. Businesses close on Good Friday. The joy of the Christmas season permeates throughout the land, not only in churches and homes but in shopping malls as well. Incidentally, the season lasts from September to December, giving everyone more time to enjoy and do good to others.

One of the beautiful customs of Philippine society is the recognition of relatives, no matter how many times removed. I will be surrounded by many who will care for me and look after my well-being. I will not be left alone in a seniors' home in Canada.

Travel in Asia would be readily accessible and affordable. Friends and relatives often go on jaunts to other parts of the country, as well as abroad. I would not want for changes in scenery.

Contrary to current thinking, we can go home again—to the familiar places, practices, palates, and people of our childhood. There is no place like the home where you were born, with many fond memories of your carefree and happy youth. 🐾

Why Canada Is the Best Place for Ageing

By Cecilia Yuthasastrakosol

October 16, 2016 – Unlike many people I know, I retired without much thought about how I was going to survive. Fortunately, Canada has old age pension and the Canada Pension Plan to rely on. To supplement income from these sources, there's the Registered Retirement Savings Plan, and supplemental income for those in need, so they don't need to rely on food banks for subsistence.

But one does not really need a lot of money to enjoy retirement in Canada. The government offers affordable ways and means for even those living below the poverty line.

In Winnipeg, as well as in many Canadian cities, any interested senior will not want for a variety of activities available to seniors—some free and others for a small fee. It is great to be able to attend classes of your own choosing, and I wasted no time in registering for classes offered by the city.

Free cooking classes were my first choice. I learned about preparing various ethnic dishes by attending Greek, Italian, Japanese, Indian, and French cooking classes. I learned how to bake the customary Christmas cookies, savoury and sweet strudel, different kinds of bread, and all kinds of pies and pastries.

While I did not become an expert, the mysteries about food we usually order in restaurants are now demystified.

Since my husband's passing, I have had to deal with car and house repairs by myself. I considered it of utmost importance to be knowledge-able about these. The City of Winnipeg offers classes in these areas as well. Now I know what is involved in changing oil or tires—and weeping tiles are not what I imagined they were. Would you believe it? At age sixty-eight, I took a class on how to use power machines, and learned how to sharpen knives?

Then there's this very domesticated avocation—sewing. I look with envy at some women who wear what they themselves sewed. But sewing definitely does not agree with me. After three sessions, I still have to finish one project. It seems that all I learned was to undo stitches. I'm not giving up yet, though.

All these classes took place in the evenings. So, how do I fill my days? I do volunteer work at various organizations. I deliver meals to the elderly and the sick through Meals on Wheels. I quit only after my osteoarthritis got worse, in winter.

Age offers the elderly the opportunity to learn or improve their command of the English language. It's a very short commitment of an hour and a half per week, and very gratifying.

For a few years now, I've been helping the Winnipeg Regional Health during the flu clinic, helping new immigrants fill out forms or directing clients where to go; sometimes, I sign up for other volunteer work when needed.

Then there's International Hope. This is an organization that collects used hospital equipment and supplies to send to third-world countries where they are badly needed. When I can, I put in about three hours a week to sort donations as they arrive. Because of this organization, I was able to send two forty-foot containers of used hospital beds and medical supplies to two hospitals in the Philippines. Indirectly, I helped get a third hospital in the Philippines similar hospital supplies when one of my helpers arranged funding from his city's government officials.

There is so much emphasis on seniors doing more physical activities to improve wellbeing, and there are a variety of activities available in Winnipeg. I have attended Tai Chi classes for several years, Aquacize three times a week at the University of Manitoba and the public pools, and free yoga classes in Fort Garry, which helped improve my mobility and enabled me to delay my knee replacement. In addition, I also attend free yoga at the Hindu Temple. My membership to the University of Manitoba Gym allows me to exercise on state-of-the-art exercise machines and the stationary bike; I walk on tracks or exercise in the pool as often as I want.

All these activities I have engaged in during retirement have definitely improved my health and my mental state. In addition to the benefits my body gets, I mingle and interact with likeminded women who, without question, improve my outlook on life and my state of well-being. I must say, what more can one want?

Cecilia Yuthasastrakosol came to Canada in 1969 with her three children to join her husband, who was studying for his PhD at the University of Manitoba. She had worked as an employment counsellor helping new immigrants find jobs, taught English in the evenings, and worked with youth at risk at the YMCA-YWCA for twelve years before retirement. Then, from 1977 to 1994, she produced and hosted a TV talk show on public access TV.

Being a Senior Is More Fun in the Philippines

By Adelaida Lacaba-Bago

Elderly citizens are entitled to many benefits under Philippine law. Photo by Jcomp/Freepik.com.

December 1, 2019 – It is an integral part of the cultural values of the Filipinos to take care of, honour, and protect their elders. In general, grandparents and sometimes great-grandparents constitute part of the Filipino nuclear family.

It is unusual for Filipino families to send their elderly to a home for the aged. This value is also shared by the government, which had already passed several laws like *Republic Act No. 7432*, amended by *RA No. 9257* (*Expanded Senior Citizens Act* of 2003), and further amended by *RA 9994*, known as the *Expanded Senior Citizens Act*, all intended to provide elderly Filipinos with senior citizen discounts and other perks to help ease their finances in their golden years.

The laws define a senior or elderly citizen as any resident citizen of the Philippines who is at least sixty years old. They provide that elderly Filipinos aged sixty and over are entitled to a 20 percent senior citizen discount and exempted from the value-added tax on applicable goods and services for their exclusive use. These privileges apply to both cash and credit card payments.

The following goods and services, as listed in the laws, are provided upon presentation of a senior citizen's card or any valid government ID that will show the age of the claimant:

- Medicines: Generic and branded medicines, vitamins, and mineral supplements (with doctor's prescription)
- Medical supplies and equipment: Hearing aids, eyeglasses, wheel-chairs, crutches, dentures, etc.
- Medical and dental services in private facilities: Lab tests such as blood tests, X-rays, etc.
- Professional fees of attending physicians and licensed health workers
- Domestic air and sea travel fares
- Public land transportation fares: Jeepneys, buses, taxis, shuttle services, MRT, LRT, PNR, etc.
- Hotels: Accommodation and amenities in hotels, beach resorts, mountain resorts, etc.
- Restaurants: Food, beverages, dessert, and other consumables for dine-in, take-out, drive-thru, and delivery orders
- Recreation centers: Rental and other fees for sports facilities such as gyms, badminton courts, tennis courts, ballroom dancing studios, bowling lanes, etc.
- Places of leisure: Cinemas, museums, parks, theaters, concert halls, etc. In some cities and municipalities, like Makati and Muntinlupa, senior citizens are able to watch movies free of charge.
- Funeral and burial services for deceased senior citizens: hospital morgue, embalming, casket or urn, cremation, etc.
- Free parking per municipal or city ordinances

Other benefits include the following:

- Income tax exemption for minimum-wage earners
- Training fee exemption on socioeconomic programs
- Free medical and dental services in government facilities
- Free flu and pneumococcal vaccinations for indigent senior citizens
- Scholarships and financial assistance for seniors' education in public and private schools
- Retirement benefits from SSS.GSIS, and Pag-IBIG
- Discounts in special programs for senior citizens
- Express or priority lanes for senior citizens in all government offices and commercial establishments grocery stores, restaurants and movie houses

PhilHealth Benefits

In many malls and some gasoline stations, separate, spacious toilets, with its own sink for the elderly provided, and with appropriate handrails installed near the toilet bowls to ensure the convenience and safety of the elderly users. Indeed, with all these perks, benefits, and privileges, the golden years of a Filipino citizen in the Philippines have a silver lining for a life well lived and appreciated.

How Catholic Filipinos Deal With Death

By Leonardo B. Cunanan

November 1, 2017 – Bereaved families find consolation in believing that death is just the beginning of eternal life, as in this prayer for a happy death:

"Lord, as years go by, I fear the yoke of sickness and pain, and I worry how my life will end. And so, I humbly ask you, Lord, that when my time comes, do not call me by sudden death, not by accident that tears the body apart, not by illness that leaves the mind confused or the senses impaired, not at the mercy of evil forces, not with a heart full of hate or a body racked with

pain; Not abandoned, lonely, without love or care, not by my own hand in a moment of despair. My dear Lord Jesus, let death come as a gentle friend to sit and linger with me until you call my name."

This prayer summarizes a Catholic Filipino's fears and acceptance of death as the will of God. The bereaved family finds consolation in believing that death is the end of all pain and suffering and the beginning of eternal life. Still, the death of a loved one always comes with grief and distress for family members.

For the survivors who are not prepared to meet the cost of funeral and other related expenses, the grief is multiplied with worries over financial obligations. To avoid these last-minute decisions when bereaved family members are most vulnerable to unscrupulous agents who may take advantage of their bereavement, many Filipinos have taken advantage of advance planning options for their demise, offered by many funeral homes. They do this through pre-need funeral plans, to lessen the burden for their family. This includes a predetermined selection of all funeral services.

Catholic Funeral Service

In Vancouver, the interment of the dead is done in privately owned or church-approved cemeteries and memorial parks or columbarium. There are four Catholic cemeteries in the Greater Vancouver area: The Gardens of Gethsemani in South Surrey, St. Peter's in New Westminster, St. Mary's Cemetery in Chilliwack, and Our Lady of Good Hope Cemetery in Hope.

The Roman Catholic Cemeteries of the Archdiocese of Vancouver is responsible for administering Catholic cemeteryregulations . Catholic cemeteries offer burial space and refer parishioners to selected funeral homes for other services.

The Gardens of Gethsemani is the only Catholic cemetery and mausoleum in the Lower Mainland. It provides in-ground burial plots, mausoleum crypts, and cremation niches—both indoor and outdoor. The cemetery is regularly open from dawn to dusk, but on November 1 and 2, it stays open late to give families more time to visit, and Masses are held throughout the day in its chapel.

In all Catholic churches in the Archdiocese of Vancouver, the fee for funeral services including Mass and interment is two hundred dollars. There are additional charges for the choir and altar servers, if needed. Personal donation to the priest by the family is voluntary.

On the day of the funeral, the body is received at the entrance of the church with prayers and blessings by the priest. The casket is then brought close to the paschal candle at the altar, while the choir is singing. If eulogy is requested, it is given by one or two members of the family, before the start of the Mass or after the Mass. After the Mass, the casket is brought to the hearse and started on its way to the cemetery. The priest or deacon may accompany the casket for the graveyard service, which includes prayers and blessing of the departed before the actual burial.

In Canada, Filipino Catholics normally hold a nine-day novena for the dead, starting a day after the demise. The prayers and viewing of the body in the funeral home is usually for one or two nights, from 6 to 9 p.m. In the Philippines, *lamay*, or all-day-and-all-night vigil, is held in the home of the deceased, so people can pay their respects. Throughout the *lamay*, guests quietly play mah jong and card games with the proceeds from the bets donated to the family to help pay for the funeral expenses. This is not done in Canada, although some funeral homes would accommodate a *lamay* without gambling on request. In Canada, it is normal for relatives and friends to give flowers, sympathy cards with money enclosed, and food for the reception. Prayers for the dead at the funeral home during the wake are led by a priest or pastor. The following day, a funeral Mass may be celebrated in a church, followed by the interment.

A Mass or special prayer is held in a church on the fortieth day after death. This memorial service is a tradition based on the belief that the souls of the dead still wander in this natural world for forty days before going to their final or transitory supernatural realm. Most Filipinos are Catholic by upbringing, but even families who are not strongly religious fall back on Catholic traditions at the time of a death. Once a death has occurred, it is considered important for those left behind to make sure the deceased is blessed by a priest, to ease the departed's journey to eternal rest.

Leonardo B. Cunanan is the founding editor of Dahong Pilipino, *the only Filipino-Canadian community and business directory in Canada. It started in 1991 and has continued to publish annually for almost thirty years. When Cunanan became an Immigration and Refugee Board of Canada member (1997–2005), his son Leo Jr. took over the* publication—but he remains editor to date.

MAD Divides the Catholic Church

By Eleanor R. Laquian

October 1, 2018 – The Vatican's *Jura et Bona* defines "euthanasia" or "mercy killing" as "an action or an omission which of itself or by intention causes death, in order that all suffering may in this way be eliminated."

After years of debate and controversial court cases, Justin Trudeau's Liberal government passed Bill C-14, decriminalizing doctor-assisted suicide in Canada, because to criminalize it was against Canada's *Charter of Rights and Freedoms.*

The bill received Royal assent in June 2016 and set out a regime to regulate who could obtain "medical assistance in dying." Immediately, it exposed the deep divisions that exist within the Catholic Church in Canada.

The bishops of Canada disagree on fundamental issues, such as whether individuals involved in medically assisted death can receive certain sacraments and a Catholic funeral. Some religious experts say the schism is the product of Pope Francis's emphasis on tolerance and compassion.

"To allow a person to die of starvation or dehydration, rather than of his/her illness, would be a form of euthanasia," wrote Archbishop Michael Miller on August 11, 2016 to Catholic healthcare professionals in the Archdiocese of Vancouver. He advocates palliative care for alleviating pain, managing symptoms, and relief from suffering.

"Doctor-Assisted Suicide is a Morally Great Evil"

In response to the new law on medically assisted death, the Catholic bishops of Alberta and the Northwest Territories issued a document entitled "Guidelines for the Celebration of the Sacraments with Persons and Families Considering or Opting for Death by Assisted Suicide or Euthanasia."

They instructed priests under their jurisdiction to deny the sacraments of confession (penance) and extreme unction (anointing of the sick) and a Catholic funeral, in certain circumstances, to an individual who helped someone die or died themselves by assisted suicide.

In a joint statement, the Catholic bishops of Alberta said, "This is not a matter of 'medical assistance in dying.' What is at issue here is state sponsored killing of the innocent. Killing is not medicine. This has no place in a just and ethical society."

Similar statements of concern were issued by the Assembly of Québec bishops, Archbishop J. Michael Miller of Vancouver, and Reverend Douglas Crosby, bishop of Hamilton and president of the Canadian Conference of Catholic Bishops.

On August 11, 2016, Archbishop Michael Miller, as shepherd of over four hundred thousand Catholics in Greater Vancouver and the Lower Mainland, reiterated the church's teaching on euthanasia and assisted suicide as a "grave violation of the commandment, you shall not kill." He clarified the false impression that the Catholic Church teaches that one must sustain and prolong life under all circumstances and at any cost. He explained that "every person has a fundamental right to refuse procedures or treatments considered 'extraordinary' or 'disproportionate'—that is, overly burdensome, painful, or of dubious effectiveness in restoring health. Likewise, the individual has the right to discontinue treatment under the same conditions."

Archbishop Terrence Prendergast of Ottawa warned Catholics that they may be denied the sacrament of extreme unction and a Catholic funeral if their death is a result of doctor-assisted suicide. "I think we have to be clear that the Church cannot condone this. It's clearly contrary to the moral teaching of everybody," he said. He called doctor assisted suicide a "morally great evil."

On the Other Hand

Cardinal Gerald Lacroix of Québec City and Archbishop Christian Lepine of Montréal both reacted differently to the new law, declaring that they would not give specific guidelines to their priests about refusing Catholic funeral services to people who requested assisted suicide.

"The Catholic Church accompanies people in every step of their life," said Cardinal Lacroix, "We do that in dialogue with every person and every family that wishes to be accompanied."

Bishop Douglas Crosby, OMI, the bishop of Hamilton and president of the Conference of the Catholic Bishops of Canada, strongly criticized Bill C-14, stating on behalf of the CCCB, "Physician-assisted suicide is an affront to what is most noble, most precious in the human endeavour, and a grave injustice and violation of the dignity of every human person whose natural and inherent inclination is indeed the preservation of life." Despite those strong words, Bishop Crosby indicated that he did not "foresee that the CCCB will be putting out guidelines" and setting out a uniform response from the Catholic Church to the new law.

"How to respond to a person who asks for euthanasia is problematic for a Catholic pastoral minister," said Bishop Noël Simard of the Diocese of Valleyfield, Québec at a provincial workshop held December 1, 2016 at the Cathedral of the Holy Family in Saskatoon. "When we are facing a complex situation, there is no black and white. There is a lot of grey zones, and it is where mercy can be expressed—in the grey zone. And I think we are called to express the mercy of God."

Dying with Dignity in Canada

Dying with Dignity Canada is a national not-for-profit organization committed to improving the conditions of dying, protecting end-of-life rights, and helping Canadians avoid unwanted suffering.

According to DWD Canada, medical assistance in dying (MAiD) is not assisted suicide, mercy killing, or euthanasia, but a safe, compassionate choice for individuals facing the prospect of a horrific death. DWD presents the following facts on end-of-life choices so people can decide for themselves:

Allowing assisted dying respects a patient's right to choose. The Supreme Court struck down the laws forbidding physician-assisted dying because they were unconstitutional and unfairly restricted individual choice. Access to aid in dying will give Canadians further control over their care and, ultimately, their lives.

Canadians want choice. More than eight in ten Canadians support physician-assisted dying. Commissioned by DWD Canada, a 2014 Ipsos Reid poll opinion poll showed that 84 percent of Canadians believe gravely ill patients should have the right to end their lives with the help of a doctor.

Making assisted dying illegal doesn't stop it. Each year, a handful of gravely ill Canadians travel to Switzerland for a medically assisted death. The cost—twenty to thirty thousand dollars including flights and accommodation—puts this option out of reach for most Canadians.

At home, laws banning assisted dying and voluntary euthanasia have led Canadians with catastrophic diagnoses to end their own lives, sometimes violently and often prematurely. These tragedies devastate families and scar first responders. It's time to stop this unnecessary trauma. DWD asserts that safeguards work. "We can provide choice for competent Canadians and protect the most vulnerable members of our society. International research has repeatedly concluded that legalized assisted dying doesn't threaten vulnerable groups, such as children, the very elderly, the poor, people with disabilities, and the mentally ill. This conclusion was upheld by the Supreme Courts of BC and was a key factor in the Supreme Court of Canada's decision to decriminalize physician-assisted dying."

Assisted dying doesn't hurt palliative care. Jurisdictions where end-of-life choice is legal are often global leaders in end-of-life care. Oregon, Washington, and Vermont were the first American states to legalize assisted dying. They also lead the US in terms of access to palliative care.

Physician-assisted dying is good for end-of-life healthcare. In places where assisted dying is legal, doctors are more likely to discuss end-of-life care with patients and their families. Legal choice in dying also forces doctors to learn more about a broad range of end-of-life options.

Who is eligible for medical assistance in dying under the new law? A Christian argument for medically assisted death justifies self-aware assisted death as a choice based on one's free will: a God-given gift to make one's own moral decisions and be responsible for them.

Under Bill C-14, two independent healthcare professionals need to evaluate an individual in order to determine whether he or she qualifies for MAiD.

To qualify, an individual must be eighteen years or older and . . .

- be eligible for health services funded by the federal government or a province or territory (generally, visitors to Canada are not eligible for medical assistance in dying);
- be mentally competent and capable of making healthcare decisions for themselves;
- have a grievous and irremediable medical condition for which death is imminent;
- make a voluntary request for medical assistance in dying that is not the result of outside pressure or influence; and
- give informed consent to receive medical assistance in dying.

Since Bill C-14 became law in 2016, about two thousand Canadians have chosen to die this way. Statistics did not indicate their religion. But for practising Catholics who believe last rites cleanse the soul of sin in preparation for eternal life in Heaven, a proper funeral is far more than an end-of-life celebration.

For the faithful questioning whether those final sacraments of penance and extreme unction are available to a loved one who has chosen a medically assisted deathurch they ask.

If There's a Will . . . Or, How to Plan for the Inevitable

By Jo Leuterio-Flach

May 16, 2019 – Do you have a will? Or would you rather not think about it? You are not alone. Shortly after we got married, Peter and I went to Berlin to visit his mother. One evening, after dinner, his mother said, "I have something to show you." She led us to her desk, pulled open a drawer, and took out a brown envelope. "If anything happens to me," she said, "open this envelope and follow the instructions." Peter and I were aghast. A very lively widow, only sixty years old, she swam several laps every morning and liked going out with her friends at night. She lived by herself and was fiercely independent. The list of instructions began with "call the lawyer," "go to the bank," etc. A will was attached—a short one, as my husband was an only child.

A year later, while my parents were visiting us in Toronto, I asked my father, "Dad, have you made a will?" He looked at me, eyebrows raised. "Why should I make a will? I know you children will not fight over any-thing." Now, Peter and I looked at each other, aghast. My parents were in their late sixties, and I was one of seven children. My dad was a lawyer by profession—a bar topnotcher for heaven's sake—and should have known better. My father was very kind, very trusting and very fair-minded (he was a judge, after all—and a very good one at that) so I did not pursue the matter further, knowing how we Filipinos do not like to talk about the inevitable. I simply said, "Don't leave me anything. I am doing fine." Neither did my sister who was a practising paediatrician in the US.

Ten years later, in 1977, a phone call came from Germany. A neighbour had found my mother-in-law on her kitchen floor; she had been dead for a while. After a night out, they were supposed to meet for lunch, but Lotte had not shown up. Peter took the next plane out. He was in a daze. Upon his arrival, he took out the instructions and followed them, step by step.

With the help of friends and neighbours, he moved in a trance-like flurry of activity: last rites and reception; apartment put on the market and sold; some paintings and sculptures, antique furniture, heirloom cutlery, and sets of dishes packed and crated by a shipping company, some given to friends, and the rest given to charity or disposed of in the trash. Six weeks later, a big container was unloaded at our house. We spent several days unpacking and incorporating the inheritance into our home; we kept and still enjoy many of these treasures, and they never fail to evoke precious memories of a beloved mother-in-law.

Both my parents died many years ago. My sister continued to live in the house, and we all would come home and visit as though my parents were still there. A cousin looked after the farms and the seasonal harvests, but when he passed away, no one took his place. In the meantime, we found out that there were no titles to some of the land properties. Notices of unpaid taxes were being received by my siblings.

Fast forward to 2019, eleven years later. I know my parents meant well, but the estate is still not settled. A lot of progress has been made, but unexpected complications have developed. My sister who was living in California passed away in 2018. She did not have a will. Because my mother also died intestate (i.e., a will was not found), the estate, administered according to law, was to be equally divided among the surviving siblings. When I reminded my siblings that I had opted out of any inheritance years ago, they all insisted I was one of them and entitled to an inheritance.

My father was right all along—no sibling rivalry here. Powers of attorney and extrajudicial settlement documents had to be executed by a lawyer to further the process. And now, even more complications. Suddenly, the lawyer wants to find out where my paternal grandfather's two sisters' families are. They both moved away decades ago, and we had lost touch. They, too, are entitled to an inheritance from their father. A search for their descendants will now begin. And so it goes.

How to Deal with an Estate

Not everyone's estate is as complex as ours. But almost everyone has an estate—you have an estate if you own a house, investments, cars, or any kind of personal effects.

Lessons are still being learned. But what I can tell you is that if there's a will, your loved ones will receive the assets in accordance with your wishes;

otherwise, the government will take charge. By naming an executor in your will, you alleviate the stresses and burdens of administering the distribution of your assets.

As you can see, having a will is not the only answer. Good estate planning is essential to minimize delays and costs in its execution. After the long, drawn-out experience with my family estate, Peter and I have decided to engage a professional who will consult with our children as co-executors. Rather than asking a friend or a relative to act as executor, you might choose to engage a professional who will consult with your children as co-executors.

An executor's responsibilities require a certain level of expertise in estate law, taxes, administration, etc. It is a job not best taken as a favour, as it comes with a demanding commitment to get the work done as quickly and efficiently as possible. It does not come without a certain amount of remuneration (a percentage of the assets), which comes out of the inheritance, but your heirs will thank you for sparing them the aggravation in the midst of grief.

So, what else can you do to make things easier for your executors, and your heirs, and save you some money in the process?

Do as Peter's mother did. Write a to-do list. Write out important contact names and telephone numbers, your passwords, and so forth : your lawyers, accountants, investment brokers, bank accounts, and safety deposit box numbers. Attach keys to safety deposit box numbers Indicate where your important documents are. Place everything together in an envelope and be sure to tell your children where it is. If you have an executor, he will guide your heirs through this process and help them get through the difficult first days of grief.

It would be wise to have a good look at your household possessions now. The Swedes have a word, *dostadning* ("death cleaning"), which refers to de-cluttering and cleaning one might do faced with the prospect of leaving this world. Do not wait for the threat of the inevitable—do it now.

De-cluttering is something we should be doing regularly in any case, as it can be overwhelming, physically and emotionally. Do you really need— or use—all those clothes and shoes crammed in your closets? Start giving away some of your jewellery to your children and grandchildren. If you have artworks and antiques, take photos of each and ask your children if they would like to have any of them.

When our children were children, we asked them to look around and tell us what they would like to inherit from us. My ten-year-old son piped up, "I want the TV." (It was a black-and-white twenty-inch screen. Today, he has a sixty-inch wall-mounted screen, and I have no idea how to turn it on.)

Friends tell me that their children don't want any of their possessions—they already have what they want, and besides, their tastes are different. In this case, get an appraisal, and keep only what "sparks joy," as Marie Kondo says.

Otherwise, everything goes to an estate sale when you're gone, appraisals have to be made, and there will be costs attached to their disposal. You can and should also give friends pieces they admire. The rest can go to charity, if in good condition, or in the trash.

Whatever you do, allow yourself a couple of hours for going through photos and souvenirs. It's easy to spend a whole day poring over memories.

Having done all this, you will be more self-aware, know what your assets are, know what you can leave to your children, and can now spend what you wish on yourself, knowing that your will is done—and your will *will* be done. So, live it up and enjoy today—you have planned well for tomorrow.

Why You Should Write Your Will

By Melissa Briones, LLB, CPHR

May 16, 2019 – For many Filipinos, writing a will is an emotional exercise. Death or dying is not a welcome thought. "Not yet, not now, can't be now" is the usual plea. After all, a will could be controversial, and leave in its wake disappointments, tensions, and conflicts that can no longer be brought under control by the will-maker when he dies. It is also, in many ways, a reflection of how a life was lived—whether family was made the priority or if it was the pursuit of material wealth. Many people do not want to know.

What If There Is No Will?

If there is no will, intestacy rules apply. In British Columbia, the Wills Estate and Succession Act dictates how estates are distributed when individuals die with no will in place.

For example, when a person who dies has a spouse but no children, the entire estate passes to the spouse. If there is a spouse and children, the first three hundred thousand dollars goes to the spouse, and the remainder is divided equally between the spouse and the children, with all the children sharing in the fifty percent. It gets more complicated with blended families.

Thus, if there is no will, the estate does not go automatically to the government. The government will search for an heir up to the fourth degree of relationship. If none is found, the estate will escheat to the provincial government.

However, hardship, delay, extra expenses, and considerable inconvenience plague the family of those who die without a will.

Instead of grieving and moving on, instead of focusing on celebrating the life that has passed—whether curling up in bed and looking at photographs or throwing a party—those who are left behind are forced to face the reality of their loved one's passing in the harshest of circumstances.

Payment of debts and mortgages leave them cash-strapped, assets are frozen or seized. Moving on becomes difficult. And because they are at their most vulnerable, some fall prey to the unscrupulous.

What Is a Will?

A will is a written and signed document that explains what a will-maker wants done with his or her property upon death. Wills deal with real estate, money, investments, and personal and household belongings.

Wills perform a fundamental role. Will-writing is estate planning, and a good wills attorney, through the help of an accountant, may be able to save the will-maker thousands of dollars in probate fees and taxes. Affairs will be put in order, and assets will be distributed according to the will-maker's intention.

If a lawyer is engaged to draft a will, the lawyer will ask the will-maker to fill out a will questionnaire, which will have the following choices:

- their choice of executor or the one who will administer the will (and a sub-executor, in case the chosen executor predeceases the will-maker);
- in the case they have minor children, who can be their possible guardians (at least three), who must be healthy, younger than the will-maker (and the spouse), and share his or her values; and
- assets owned, to whom they should be given, and when.

At the appointment, the lawyer will discuss planning tools (joint tenancies, life insurance, RRSP, RRIF, trusts, charitable donations), probate fees, and tax issues. The lawyer will then obtain instructions from the will-maker and prepare supporting documentation so it won't be vulnerable to a wills variation claim.

The cost of preparing a will varies according to its complexity. Simple wills cost about $350, more complex wills start at $2,000.

Wills should be reviewed every three to five years, or when circumstances change, such as a change in financial circumstances, or a new marriage, birth, or death in the family.

A will could be a final act of grace, of benevolence, of saying goodbye, or a way to make things right. It could be a last heave before a person and his words go kaput. It can transmit hopes and dreams to people one does not wish to leave too soon.

It is part-love letter, part-goodbye letter. It is an emotional exercise and a practical one. It puts one's affairs in order so that those who will be left behind will be spared additional grief and expense at one's passing. Most people would prefer not to look, but in not looking, they do not know that they might be doing themselves—and the people they love—a disfavour.

CFNet Honorary Legal Counsel

Melissa Briones, barrister and solicitor, is a lawyer licensed to practice law in British Columbia and the Philippines. A graduate of the University of the Philippines College of Law, she also received a degree in HR management at Ashton College (with honours) and obtained a Chartered Professional in

Human Resources (CPHR) designation. A lawyer for ABS-CBN Broadcasting Corporation, she became the first editor-in-chief of the Philippine Canadian Inquirer, *a nationwide publication that focuses on the Filipino diaspora, when she arrived in Canada. She is a director and member of the Rotary Club of Vancouver Mountainview and a former UPAABC president. She practises corporate, employment, real estate, wills and estates, and family law at her Vancouver law firm, Northam LawCorporation*

Searching for Lola

By Carissa Duenas

November 1, 2018 – I was eleven when my *lola*, or grandmother, passed away. My entire childhood, the complete gentleness of those years, is associated with her, my lola.

The routine was established early on: my parents dropped us off at her home in Pasay, usually in the early morning, before heading off to work. We remained under her care until school was over for the day. We'd run up the stairs as soon as we got back from school, sit around her favourite chair, and regale her with stories about what had transpired in class. She lovingly listened, amused, I imagine, by our little, happy lives. I loved her. But I also adored her, as so many other people did. Selfishly, I was grateful to have access to her heart—and she, mine—in ways that others didn't. Our bond was sacred.

And so, when she passed after a six-month battle with cancer, I was devastated. To this day, I can't recall a sadder moment than the day my lola died. I was grieving the first death in my family. In the immediate aftermath of her passing, I recall sitting at her sala, enveloped by heartache, confronted by an emptiness I have yet to feel again.

Equipped with the curiosity of a child, I wondered about where my lola had gone. I didn't know where to begin searching for the answers.

My parents told me stories of my lola being in heaven with God and the angels. The priest and my teachers told me the same. Having been raised in the Philippines with a deeply Catholic upbringing, that made sense. I lived with this belief throughout many years, at peace and comforted by what I had been told.

But it's been over two decades since my lola passed. And today, I find myself in a country where religion isn't necessarily shared by many, and individuals hold personal, differing philosophies about what gives meaning to existence.

Many people have come and gone since my lola's death, but there's a sense of closure—a need for certainty, still—that I seek today. An explanation distant from religious dogma.

Nobel Prize-winning physicist Arthur H. Compton believes that it takes an entire lifetime to attain a noble life. He says: "The adventures and disciplines of youth, the struggles and failures of success, the pain and pleasure of maturity, the loneliness and tranquility of ag—make up the fire through which he (the individual) must pass to bring out the pure gold of his soul." He claims if nothingness is the ultimate destiny of all this, it would be such a waste. He chooses to believe that the soul moves on to a greater place, where it returns to the Creator with "the work he had here begun."

Dr. Wernher von Braun, a space physicist, asserts his belief that death is the process of evolution. Science tells us that nothing can disappear without a trace—nothing ever leaves this universe. Everything merely transforms. And he asks, if "God applies this fundamental principle to the most minute and insignificant parts of the universe, doesn't it make sense that he applies it to the human soul?"

I have returned to the words of these brilliant men, and they have led me to my own answers. My understanding of grief and loss has taken to a new dimension.

When someone passes, science teaches us it's the end of any physical manifestation of the individual. But I have wondered about the moments when I sat under my lola's beautiful, old mango tree, and felt enveloped by a love that can't be spoken of.

I have thought of the moments when I cried to and for her, in prayers and dreams, and felt a quiet peace descend on me. There are moments when I offer help to people in need solely because of the memory of her. If she is truly gone, then why do I feel she is with me?

I now know, from these slivers of experiences, that there is something beyond life as we understand it. My lola has transformed, as Dr. Wernher von Braun put it.

And although I cannot grasp the complexities of the vast and cosmic universe, nor the laws that tame it, I hold in my heart one of its certainties: That each of us has the power to be immortal, to transcend the barriers of human existence and still exist.

This is the miracle of life, of living. Though this may not be the philosophical belief of an astrophysicist or a theologian, but that of a granddaughter, it is my sacred truth. For this was the story of my lola, who lived and died.

And lives. Her spirit endures, be it in the presence of the golden angels soaring in the high heavens or in the small confines of my heart. Of that I am certain.

Pondering Our Mortality: Is Quality of Life Possible in Ageing?

By Eleanor R. Laquian

November 1, 2020 – When family and friends have a birthday, we often wish them many more birthdays to come, as though a long life is a great gift. Is it always desirable?

I have many relatives who lived long lives. My grandparents died at ages ninety-five and eighty-eight in Pila, Laguna. My husband's grandmother died at age 103 in Apalit Pampanga. My godmother, the younger sister of my mother, died at 103, and her husband at 101 in Guimbal, Iloilo. But my mother, who moved from Guimbal to Manila when she was eighteen to study nursing, then got married and raised a family there, died at age fifty-six, while my father, who left Pila while still in high school to study in Manila, and settled there for good, died early, at age fifty-two.

It would seem that the simple life and clean environment of rural Philippines were more conducive to long life than the hectic and stressful life in the city. Now, advancement in technology and medicine has made long life possible even in urban areas. But does quality of life also come with a long life—whether on the farm or in the city?

Sadly, for many Filipino seniors in Canada, their golden years may not always glitter like gold. Senior Filipinos who were sponsored by their children to take care of grandchildren are less financially secure if they were not employed outside the home, and entitled to a pension and other benefits in retirement. Not being fully acculturated to Canadian life, they may feel lonely when left alone all day while the rest of the family goes to school or work. They may suffer from severe isolation and depression if their children are forced to put them in a nursing home—perhaps because all the adults in the family need to work to make ends meet, so nobody is home to care for an elderly parent. Or their place may not be suitable for a disabled's wheelchair and safety.

To have a decent quality of life in old age in Canada, one must be mentally alert and aware, physically strong and healthy, and financially secure and independent. Caring for a mentally incapacitated or physically handicapped parent is a huge burden to impose on anyone. Most parents know this, and do not wish to be such a burden to their children, so they may agree to go to a home.

Long-Term Care Homes

Nursing homes, no matter how fancy and expensive, are virtual prisons. And low-cost homes are often short-handed, with poorly trained staff and horrid sanitary conditions that should be condemned—but they continue to operate.

In nursing homes where residents require twenty-four-hour care, the residents are locked in for safety. They are not allowed to wander outside the building on their own, for fear they would get lost or hurt themselves. There had been news items about residents who had walked out in their pajamas in the middle of a snowy winter night and later been found dead from hypothermia on the sidewalk, not far from the nursing home. Thus, for their safety and because of the staff's concerns, residents, like children, are constantly told what they can and cannot do.

Most low-cost nursing homes are more concerned about making the job easy for the staff than making life pleasant for the elderly residents. Mealtimes are regulated, and served only at specific hours. Meals are usually bland—balanced enough to nourish the body, but not the soul. Nor do they satisfy an occasional craving for salty, sweet, rich, fatty, spicy, or high-in-cholesterol favourites. Troublesome foods are not served, to prevent gagging and diarrhea, which could embarrass the resident and cause more laundry and cleaning-up for the staff.

Bothersome and complaining seniors are often mildly sedated to keep them quiet and peaceful for the safety of other residents. Television sets are on all day so residents can have something to look at, even though they don't understand what they are watching.

Organized activities are mainly to keep them visually occupied, but not necessarily to stimulate their minds. The main purpose of these institutions is simply to keep the residents reasonably pain-free, comfortable, and safe from each other—not necessarily to improve their quality of life.

Bahay Dona Rosario is a nursing home for seniors in Muntinlupa, in the Philippines. Photo by Braintree Care Services & Senior Residences.

Many Filipino seniors who came to Canada in the prime of life, worked, and retired with pensions are opting to spend their retirement years in the Philippines, where their pensions last longer. Those who choose to remain in Canada to be close to family may eventually face the question of how to spend the final years of their life in this country.

Growing Old in Canada

Ideally, if they can retrofit their home to be invalid-safe and afford to have caregivers looking after them day and night, Filipino seniors can grow old at home until the final days of their life. But even in this ideal situation, if they suffer from chronic or other illnesses, all their visits to doctors and hospitals will only prolong their rapidly deteriorating condition, while keeping them as physically comfortable and pain-free as possible.

There is no regard for the life of the mind at this stage because once dementia sets in, the mind dies with age, long before the body does. Thus, when people of a certain age with serious illnesses are institutionalized or hospitalized, their family is routinely asked to sign a statement indicating whether or not to resuscitate the patient or use artificial means to prolong life should such a question arise.

How Life Ends

As people ponder the end of life, they need to ask themselves: how much are they willing to spend in time, money, and effort just to have a few more years of merely breathing but not really living?

Some would probably just leave it all to God and fate. Others may prefer to end life on their own terms through medically assisted death, now legal in Canada. It's a decision we all must make when the time comes. And it's something to think about as we age and come face to face with our mortality.

Cold, dark, and dreary November must be the saddest month of the year. The sky is grey, the trees are bare, the ground is brown, and people go around in dark clothing as though in mourning. Even the holidays of November are sad—All Saints' Day, All Souls' Day, Remembrance Day—all prompting thoughts of dying, death, and departed loved ones.

One early evening, as I sat in the dark watching the dusk take over the last lingering sunrays of day, I wondered if the end of life happens in the same way—like the gradual surrender of light to the dark unknown.

I thought, then, that dismal and grey November must be one of the reasons why Christmas is such a highly anticipated joyful season. After November 1, even I can barely wait for December to come around, when carols fill the airwaves and shops start counting the days before Christmas.

Chapter 8:
EARNING THEIR KEEP

Chapter 8 looks into the contributions of Canadian Filipinos to the development of Canada's multicultural society and its prosperity and stature in the world. Early Filipino migrants, coming from urban areas in the Philippines, flocked to big cities in Canada, where they found employment opportunities for their special training and education. More recent Filipino immigrants have discovered that they could make a difference in small towns in Canada where their skills and services are more needed.

While a majority of Filipino immigrants came via the healthcare worker route, recent years have seen more and more of them making their marks not just in the labour force, but in the fields of arts, sciences, community development, socially conscious businesses, and politics at all levels of government, where they bring their unique Filipinoness to whatever they dare to undertake.

In this chapter, a CFNet editorial explains how Filipino values contribute to Canada's Asian heritage. Also featured are stories of support groups, such as the Committee for Domestic Workers and Caregivers Rights which has been serving the community for over thirty years and the Victoria Filipino Canadian Association—which has been serving the community for over fifty years.

Highlighting Filipino contributions to the arts are stories about Eleanor Guerrero-Campbell, author of *Stumbling Through Paradise*, and Catherine Hernandez, for her novel *Scarborough*.

Leading the list of a new breed Filipino entrepreneurs are Macario "Tobi" Reyes, a Vancouver property developer, and Gelaine Santiago, champion of Filipino artisans who fills her Toronto shops with arts and crafts designed and handcrafted by select Filipino artists and artisans in the Philippines. Also, Pura Tolentino's Saskatoon restaurant and bakery and Jay-R and Rose Lacsamana's Global Pinoy Food Store which serve as community hubs for Filipinos in Saskatchewan.

Filipino Values Contribute to Canada's Rich Asian Heritage

By Eleanor R. Laquian

May 1, 2018 – The 2016 Census showed that Canada is home to over 4.6 million people of Asian heritage out of a total population of about 36 million. More than 15 percent of Canada's population identifies as being of Asian descent. The Asian continent, the most populous, is the largest source of new immigrants to Canada today. And the Philippines, being the only Catholic country in Asia, has contributed immensely to the fast-growing Catholic population of Canada. They have filled up once empty churches and introduced their religious traditions, such as *Salubong* and *Simbang Gabi*, to parishes attended by many Filipinos.

According to the 2016 Census, Filipinos in Canada number 837,130. They represent 2.3 percent of the Canadian population. Based on the 2016 Census results, Filipinos comprise the fourth-largest visible minority group in Canada. Their national language, Tagalog, is the fastest-growing language in Canada. As such, they can shape the country's character and heritage in more ways than ever before.

The history of Asian immigration to Canada can be traced back to more than 150 years ago, when Chinese workers arrived on the West Coast to build the Pacific Railway in the mid-nineteenth century. Since then, Asian-Canadians not only physically helped to build Canada, but also culturally enriched its diversity, a characteristic of Canada which has been admired worldwide.

Asian immigrants, however, have experienced varying levels of racism throughout Canada's history. Currently, many Filipino workers come through the government's Temporary Foreign Workers Program, which has been greatly expanded over the last decade despite its racist undertone.

Temporary workers, mostly from poor developing countries, have limited pathways to permanent residency and citizenship, and do not have the same access to labour standards, benefits, and other protections that other workers in Canada have. Their jobs are low-paying and precarious, and force them to be tied to a specific employer, which leaves them open to abuse, with little oversight.

Of Dreams and Hardships

Although significant, Filipino immigration to Canada only started in the 1960s—but Filipinos now constitute the largest group of Southeast Asian Canadians. The Philippines also ranked first as country of birth among people who immigrated to Canada between 2011 and 2016. Since 1992, Filipinos have consistently ranked first in the "independent immigrants" category, a group selected on the basis of skills and ability to contribute quickly to Canadian society and the economy. In 2014, the Philippines became the principal source of immigrants to Canada, which welcomed more than forty thousand permanent residents from the country that year.

The story of Filipino immigration to Canada is one of dreams, hardships, sacrifices, resilience, survival, and eventual success. Many Filipinos have had to work hard to bring their immediate families to Canada. Oftentimes, they first come as TFWP workers, leaving spouses and children behind. They can bring their families to Canada only when they become permanent residents. But many years of separation takes a toll on family relationships, and many problems ensue.

The Filipino Community Profile

Statistics Canada's profile of the Filipino community shows a young population of more women than men, the large majority of which is Catholic. Almost all can converse in one of Canada's official languages (English), only a few live alone, especially among seniors, most of them have a university degree, most live in urbanized areas, and most are employed.

Filipinos arrive ready to contribute their talents and skills to Canada's progress. In addition, they bring to Canada their rich cultural heritage in the arts and religious traditions, also in food, music and dance. They contribute to every aspect of life in Canada—artistic, cultural, economic, political, and social—from the arts and sciences to sports, business, and government.

As they transition from being Filipinos to becoming Canadian Filipinos, it is through their personal and social relationships that they show and share the innate values that identify them as Filipinos: compassion, gratitude, kindness, honesty, hospitality, reciprocity, respect for the aged, and their deep-seated commitment to family honour, education, and the church.

Filipinos value honour and dignity more than wealth; they cherish education and dream of their children having professional careers. They care for their elders at home and consider putting them in institutions a dishonour to the family. They avoid conflict by being sensitive to the feelings of others. They smile through hardships because their religion sustains them. As warm, cheerful, helpful, and outgoing people who tend to socialize outside their ethnic group because of their English capabilities, Filipinos can be a unifying force in the community and eradicate racial barriers between the peoples of different nationalities that make up Canada's society today. 🖐

The Philippines Deepens Economic Relations with Canada

By Mary Ann Mandap

April 16, 2017 – The Philippines is looking to deepen its economic relations with Canada, and took a significant step with the recent re-opening of the Philippine Trade and Investment Centre in Toronto.

Both the Philippines and Canada stand to benefit from strengthened economic cooperation, as the Philippines, which is centrally located in the Asia-Pacific region, can serve as Canada's gateway to the region.

Senior Trade Commissioner Roseni Alvero, who will head the PTIC, said the prospect of an ASEAN-Canada Free Trade Agreement is high on the agenda of both countries, after the prospects for a bilateral PH-Canada FTA dimmed following Canada's expressed preference for a more comprehensive regional trade agreement—key to its strategic re-engagement with Asia.

The expansion of trade presence is likewise part of the Philippine Department of Trade and Industry's response to Canada's designation of the country as a priority emerging market for trade and investment promotion under Canada's Global Market Access Plan, according to Alvero.

The new office is tasked to promote and implement the initiatives of the DTI, specifically on trade and investment promotions, as well as actively participating in trade policy and gathering of market and commercial intelligence. "We will work closely with trade associations, special interest councils, business organizations, and relevant agencies to connect Philippine companies with their counterparts in Canada," Alvero said.

She added that PTIC will also provide assistance to Filipino-Canadian entrepreneurs interested in investing in the Philippines.

Alvero said the priority products for trade and investment are:

- IT/business process management—specifically game development and animation (British Columbia, Ontario, and Québec);
- Manufacturing: aerospace, electronics, agri-based and food products; consumer products (Québec, Alberta, Manitoba, and Ontario);
- Food—specifically seafood, processed fruits, Filipino ethnic food, coconut products, and halal, natural, and organic food (British Columbia, Calgary, Winnipeg, and Ontario;
- Start-ups and innovation (British Columbia, Ontario, and Québec);
- Furniture and furnishings/design-driven products (British Columbia, Alberta, Ontario, and Québec)

"Canada is the twenty-first major trading partner of the Philippines, fifteenth-biggest export market, and twenty-fourth import supplier," according to Alvero. "It is the Philippines's sixth top partner for development assistance. Top export products from the Philippines are wiring harnesses, coconut (crude oil and desiccated), and electronic products, while top imports from Canada are wheat, wood products, chemicals, and pork." Canada has strong presence in trade, manufacturing, mining and the Business Process Outsourcing industries in the Philippines.

In 2016, total bilateral trade was only a measly 1 billion USD, with the balance of trade in favour of the Philippines. Alvero predicts total exports to reach 1 billion USD in 2025 from the 2015 level of 563.5 millionUSD. "I predict total trade to be at the level of 1.7 billion USD. Registered Canadian investments will peak at 500 million USD during the ten-year period, with investments in the manufacturing sector playing a significant role," she said. 🖐

The CDWCR Story: Caring for Caregivers

By Eleanor R. Laquian

August 1, 2017 – Since 1982, domestic workers and caregivers (CDWs) from developing countries have come to Canada to take care of the young, the elderly, and the disabled. Their work is strenuous, their responsibilities, heavy, and their pay, minimal. So, who takes care of them when they are cheated by recruiters, are abused by employers, and eventually grow old alone?

In Vancouver, the Vancouver Committee for Domestic Workers and Caregivers Rights (CDWCR) was established in 1992 as a community-based non-profit to help CDWs improve their employment conditions and immigration status. It was started by domestic workers and their community supporters. It assists CDWs through counseling, lobbying, and information. The organizers often spend personal funds to cover costs.

The Vancouver Committee for Domestic Workers
and Caregivers Rights was established in 1992.

In 2007, CDWCR received a grant from Vancity Credit Union for a project to conduct a series of workshops to improve CDWs' skills while adjusting to life in Canada.

The series included training in first aid, CPR, childcare, and eldercare, as well as financial and career planning after the two-year LCP program. Former caregivers Julie Diesta and Lorina Serafico, who helped create the CDWCR, were volunteer coordinators.

When the Vancity grant expired, other groups continued to fund the project—the BC Government and Service Employees Union, the BC Hospital Employees Union, the Movement of United Professionals, the Health Sciences Association of BC, the West Coast Domestic Workers Association, and the Immigrant Services Society.

In 2013, the musically inclined CDWCR members formed "The Singing Nannies." Filipino musician Kimwell Del Rosario trained and practised the group for a successful fundraiser called "Pasko na Naman!" (It's Christmas Again!) at the UBC Asian Centre Auditorium.

In 2014, supported by the Annual Vancouver Jewish Film Festival and Scotiabank, CDWCR presented a movie, *Transit*, about Filipino caregivers in Israel, to raise funds for a CARE Centre to serve as a respite place with temporary accommodation for CDWs between jobs, as well as a CDWCR office for counseling and referral services. It opened in 2015.

In 2014, the City of Vancouver also gave CDWCR a grant for various studies to support the CARE Centre. The additional funds were used to upgrade their website, create a logo/brand, pay for a feasibility study for a caregiver-referral business, and other activities. Unfortunately, the rental money for the CARE Centre ran out in 2016, and it was closed.

Yet CDWs from the Philippines continue to arrive in Canada, needing support, counseling, and information. At the same time, those who arrived in the early 1980s continue to struggle to achieve economic and social upward mobility. By 2018, many of them will be reaching the retirement age of sixty-five.

The Ageing of CDWs

From 1981 to 1989, under the Foreign Domestic Movement program, 30,279 CDWs were admitted to Canada as temporary workers eligible for permanent residency. Almost all of them became permanent residents after five years. It was estimated that about 14 percent of them—or 4,239—were in British Columbia. (Immigration, Refugees and Citizenship Canada website).

The FDM was replaced by the Live-In Caregiver Program in 1992. While eligible to apply for permanent residency after two years, it then took them an average of eight years to become permanent residents and save enough to bring their families to Canada.

From 1993 to 2009, 52,493 CDWs landed in Canada under the LCP. From 1993 to 1997 (a five-year period when information on the age of CDWs was available), about 7,000 of them were thirty-one to forty years old. They would be about fifty to sixty years old by now. About 2,200 caregivers aged forty-one to fifty arrived in Canada from 1993 to 1997. They are now more than sixty years old (Source: Profile of live-in caregiver immigrants to Canada, 1993-2009, Toronto Immigration Employment Data Initiative (TIEDI).

Why Ageing Caregivers Need Care

Because CDWs were not allowed to bring their family while on temporary status, they were separated from their families for many years. Some were unable to bring their family because they were single parents whose children had exceeded the eligibility age, or a vengeful ex-husband was unwilling to sign off on child custody. One of the unfortunate results of the LCP is broken homes and families. Many were also never married, and were the sole support of ageing parents back home. As a result, many CDWs end up living alone in Canada.

The work of CDWs is physical, involving long hours. Because of the low pay, they often need to work two jobs, resulting in physical strains, injuries, and long-term physical illnesses. They received only forty dollars a day, regardless of how many hours they worked. It was only in 1994 that they got minimum wage, plus overtime after eight hours of work. They paid taxes on their meagre earnings.

Under the FDM and LCP, CDWs were allowed to work only with the employer specified on their work permit; part-time work was illegal. Most of their income was used for board and lodging, and family support. Their low income entitles them to only a small pension under the Canada Pension Plan. Their Old Age Security may also be reduced if they do not meet the forty-year residency requirement, so most of them work after age sixty-five.

After spending the prime of their lives in Canada on work that ordinary Canadians do not want, they have yet to see the better future they hoped to find forty years ago. Many ageing CDWs now face mental, emotional, and physical challenges. CDWCR has launched a project to identify problems and develop programs to solve them. They need funds to help CDWs grow old, with the security they deserve after years of contributing to this country.

To support CDWCR, visit *CDWCR.org*.

Canadian Filipino Authors Featured in 2017 LiterASIAN Festival

By Rachel Ramos-Reid

September 1, 2017 – Two Filipinos are among eight Asian authors featured in this year's LiterASIAN Literary Festival, to be held in various Vancouver venues from September 21 to 24.

"This year's featured authors represent some of the most stellar titles being published by the Asian Canadian writing community," said Allan Cho, LiterASIAN festival director.

Cho noted that this year's festival theme, "Storytelling and the Art of the Novel," is truly special, as this was founder, Jim Wong-Chu's, final "masterpiece" before his recent passing this July. He added that Wong-Chu "spent numerous hours on the schedule and program, which features quality writers at this year's festival.

Wong-Chu also founded *Ricepaper Magazine* before establishing LiterASIAN as the first Canadian literary arts festival featuring writers of Asian descent. The Filipino writers selected this year are Eleanor Guerrero-Campbell and Catherine Hernandez.

Eleanor Guerrero-Campbell immigrated to Canada in the late seventies, bringing with her a degree in English and comparative literature and a master's in urban and regional planning. She worked as urban planner for cities in BC and Alberta. It was when she co-founded the Multicultural Helping House Society in Vancouver that she became aware of the issues surrounding new immigrants' integration into the Canadian workforce and their inability to find work related to their past job experience and credentials. Such was the inspiration for her novel, *Stumbling Through Paradise*, which follows the struggle of a Filipino family who left their home country in search of a better life in Canada.

Stumbling Through Paradise is the story of the fictional Del Mundo family, through three generations, and their struggle to find their place in Canada. Unable to find work based on their skills and experience, the Del Mundos must choose between pride and practicality, survival, and surrender.

Writing fiction was a promise Guerrero-Campbell made to herself when she retired in 2012. Working with multicultural groups throughout her career, she witnessed the "effects of underemployment of many of our *kababayans*—engineers, doctors, nurses ending up cleaning floors." Her years working with various cultures helped shape the characters of the novel.

Guerrero-Campbell found her writing voice in 2000, when creative writing guru Natalie Goldberg prompted her to seriously pursue writing fiction. "I thought fiction based on reality would be a powerful way of bringing the issue [of labour market integration) realistically to people and move them to understand and act."

Eleanor Guerrero-Campbell and Catherine Hernandez are first-time novelists, but are no strangers to the Filipino diaspora.

Catherine Hernandez is a proud queer woman of colour, prolific playwright, theatre practitioner, activist, children's book author, artistic director, and former owner of a daycare run out of her home—the venue in which her novel, *Scarborough*, saw its beginnings.

In an interview with *NOW Magazine* earlier this year, Hernandez recalls, "I'd wake up at 5:30 a.m., then start to write at 6, until parents dropped off their kids. Then, I'd write again when the kids napped. When I'm doing laundry, feeding a baby, changing diapers, I'm thinking. Then at night, I just write, write."

Hernandez's debut novel bears the namesake of suburban Ontario's low-income and culturally diverse East End. It follows the story of three children brought together under a Scarborough school's literacy program. Hina is the hijab-wearing program coordinator who has made it her mission not only to improve the children's language skills but also to offer an environment safe from the community's crime, poverty, and racism. The interconnected stories of Bing, a boy struggling with his own sexual identity, Laura, a victim of her mother's neglect and soon to suffer from her father's neglect, and Sylvie, a special needs child who lives with her family in a shelter, provide a snapshot of the Scarborough community that Hernandez herself grew up in and is thankful for.

Born and raised in Canada by parents who are Filipino immigrants, it is with the character of Bing's mother, Edna, that Hernandez intimately identifies.

It is this constant longing for a Filipino connection that Hernandez wrote the plays *Singkil*, *Eating with Lola*, and *Kilt Pins*. In 2012, to help raise funds for flood victims in the Philippines, Hernandez lay in a raft as part of an art performance at a storefront space in Toronto for twenty-four hours, without food, while artists and storytellers performed around her. "'Operation Lifeboat,' for me, was my connection to this country as someone born in Canada taking responsibility for Canada's hand in such disasters, and as an act of love for my own culture," Hernandez reflects on her activism.

Hernandez considers being part of this year's festival "bittersweet," in that she considers Jim Chong-Wu her much-valued and well-respected mentor.

"I thought I was going to attend the festival and report back to my mentor about all the success my novel had. While it is unbearably sad that he will not be physically there, I know that he will be proud of me and all of the countless Asians he has guided to literary success." Hernandez sums up, "Every word I write now has his fire, his passion behind it."

Progress of Filipino Businesses in Canada

By Prod Laquian

April 1, 2017 – Most Filipino entrepreneurs in Canada did not immigrate specifically to engage in business. In the 2006 survey in connection with our study of Filipinos in Canada, only 2.7 percent of 514 respondents had business experience before arriving in Canada. Many early Filipino businessmen, then, started out as "accidental entrepreneurs." They saw business opportunities and pursued them in typical *bahala na* ("let's just see what happens") fashion.

Many of these early Filipino entrepreneurs went into business because they could not find salaried jobs that were satisfactory. Others wanted to be their own boss. A few had special talents and decided to use them. Many were simply *gaya-gaya* (copycats), who saw others doing well in a certain type of business and felt they could do as well, if not better.

The interesting outcome is that whatever their motives, and despite their lack of experience, quite a number of these Filipino entrepreneurs did quite well through ups and downs over the years.

For example, Filipinos in the 1970s got into business largely by accident. Noticing the lack of certain services needed by their *kababayans*, they filled the gap. For the last fifty years, Filipino Canadian businesses have followed the same pattern.

Other problems faced by Filipino businesses were (1) poor choice of business venture, (2) unsuitable location with no parking, (3) failure to maintain quality and high standards, (4) unwilling to pay (probably due to lack of funds) for services needed to ensure success in business such as legal fees, accountancy, and marketing/promotional consultancy.

Many dismissed the need for such services as unnecessary because *kaya na namin yan, kami na lang ang gagawa* (we can do it so we'll just do it ourselves). (5), lack of professional service orientation toward their clientele such as an unbusiness-like attitude of *maghintay sila, kailangan nila tayo* (let them wait; they need us anyway).

Many small grocery stores owned by Canadian Filipinos have come and gone in Metro Vancouver over the years. Photo from MaxPixel.FreeGreatPicture.com.

Some Filipino businesspeople who survived those early years of entrepreneurship did so because they learned their lessons quickly and adjusted their business conduct accordingly. They realized that they must consider several factors before going into business: personal interest and motivation, availability of sufficient capital, and a realistic business plan that budgets for the lean period until the business turns a profit and becomes a self-sustaining venture. Many of the early *sari-sari* stores and *turo-turo* restaurants in Toronto, for example, killed each other through cutthroat competition.

Over the years, the growing Filipino population in Canada has produced a new breed of Filipino entrepreneurs. They are young, info-tech-savvy, and business-oriented. The highly educated ones have MBAs, while tradespeople learned their skills and earned their training and apprenticeships through Canadian trade institutions like BCIT and Langara. They all know how to do business the Canadian way, as demanded by their Canadian consumers. They aim to serve Filipinos as well as mainstream Canadian society, and offer goods and services to suit their common needs. 🍎

Introducing a New Breed of Filipino Entrepreneurs

April 1, 2017 – Filipinos are found in the seven continents of the world. And everywhere they go, Filipinos are proud to say that they can compete with the best.

Here in Canada, Filipinos are found in various fields, from the professions to the arts and trades. Many of them are successful in their own right, proving that Filipinos can indeed shine among the finest.

But aside from mainstream politics, it seems that there is one ground that Filipinos in Canada have a hard time cracking. That's in the area of business and entrepreneurship. It's often said that there aren't enough Filipino entrepreneurs, just like there is a scarcity of Filipinos active in electoral politics.

Although a March 2016 study released by Statistics Canada doesn't provide specific numbers about Filipinos in business, it is a good starting point to see how Filipinos fare in this field.

According to *Immigration, Business Ownership, and Employment in Canada*, immigrants in general are entrepreneurial, though their degree of expertise varies depending on where they came from.

The study, which was the first of its kind, found that immigrants from English-speaking countries like the US, Australia, New Zealand, South Africa, Ireland, the UK, and others in Western Europe had the highest likelihood of being business owners. Roughly 7 percent of these immigrants owned a private business.

Next are immigrants from India and China, with proportion of business ownership at around 6 percent and 5 percent, respectively.

The lowest rates of business ownership were observed among immigrants from Southeast Asia (the region where the Philippines is located), 3 percent; Latin America, 1.6 percent; and Africa, 1 percent.

There are a number of possible explanations why Filipinos and similarly situated immigrants are struggling in entrepreneurship.

Some of these can be learned from the results of a 2013 survey conducted, by the North York Community House and Public Interest Strategy and Communications, of around a hundred businesspeople from six immigrant communities in Toronto.

The respondents, who included Filipinos, said in the survey results, later incorporated in the study titled 'DIY: Immigrant Entrepreneurs are Doing It for Themselves', indicated their need for enhanced English language skills, more knowledge about finances, networking, and mentorship.

It appears to be the same elsewhere in Canada—particularly in British Columbia, where the rise and fall of many a Filipino business has been witnessed by Leonardo "Ding" Cunanan, publisher and editor of *Dahong Pilipino*, a business directory.

Cunanan was interviewed by Eleanor R. Laquian for a piece about how his *Dahong Pilipino* business directory is supporting community businesses, and he noted that Filipino entrepreneurs who succeeded had a good knowledge of their numbers, developed a sound strategy, and enjoyed good relations with their clientele.

Prod Laquian, in a separate piece for this April 2017 edition, observed that a number of businesses failed because of a lack of professionalism and an aversion to hiring expert staff. But as Prod and Eleanor Laquian noted in their articles, a new breed of Canadian Filipinos is emerging. They're young, tech-savvy, educated in Canada, and professionally trained to do business the Canadian way.

Moreover, Canadian Filipinos are branching out to businesses that cater to needs that are not specific to Filipino or immigrant communities. They're going mainstream. While the community will continue to see businesses like Filipino grocery stores and restaurants, and immigration consultancies, new businesses owned by Filipinos are now in fields like arts services and information technology management.

Much attention has been given to immigrants who are seeking employment in the fields in which they have been trained in their native countries. This effort should continue, and at the same time, more awareness needs to be given to ensuring the success of those who want to become entrepreneurs.

As Canada will remain reliant on immigration for its growth, the success of immigrant entrepreneurs is important. By creating businesses, entrepreneurs generate employment, and with jobs, come a vibrant economy that supports all Canadians.

Since starting a business is a major challenge for many, attention should be paid by governments and other stakeholders in supporting new entrepreneurs on a range of things, from individual mentoring to business incubation and financing.

The CFNet Editorial Board

Filipino Community Hubs in Saskatoon

By Rachel Ramos-Reid

March 23, 2016 – Two stories by the CBC highlighted an important role played by family-run retail businesses in the Canadian Filipino community in small town, which is quite often overlooked because there are few Filipinos living there.

Reporting in March 2016 from Saskatoon, the national broadcaster focused on a restaurant and general store that do more than just sell familiar food and products. They also serve as hubs for the growing Filipino community in the city.

One such a store is Cesar's Cakes and Café, a restaurant and bakeshop that was started by the Tolentino family more than twenty years ago. According to the CBC, when Filipinos arrive in Saskatoon, Saskatchewan, the Tolentino establishment is one of the first places they visit.

They come not only for the cakes and breads, but for the friendly welcome, and for catching up on news about the home country. There are always other Filipino customers there who come for bread and news about the community.

Pura Tolentino is proud of the welcoming atmosphere in the restaurant: "It feels like home. You speak the same language and you have the same experiences from back home. So you don't miss the Philippines as much."

Since the bakery opened twenty years ago, it has attracted quite a loyal following.

Pura noted in the CBC report that Filipinos in Saskatoon are not their only clients: "People come here from out of town. Their only purpose for the trip is to come here. They have lunch and buy their breads here, because we are the only Filipino bakery in Saskatchewan."

Another Gathering Place

The CBC also reported about Jay-R's Global Pinoy Food Store, which is owned by Rose Lacsamana and her spouse, Jay-R.

"We opened the store in 2008 when the Saskatchewan Immigrant Nominee Program started," Lacsamana said. "So, a lot of people from the Philippines came over as temporary foreign workers, and there was a demand for Filipino products."

Cesar's Cakes and Café makes its Saskatoon version of bibingka, or rice cake, minus the banana leaf wrap.

The store's popular products include *longanisa* and ube ice cream. According to Lacsamana, food plays a big role in making new immigrants feel at home.

"It's important. because we miss home," Lacsamana said in the CBC report. "So, when we have access to all these products, we bring a little bit of what's home to Saskatoon."

Macario "Tobi" Reyes in Vancouver Property Development: How Does He Do It?

By Eleanor Guerrero-Campbell

Vancouver-based Macario "Tobi" Reyes founded his PortLiving property development company in 2003.

April 16, 2017 – "Good real estate is the successful merging of vision, economics, talents, timing, and relationships. "With the right personal strengths, combined with a great set of people who work at and with PortLiving, the business of development has been fun, creative, and fulfilling," said Tobi Reyes.

A 1.5 generation Canadian Filipino, Tobi Reyes has splashed into the tricky waters of Vancouver real estate development with, interestingly, a nautically themed condominium building at the foot of the Cambie Street Bridge, a gateway to the downtown peninsula. This boutique condo project, called South Creek Landing, consists of fifteen homes. It won two awards in 2016: the Georgie Award for the Best Multi-Family Mid-/High-Rise, and the Lt. Gov. Special Jury Award for Contextual Innovation.

This building is now an icon in Vancouver's glittering "condoscape."

Tobi Reyes was born in Manila, and moved to Vancouver in 1979. He studied at St. George's School, then took up psychology and history at Queen's University. Ever since he could hold a pen, he loved to draw, and this artistic bent evolved into a broader interest in art, design, environmental sustainability, and entrepreneurship. His first adventure as an entrepreneur was a dial-up internet service provider in the Philippines (Impact Information Systems). Tobi's first taste of Vancouver real estate was in the commercial sector, when he, along with partners, purchased a warehouse in Mount Pleasant.

This led to the creation of PortLiving, and eventually, their first residential project South Creek Landing. Founded by Tobi in 2003, PortLiving has twelve residential projects and three commercial projects being built.

With current projects in Vancouver, Seattle, and Toronto, PortLiving's portfolio consists of award-winning developments, ranging from low-rise buildings to innovative towers, totalling more than a million square feet of space. What strategies did Tobi use to transition from a major in psychology/history to a tech entrepreneur, to success in a highly competitive real estate/property development market such as Vancouver?

"I loved the application of skills needed to create a successful real estate company. Since the earlier days related to founding a tech business, pursuant to endeavours in commercial and residential real estate, I have always benefited by collaborating on diverse projects alongside great teams. Real estate is a process that requires the involvement of many people, with various talents and abilities, and we're always searching for better combinations and better ways of solving problems to make smarter real estate decisions." Tobi's vision is encapsulated in PortLiving's mission, which includes "a commitment to innovation, craftsmanship, and building neighbourhoods."

To achieve business success, Tobi offers some advice:

- "Know yourself and build a team. Know what you're good at and what you're not. Identify the same in others, so they can complement you."
- "Keep learning. School is just the beginning, and experience will become your teacher for the rest of your life."
- "Be credit-worthy, and build a brand. Whether it's in your name or your company's name, give people a chance to respect you . . . trust is the key to all relationships. Business requires trust."

Tobi attributes his success to his Filipino roots, such as:

- "Being grounded by a strong sense of family . . . as the backbone of almost all our daily activities, family has given me the love and confidence to grow and serve others."
- "The golden rule and empathy. Treat others the way you would expect to be treated yourself. This applies to your team and to your

customer . . . applying empathy to real estate helps one consider several factors, such as design, livability, and affordability."

- "Hard work—take nothing for granted. We find ways to smile in the face of adversity. Failure is commonplace. Through hard work, constant effort, and acknowledging each success as a blessing, I find that it is easier to contribute positively and evenly through ups and downs."

When asked about the ongoing dream of a Filipino community centre in Vancouver, Tobi says: "The Filipino community is one of the largest groups in Canada, but also potentially the most disenfranchised. We are a community without a home, without a face, and without a voice. I would love to develop a centre we can be proud of—and one which potentially serves as a model for other cities. I hope to kickstart this commitment with my own resources, but ultimately, we will need funding, leadership, and resources."

Further, Tobi states, "I have some space in Mount Pleasant which may be useful as an interim platform for the centre. For the moment, there is no official status, no official members/supporters, and no plans committed. But I would like to engage the community sooner rather than later through this temporary space, to offer some services—but primarily as a beachhead to help begin the process for the permanent space."

Victoria Filipino Canadian Association's Legacy of Service

By Ben Pires

April 16, 2019 –Almost fifty years ago, on February 10, 1969, fifteen Filipino immigrants—all women, mostly in the healthcare field—signed an application for incorporating the first Filipino Canadian association in the country: the Victoria Filipino Canadian Association. It has been busy since. Its membership has grown, as well as its activities. Some of the reasons for its success are:

1. The number of Canadians of Filipino ancestry in the Capital Regional District was comparatively strong and there was a need for a united group.

2. The association focused on showcasing Filipino culture: folk dancing, music, arts, fashion, and food. Since 1972, it has participated in the Victoria Day Parade, and in 1991 and 1994, it sponsored a Philippine Musical Extravaganza. Alongside a long list of cultural programs, it also hosted visiting performers from Himig ng Lahi, the Bayanihan Dance Group, the Philippine Educational Theatre Association, the Alumni Ensemble of the Philippine Madrigal Singers, Pilita Corrales, Powerdance, Kontra-GaPi, and the Manila Concert Choir.

3. It hosted high-profile guests: Philippine President Diosdado Macapagal and his family in 1970 and Philippine delegates to the APEC conference ministerial and senior officials in 1997.

4. It hosted the second conference of the Filipino Canadian Association of BC in 1989.

5. A determined effort is made to avoid any conflict of interest or even the slightest perception of it. No individual, whether an official or member, has special privileges or status; all are equal and are expected to work for the community's benefit.

VFCA Food Kiosk - In 1980, VFCA introduced its Filipino food kiosk, which members built in three days, at the annual Folkfest. However, in 2006, after twenty-six continuous years, the Inter-Cultural Association of Greater Victoria, organizer of the event, terminated the event due to escalating costs. Since then, the VFCA has been taking its food kiosk to the three-day Saanich Fall Fair at the fairgrounds in Central Saanich. It has been returning to the fair every year.

VFCA's Carolers - In 1978, VFCA shared the joys of Christmas caroling with the Filipino community and fundraised for the future Bayanihan Community Centre.

The Victoria Filipino Canadian Association has a long tradition of nurturing the Canadian Filipino community on Vancouver Island.

VFCA's Sampaguita Folk Dancers- In 1971, VFCA established the Sampaguita Folk Dance Group. Each year, the VFCA Sampaguita folk dancers join the Greater Victoria Performing Arts Festival. Over the years, the children under fourteen, the youth, and the adult dancers have received awards and performed at the Honours Performance. It also performed at the Vancouver EXPO 86 stage, and at the opening ceremonies of the XV Commonwealth Games in Victoria in 1994.

Victoria Filipino Canadian Caregivers Association - The need to discuss childcare standards, domestic services duties, human rights, employer and employee contracts, immigration rules, and assertiveness training prompted a group of caregivers to establish the International Childcare and Domestic Services Association, under VFCA's auspices and full support. By February 1989, the association was registered under the Society Act. In 2001, the association changed its name to the Victoria Filipino-Canadian Caregivers Association. Its purposes, however, remain unchanged.

Victoria Filipino Canadian Seniors Association - In April 1988, a group of elderly new immigrants from the Philippines and Canadians of Filipino ancestry got together to form an organization, under the auspices of VFCA. The next year, the group was formally registered under the *Society Act* as the Victoria Filipino-Canadian Golden Age Association. In 1995, they amended the constitution and changed the name to the Victoria Filipino-Canadian Seniors' Association. The VFCSA sponsors the annual Halloween Dinner Dance and organizes trips and social events for seniors.

Bayanihan Cultural and Housing Society - On February 16, 1991, VFCA officers took the bold step of combining the Bayanihan Cultural and Housing Society to focus on acquiring a building for a cultural centre. To ensure the integrity of BCHS as an arm of the VFCA, with support from the VFCCA and the VFCSA, and that it would not succumb to any individual's or group's personal ambitions, the society's membership was limited to sixteen members: seven ranking VFCA officers; one representative each from the VFCCA and the VFCSA; and five other individuals appointed by VFCA—two of whom must be VFCA directors for the year and three from the VFCA membership.

BCHS was incorporated under the *Society Act* on April 12, 1991.

On April 30, 2001, it acquired the property at 1709–11 Blanshard Street for $395,000:

- from 1991 to 2001, BCHS raised, $120,000 for a centre.
- The City of Victoria gave the green light for BCHS to apply for a building permit and to operate a community centre.
- The provincial government gave a "Community Partners Program" grant of $215,000 on March 26, 2001.
- A credit union authorized a mortgage of $310,000 on April 27, 2001.
- Capital Health Region (now Vancouver Island Health Authority) approved the operation of a commercial kitchen in the building on April 11, 2001.
- The cost of renovations of the building plus permits was $71,746.80. Volunteers helped minimize the renovation costs by contributing their skills, labour, time, and effort.
- The total cost was $471,748.80 (a total of $335,000 raised from donations, including the $215,000 provincial grant).
- Bayanihan Community Centre was formally opened on November 3, 2001.
- On April 26, 2002, BCHS was designated by the Canada Customs and Revenue Agency a "charitable organization," allowing donors to get an income tax deductions for their donations to BCHS.
- On January 2, 2007, BCHS paid off the mortgage for the centre, and on January 28, 2007, they held a mortgage-burning ceremony.

Bayanihan Community Centre - The Bayanihan Community Centre is the venue for:

- Sunday Open House Lunch;
- Charitable programs, such as "Feeding the Needy," and helping others here and abroad;
- Fundraising for disaster victims (Typhoon Haiyan in the Philippines — $63,125.88 as of December 13, 2013 —and the Nepal earthquake);
- The annual Filipino Food Fiesta;
- Philippine Consulate Outreach Services (passports, visas, affidavits, etc.);
- Leadership, FoodSafe, CPR, and other training programs, as well as information workshops for caregivers and Temporary Foreign Workers;
- Tagalog classes;
- Supporting annual dinner-dances of the three organizations, dancing lessons (folk dancing, ballroom dancing, line dancing); and
- Programs with the InterCultural Association, Victoria Immigrant and Refugee Centre Society, and the Community Partnership Network;and more.

Maharlika (Nobility) Award to VFCA for an Outstanding Filipino-Canadian Association, 2010

The VFCA was singled out as an outstanding Filipino association for establishing the Bayanihan Cultural and Housing Society, and, with its strong support, the BCHS successfully acquired property to establish the Bayanihan Community Centre.

The Maharlika (Nobility) Award for Outstanding Filipino Canadian Association(2014) went to the Bayanihan Cultural and Housing Society in January 2015, for its many charitable and fundraising efforts for victims of natural disasters.

BCHS Sponsors Syrian refugee family - BCHS welcomed a Syrian refugee family from Aleppo to Victoria on April 27, 2017.

BCHS Looking at Options for Centre - While the centre is financially stable, with the mortgage having been paid off in five years and about fifteen thousand dollars in the bank, BCHS is looking at options for the future. The centre has a prime downtown location near major bus routes. The building is ageing, and requires an expensive, seismic upgrade, and better heating/cooling indoors.

Operating the Centre for the Last Sixteen Years

They are now in their sixties and up, and are getting burned out by their volunteer work. There are only a few new volunteers, despite a dramatic increase in newcomers (immigrants, caregivers, skilled workers) to the Capital Regional District in the past decade.

Four in ten Canadians volunteered in 2013, down by 4 percent from 2010. Decline in the volunteer rate is most pronounced among persons aged thirty-five to forty-four, with a 6 percent decrease from 2010 to 2013. There are fewer newcomers who volunteer than those who are Canada-born. The options for the future are on the centre's website at *Bayanihan. ca/community-future.*

Gelaine Santiago Champions Filipino Artisans

By Rachel Ramos-Reid

September 16, 2019- In her company blog, Gelaine Santiago second guesses herself. "I remember [being] in my early twenties. I would read about the award-winners in business and think how accomplished everyone was. I hoped that one day I would be deserving of this award, too." Santiago is this year's lone Filipino recipient of the RBC Top 25 Canadian Immigrants Awards. "Now that the day has come, my reaction is not what I expected."

Santiago is the co-founder of Cambio and Co., an e-commerce fashion retail company that features products designed and handcrafted in the

Philippines by select Filipino artists and artisans. She also co-founded the recently launched Sinta and Co., which sells wedding paraphernalia, also made in the Philippines.

In 2012, she also co-founded the non-profit *ChooseSocial.ph*, a digital platform connecting Filipinos in the diaspora with social enterprises in the Philippines.

Santiago was only three when her family moved to Canada in the early nineties. "My parents chose to leave the Philippines because, at the time, they didn't have stable employment." Gelaine toldher story to *Canadian Filipino Net* (CFNet) which has supported Gelaine's business undertakings since the early years of Cambio and Co. "They wanted to live in a country with higher wages and stable employment opportunities, all the things they would want for their children," She said of her parents.

The Santiago family of five began their new lives in a cramped apartment in the city of Toronto, where an aunt already lived. It was two decades before Santiago went back to her birth country.

Gold filigree bracelet and wedding pillow - A new online bridal boutique aims to provide customers with a true Filipino wedding. For more information: www.shopsinta.co.

In 2013, she and her then boyfriend (now husband and co-founder) Jérôme Gagnon-Voyer travelled to the Philippines, an experience that jump-started the idea of a business that does social good. Santiago told CFNet, "While there, we ended up learning about an amazing community of entrepreneurs using fashion to provide sustainable livelihood for Filipino artisans who were creating quality products but simply lacked access to the global market."

Both Santiago and Gagnon-Voyer were unhappy with their corporate jobs back then. "We wanted more meaning, so we decided to quit our jobs in pursuit of creating a business together," she reminisces. Their shared Philippine experience in 2013 sparked the inspiration to establish Cambio and Co. "We knew we wanted it to be a business with meaningful impact."

When the two got married in 2018, they wanted to celebrate both their families' Canadian and Filipino heritage. Putting together a wedding that

speaks of both families' cultures made them realize they were not alone in such an endeavour and that there are couples around the world who would wish to celebrate a union of not just two people but also of two heritages and cultures.

In July this year, Sinta and Co. was born, with the same ethical principles that its sister company embodies.Gelaine Santiago (left) and Jerome Gagnon-Voyer believe that businesses should have a social conscience

In sourcing the products, the founders are particular about selecting both the prospective business partners and the products themselves. Aside from selecting products based on quality, craftsmanship, and authenticity, they made sure that the business employs and supports artisans and whether the pieces represent Philippine culture in some way. Santiago asks them: "Do they share a part of our history and preserve our heritage? Are they telling a meaningful story?"

The co-founders also place significant value on sustainability: where the materials come from and to what extent such ethical principles embedded into the partners' business models.

Santiago and Gagnon-Voyer avoid companies that "greenwash" (using sustainability as a mere marketing ploy but not actually committing to the cause), and make sure they meet each partner to try to understand their business models. In short,they make sure these companies walk their talk.

Santiago initially felt undeserving of the RBC award because she grew up in Canada, unlike the other awardees, who had a tougher time adjusting to a new way of life.

She cites her parents and her family's humble Canadian beginnings, the Filipino neighbours who would babysit Santiago and her siblings, and Filipinos in Canada, whose tireless work has led to the declaration of June as Filipino heritage month. "It's because of them that stories of younger Filipinos like me can be shared and celebrated on a national platform."

The journey to operating a business with a social conscience was a leap of faith, and here is what Santiago would advise CFNet readers: "There's no such thing as a perfect idea or an ideal moment to be an entrepreneur. If you wait for those moments to come, you'll be waiting for a long time. Don't be afraid to make mistakes, and always be willing to learn and grow."

Chapter 9:
ISSUES TO PURSUE

The seeds that were planted to bring this nationwide online newsmagazine to life were not out of whim, as the work involved was completely voluntary. But what brought *CanadianFilipino.Net* to life was a genuine desire by the founding members of the Maple Bamboo Network Society, its publisher, to inform, engage, and connect Filipinos all over Canada and shed a light on the valuable contributions of this indomitable people. CFNet's mission is to let Canadian Filipinos know what other Filipinos are doing to contribute to Canadian society.

However, despite having built up an undeniable and palpable presence in Canada for a number of years, issues that haunt Canadian Filipinos continue to set back their progress, individually and as a community. These are issues that beg government intervention, such as credential recognition for new immigrants, landed status on arrival for domestic workers and caregivers, affordable higher education for deserving students, closing the gender equality gap, promoting diversity and multiculturalism, and elimination of racism against people of colour.

Statistics Canada reported in the 2016 Census that those with Filipino heritage comprise more than 2 percent of Canada's population. As such, they should have at least six MPs to represent them proportionately in parliament. At present, they have only one. They are also underrepresented in local politics and government jobs. These issues are discussed by editorials in this chapter.

In fact, Filipinos, although recent immigrants compared to the Chinese and South Asians who arrived in the 1800s, are now the third-largest and fastest-growing immigrant group in Canada, following India and China.

A census in 2021 showed that they will hit the one million mark. Would this bring a positive response from those in power to the issues close to a Canadian Filipino's heart? 🖐

Editor's note: The editorial for the first issue of CFNet *on July 1, 2016 explained its purpose. Succeeding* CFNet *editorials discuss issues that occupy the minds of its current editorial board, which future generations may pursue while making their own history in Canada's diverse society.*

A Website for Thought and Action

July 1, 2016 – Starting a new website in a crowded field of millions competing for the highest number of "hits" and the most "likes" is a daunting task in this fast-paced digital world. However, with the number of Filipinos in Canada approaching a million, a website inviting readers to pause, reflect, and do something about issues that affect their lives is timely and fitting.

Fortunately, there are more positive than negative factors in Filipino culture, values, and traditions. And Canada's inclusive society makes it easy for the mostly Christian, family-oriented, peace-loving, compassionate, caring, industrious, and law-abiding Filipinos to succeed, as indeed they do.

The goal of this *CanadianFilipino.Net* website is to connect Filipinos all over Canada in order to focus on their issues as a community, highlight their heritage and social, cultural, and economic contributions, and promote their engagement in Canada's multicultural society.

The Mission of this biweekly *CanadianFilipino.Net* is to inform, engage and facilitate interactions among self-aware and involved Filipinos in Canada. To provide them a platform to express their views, needs, and issue through digital media. To share their values and culture with other Canadians and promote better understanding and collaboration with other Canadians.

CFNet website uses "Canadian Filipino" instead of the more common, hyphenated "Filipino-Canadian" in order to emphasize the Filipinos as Canadians, their experiences in Canada, and their impact in Canada as Canadians but still Filipinos at core.

Canadian Filipinos Will Thrive under Two Flags

By Eleanor R. Laquian

January 1, 2017 – According to estimates from the Commission on Overseas Filipinos, in 2013, out of a total Philippine population of about 97 million, about 10.2 million Filipinos were living outside the country. They were found in 288 countries all over the world.

In 2016, the country's total population rose to almost 103 million, and it is safe to conclude that more Filipinos have also left the country to live and/or work abroad.

Due to their colonial history (more than three hundred years under Spain, which Christianized the Filipinos, and fifty years under the United States, which promoted democratic governance and public education), most Filipinos are familiar with Western culture and are at ease in a Western milieu. They have no trouble with cultural assimilation and social integration. Wherever they may live in the world, they easily become global citizens.

But breathes there a Filipino, wherever he may be, who does not feel a lump in his throat, a tug at his heartstrings, and shivers running down his spine when he hears the haunting lyrics of "Bayang Magiliw"? And when he tries to join in the singing of the national anthem, does his voice break in mid-sentence as he is overcome by feelings of longing, loneliness, nostalgia, and latent patriotism?

Even Filipinos who have become naturalized citizens of other countries like Canada feel this aching homesickness for the old country when they hear the national anthem after being away from the Philippines for many years.

Some naturalized Canadian Filipinos opted for dual citizenship after the Philippines passed the *Dual Citizenship Law* in August 2003, just so they could sing the national anthem "with fervour burning" as Filipinos once again.

Even those who have no plans to return to the Philippines feel this emotional reaction to "Bayang Magiliw." Some reacquired their Filipino citizenship for sentimental reasons, such as to regain the right to be called "Filipino" by citizenship, and sing the anthem as one.

Although dual citizenship has many advantages for Canadian Filipinos, not many of them have taken advantage of it. Older naturalized Canadian Filipinos don't feel the need to reacquire their Philippine citizenship because they had decided to stay in Canada permanently, and are able to visit the Philippines as *balikbayan* whenever they wish anyway.

Others are concerned because of the recent extrajudicial killings under the virtual dictatorship of President Duterte and the perceived unstable political, social, and economic conditions in the country. Still others are unaware of the rights and privileges they would enjoy as dual citizens.

Aside from the lack of information, there is also disinformation among the uninformed, about imagined problems and situation that may never occur, such as a war between the Philippines and Canada, or the Canadian Embassy in Manila refusing to assist or rescue Canadian Filipinos because of their dual citizenship.

Only a few countries grant dual citizenship without restrictions and pressures to integrate or intermix with the mainstream population. Some of these countries are Australia, Canada, New Zealand, and the United States. They believe in multiculturalism, which brings about a more interesting and diverse society with an enriched culture of new traditions and ideas.

In the diverse Philippine society, naturalized Canadian Filipinos play an important role in passing on their Canadian values and beliefs to Filipinos they encounter when they visit the Philippines, by encouraging them to follow Canadian practices in human rights, social justice, and clean government.

In a world that is dangerously turning exclusive, ultra-right, and conservative under a strongman rule, Filipinos in liberal and democratic Canada are fortunate to have the opportunity to become citizens of two countries that allow dual citizenship.

Naturalized Canadian Filipinos, who still have some ardent feelings for their native land, now have a chance to become Filipino citizens as well. They just have to seize the opportunity available in any Philippine Consulate in Canada and the Philippine Embassy in Ottawa.

Dual Citizenship: All Pros and No Cons

By Attorney Anthony A. L. Mandap

January 1, 2017 – Juan Alim, seventy-eight, a former Filipino citizen who was naturalized as a Canadian citizen in 1998, arrived in Manila last year to celebrate Christmas with relatives. He enjoyed his stay so much that he decided to live there for the rest of his life. However, he's worried that one year after his date of arrival, he would be declared an "overstaying alien" by the Bureau of Immigration and charged exorbitant fees.

While Juan is weighing his options, another former Filipino citizen, Jericho Mercado, a licensed architect in the Philippines before migrating to Canada, is interested to know how he can resume the practice of his profession and capitalize on the construction boom in the Philippines.

What's the best solution to the two gentlemen's dilemma? Simple: dual citizenship.

The Philippine *Dual Citizenship Law*, otherwise known as the *Citizenship Retention Act* of 2003 (*Republic Act 9225*), is a law that allows natural-born Filipino citizens who have been naturalized as citizens of another country to regain or retain their Philippine citizenship and all the benefits and privileges. It was passed by Congress in 2003, principally as a means to open up the Philippine economy to former Filipinos who are willing to contribute to its growth and development.

Rights and Privileges

It goes without saying that once a person reacquires his Philippine citizenship, he also regains virtually all the rights and privileges he had previously lost when he was naturalized as a foreign citizen, including the following:

- the right to be issued a Philippine passport;
- the right to live and stay in the Philippines, visa-free, and for an indefinite period of time;
- the right to practice one's profession;
- the right to engage in business, including investment in areas or industries reserved wholly or partly for Filipino citizens or Philippine companies;
- the right to register and vote in Philippine elections;
- the right to own real property, beyond the legal limits prescribed for former citizens; and
- the right to be appointed or elected to public office, under certain conditions;
- the right to indefinite stay, start a business, practice of profession

In the case of Juan mentioned above, reacquisition of dual citizenship will entitle him to stay in the Philippines beyond the one-year limit fixed for former Filipino citizens under the old *Balikbayan* program. Why? Because he is now a Filipino citizen again, and no government authority, including the BI, has the authority to treat him as an alien and impose penalties for "overstaying."

In the case of Jericho, practice of his profession in the Philippines will violate no law, including the 1987 Philippine Constitution (which restricts practice of profession in the Philippines to citizens of the Philippines one hundred percent), since legally, he retains or reacquires his Philippine citizen once he takes his oath of allegiance under *RA 9225*. He then only needs to secure or renew his professional license from a regulatory agency—which, in most cases, is the Professional Regulation Commission.

The framers of the law anticipate substantial gains for the country in terms of investment in real property and the identified priority investment areas.

Among the more business-minded overseas Filipinos, it is an opportunity to be productively involved in the Philippine economy. Hence, former Filipinos who wish to invest in areas like retail, advertising, mass media, public utilities, or exploration of natural resources but have been barred by nationalization laws would have the means to legally come in and infuse their capital.

To the framers of the law, this is clearly a win-win situation, where expatriate Filipinos find new opportunities for profit, while the Philippine economy and the rest of the Filipino population benefit from their investment in terms of new jobs and incomes.

Suffrage and Public Office

For the more politically minded, dual citizenship is a vehicle that allows them to participate in the shaping of the country's political destiny, particularly by voting in Philippine elections.

The passage of the *Dual Citizenship Law* complements the *Overseas Absentee Voting Law*, or *RA 9189*, enacted earlier in the same year. Where *RA 9189* limits its application to overseas workers permanent residents and other Filipinos living or working in other countries who have not taken up another citizenship, *RA 9225* broadens the scope of overseas voting to include dual citizens.

A question that's frequently asked is whether a dual citizen can run for an elective position in the Philippines. *RA 9225* says yes, but with a big *if*—and that is, if the candidate renounces his/her other citizenship upon filing his/her certificate of candidacy with the Commission on Elections. Indeed, it's a tough choice to make. But Congress justifies this requirement as a way of ensuring an elected public official's undivided loyalty to the Republic of the Philippines.

A similar rule applies to those accepting an appointment to public office: they must renounce their oath of allegiance to the country where they were naturalized.

Now this sounds like it creates a disadvantage for those who have ambitions of holding public office in the Philippines. In reality, it gives them an advantage—an option which did not exist before, when dual citizenship was not yet legislated.

In addition, it must be stressed that the right to vote and be elected or appointed to public office is not available to the following: (1) those who are running for or occupying public office in their other country of nationality and (2) those who are in active service as commissioned or non-commissioned officers in the armed forces of that other country.

Property Rights

One of the most significant changes brought about by *RA 9225* is the exemption of dual citizens from the legal limits to private land ownership in the Philippines. While *RA 9225* does not explicitly mention it, this conclusion logically flows from the fact that a dual citizen under this law is a Filipino citizen; therefore, the constitutional or statutory prohibition on account of nationality ceases to apply to him.

The Philippine Constitution generally prohibits non-Filipino citizens from owning private lands in the Philippines. The *Foreign Investment Act* of 1991, however, allows natural-born Filipinos who have been naturalized as foreign citizens to own up to five thousand square metres in the case of urban lands and three hectares in the case of rural lands.

The reacquisition or retention of Philippine citizenship under *RA 9225* renders these limits moot and academic, meaning that dual citizens may legally invest in private land with no size limits, except in the case of agricultural land covered by agrarian reform laws.

Parenthetically, since both the Constitution and the *Foreign Investment Act* speak only of "land," it follows that foreigners—natural-born Filipinos or not, dual citizens or not—may legally own condominium units in the Philippines.

Minor Children

Another benefit extended to persons wishing to retain or reacquire Philippine citizenship under this law is the derivative citizenship conferred on their minor, unmarried children. *RA 9225* specifically provides

INDOMITABLE CANADIAN FILIPINOS

that such children, whether legitimate, illegitimate, or adopted, "shall be deemed citizens of the Philippines."

In order to take full advantage of this provision, applicants for dual citizenship are advised to include such children in the application, specifying their names, ages, and dates of birth. This is particularly important to those who intend to send their children to school in the Philippines and protect them from discrimination, or from being categorized as "aliens" or "foreign students."

Dual citizenship in this context is also a convenient means for children of mixed parentage to regain the opportunity to participate in sports competitions in the Philippines, such as the Philippine Basketball Association, where a number of "Fil-Foreigners" have risen to stardom playing in the pro league.

Others, like the "Fil-Brits" who play for the national football team the Azkals, get the chance to represent the country in international competitions.

Taxation

Another common concern is the matter of taxation. Some individuals worry that when they reacquire their Philippine citizenship, their income abroad shall be assessed for income tax by the Philippine government. This is not true. As the authors of *RA 9225* have repeatedly explained, Philippine tax laws, particularly the *National Internal Revenue Code*, explicitly limit the definition of "taxable income" of Philippine citizens residing overseas, including overseas contract workers, to all income earned "from all sources within the Philippines." Thus, dual citizens, for as long as they are considered "residing outside of the Philippines," shall be exempt from paying income tax on their income earned abroad.

Moreover, there is an additional level of protection for Filipinos earning income in countries like Canada, United States, and other countries with which the Philippines has an existing treaty on the avoidance of double taxation. Broadly, any such income tax paid to the government of either country "shall be deducted" from the tax payable to the government of the

269

other country, meaning that in no instance shall an individual subject to taxing by both countries be required to pay tax twice on the same income.

In conclusion, therefore, there is sufficient protection for dual citizens against being taxed twice for the same income. In the first place, the law, *RA 9225*, cannot be interpreted in a manner that would defeat its purpose, which is to attract and encourage former citizens to rejoin the Philippine mainstream society and participate in its economic growth and development. It cannot be interpreted as imposing a heavy burden on anyone wishing to embrace the Philippines once more as his or her country of nationality.

Application Requirements, Fees

Applying for dual citizenship is pretty simple, quick, and inexpensive. Applicants are basically required to present two things. The first is proof of being a natural-born Filipino citizen, which could be a birth certificate, baptismal certificate, Philippine passport, or any other Philippine government-issued document, at the discretion of the consular officer. The other is proof of naturalization as a foreign citizen, which could come in the form of a certificate of naturalization or a citizenship card.

The fee is fixed at $57.50 CAD for every applicant, with an additional fee of $28.75 CAD for each minor dependent child, if applicable.

The application form and all relevant information may be downloaded from the Consulate General's website at *VancouverPCG.net*.

All Advantages, No Disadvantages

There are at least sixty countries that expressly allow or recognize dual citizenship, and Canada is one of them. Filipino-Canadians can consider themselves fortunate that the government of Canada explicitly allows dual or multiple citizenships. "Canadian law permits dual or multiple citizenships: you can be a citizen of another country and still be recognized as Canadian," says the website of the Department of Foreign Affairs and International Trade of Canada.

The same website provides information and practical advice on dealing with situations where dual citizenship could cause some problems or inconveniences. But on the whole, it is reasonable to conclude that there are no real disadvantages in having both Philippine and Canadian citizenship.

For sure, there could be situations where, for instance, possession of two passports could cause some confusion or delay, or where taxation could create some false apprehensions. This is why it is important to distinguish fact from myth and information from mere opinion, and to develop a clever and practical way of making the most of one's dual citizenship.

In truth, dual citizenship is a means for further empowerment. It can only add to what a naturalized Canadian citizen already enjoys, and cannot take away anything in terms of benefits, rights, and privileges.

In a very real sense, it is a way to have the best of both worlds.

Attorney Anthony A. L. Mandap is the Deputy Consul General at the Philippine Consulate General in Vancouver, BC.

Is Education an Equalizer for Filipinos in Canada?

By Maria Veronica G. Caparas

September 1, 2018 – This question segues to the more intricate nature of education as a leveler for Filipinos in Canada and leads to a number of proofs of how Philippine-earned credentials can level the playing-field.

The answers to the "how" question can be summed up, to wit: 1) highly skilled Filipinos in healthcare, engineering, education, and business administration in Canada act as silent Philippine ambassadors; 2) the silent ambassadors among long-time Filipinos in Canada negotiate spaces for aspiring immigrants and residents through policies and means, just and fair; 3) with their Philippine-earned degrees spiced up with Canadian credentials, deep-seated values, and hard work, Canadian Filipinos pave the way for future *kababayan*s to join the crème de la crème of equalizers; and 4) these Filipinos rank similarly with well-credentialed immigrants from other countries like India and China whose efforts can only go as far as Canada would allow.

The University of the Philippines in Diliman, Quezon city

Alas! Canada's criteria as a labour-receiving country are confusing on so many levels. Highly skilled Filipinos find that they still have to take courses and pass exams before they can qualify for professional practice in Canada.

Compared with first wave Filipino immigrants, today's Filipino immigrants go through the eye of the needle to get good jobs. In hindsight, Philippine education is largely patterned after the US public school system, and this may be a factor in why the US is more welcoming than Canada to Filipino immigrants. Filipinos do find that entry to the US is easier than to Canada; however, many of them choose to go to and stay in Canada, where healthcare system is deemed better and where they get reunited with their families who moved to Canada a generation or two ahead of them.

Those who decide to stay in Canada turn deaf to the Philippines' complaint of brain drain and demonstrate their competitive advantage with equally well-credentialed immigrants from other countries. A good number of them have joined the ranks of Canada's tenured university professors, licensed engineers, professional healthcare workers, and bank managers. Some choose to earn more credentials, challenge Canada's undelivered promises, organize assemblies to lobby for critical changes, and strive to go back to the Philippines at a summons of patrimony.

Those who opt to get reincarnated in a different profession or learn a new skill for a job considered to be at the lowest rung in Canada's totem pole can only sigh, shed a tear or two, and aspire for a good life for their children or young relatives back home. They know that these temporary jobs at stores and fast-food chains put victuals on their tables. Their primary concern remains economic and social.

Filipinos' home-earned education has molded them into discerning and willful individuals who, as silent ambassadors, have leveled the playing field. After all, the marks of true education goes beyond those displayed on walls or those two- or three-letter titles attached to one's name. Many Filipinos have proven to be really educated in more ways than remaining still in Canada; they continue to conquer what they deem essential to their circumstances.

Filipinos Now Third-Largest Immigrant Group in Canada

April 1, 2021- In the 1990s, the UK, Italy, and the United States were the major country sources of immigrants to Canada. By 2007, China exceeded the UK in the number of immigrants to Canada and was the number-one source of immigrants to Canada.

But by 2012, China, India, and the Philippines were competing for top place, with China still slightly ahead. From 2016 to 2020, India succeeded in replacing China as the major source of Canadian immigrants, followed closely by China and the Philippines, with India ahead by only a few thousand more immigrants. In a few more years, the Philippines may be able to surpass both India and China in supplying Canada with competent, highly educated, professional, industrious Filipinos with exemplary work ethics who, when they arrive, hit the ground running.

What Canadians Want in Immigration

In a newspaper article about what native-born Canadians want regarding immigration, the majority said that they consider immigrants necessary for diversity, which they consider an asset and a good characteristic of Canadian society. However, they also said that immigration should not have the effect of substantially changing the Canadian society native Canadians are used to.

There was also a widespread agreement among them that immigrants should know one of Canada's official languages (English or French), make a concerted effort to integrate into the society into which they have moved, and should not seek to form enclaves that amount to a mini-version of their own country, transplanted geographically. Also, that they need to leave behind customs and values that are incompatible with Canadian values such as preference for boy over girl children, bride burning for lack of dowry, and pre-arranged marriages.

What Filipino Immigrants Bring

Almost all Filipino immigrants to Canada are Christian, and the majority of them are Roman Catholics, because the Philippines was a colony of Spain for over three hundred years and the only lasting effect of that colonization was the conversion of Filipinos to Christianity. Then, the United States took over Spain and occupied the Philippines for fifty years, finally giving it its full independence on July 4, 1946. America's greatest contribution to the Philippines was the introduction of the public-school system, with English as the means of instruction, because the early teachers were Americans, and the textbooks were from the US.

Although the United States colonized the Philippines for only a short time, its influence on the Filipino way of life has been tremendous. Every Filipino, even the illiterate and the uneducated farmer in the rural area, understands and speaks some words of American English. But those who went to school when English was the means of instruction spoke with better grammar and vocabulary. They can easily pass Canada's English requirement exams for citizenship.

Although Filipinos can be found in large numbers in five Canadian cities: Toronto (Ontario), Vancouver (British Columbia), Winnipeg (Manitoba), Calgary (Alberta), and Edmonton (Alberta), there are no Filipino or Pinoy Towns, like Chinatown or Little India, in those cities. That's because all Filipinos dream of owning their own home. As soon as they can afford the down payment, they buy a house in whatever neighbourhood they can afford. As their financial situation improves, they move to a better neighbourhood.

Because Filipino immigrants come in all categories, their incomes vary. Some Filipino families live in very expensive neighbourhoods, others in low-income neighbourhoods, and the majority of them somewhere in between. There are no large groups of Filipinos living closely together, though Filipino entrepreneurs may have businesses located close to each other and other Asian businesses in certain commercial places.

Because of their Western colonizers, most Filipinos grew up with a Western lifestyle very similar to Canadian ways of living. They do not practice harmful traditional rituals like other immigrants. When they immigrate to Canada, they bring their professional knowledge, technical skills, entrepreneurship, community spirit, political awareness, and Filipino values of religiosity, hospitality, care of elders, appreciation of education, and respect for the law.

They share their Philippine heritage, arts and culture, religious rites, and traditions with other Canadians as they integrate into Canadian society and make Canada their home. Because of Canada's family reunification program, all their family members are in Canada, so they are here to stay while significantly contributing to Canada's development and multicultural image.

Without Filipinos, there will be less music, dance and joy to celebrate Canada's diversity and less art to enrich Canada's multicultural collage.

The CFNet Editorial Board

Gender Equality: An Unfinished Global Task

March I, 2020 – The world marks International Women's Day on March 8, 2020. According to the United Nations, the theme of this year's celebration is "I Am Generation Equality: Realizing Women's Rights."

The international body notes online that International Women's Day is a "time to reflect on progress made". It is also a time to "call for change and to celebrate acts of courage and determination by ordinary women who have played an extraordinary role in the history of their countries and communities."

The UN points out that while the world has made "unprecedented advances, no country has achieved gender equality." It notes that women earn 23 percent less than men globally. Legal restrictions have kept 2.7 billion women from accessing the same choice of jobs as men. Women spend three times more time than men doing unpaid care and domestic chores.

A total of 750 million adults worldwide are illiterate, and two thirds of them are women. Women occupy only 24 percent of parliamentary seats worldwide. One in three women experience physical or sexual abuse.

Here in Canada, the country has a self-declared feminist for a prime minister in Justin Trudeau. According to the Trudeau government, advancing gender equality is one of its most important priorities. When the country marked Gender Equality Week in September 23–27, 2019, the federal government declared that it had made progress in advancing gender equality in Canada and around the world.

The government cited Canada's first gender-balanced federal Cabinet, as well investments in programs for women and girls in the country and abroad.

Another example mentioned is the investment of forty billion dollars in a National Housing Strategy, with at least 25 percent of projects supporting women, girls, and their families.

The government also pointed to its two-hundred-million-dollar investment across government bodies to prevent gender-based violence, support survivors and their families, and create more responsive legal and justice systems.

The government has launched Canada's *Feminist International Assistance Policy* to respond to the needs of local women's organizations in developing countries.

On October 28, 2019, the Canadian Centre for Policy Alternatives and a network of more than fifty women's rights and equality-seeking organization released a report highlighting the work that still needed to be done. The report is aptly titled "Unfinished Business: A Parallel Report on Canada's Implementation of the Beijing Declaration and Platform for Action."

The study assessed Canada's progress in meeting the goals for gender equality identified in the Beijing Declaration. According to a media release about the report, the Beijing Declaration is the "most progressive global blueprint ever for advancing women's rights." The declaration was adopted unanimously in 1995 by 189 countries, including Canada.

The report noted that between 2006 and 2018, Canada's gender gap in economic participation and opportunity had inched forward an average of 0.2 percent per year. At this lethargic rate, it will take 164 years for Canada to close the economic gender gap.

Men outnumber women in public and private sector management positions by two to one. In the political arena, only 29 percent of members of the federal parliament are women.

The latest available Statistics Canada data on gender, diversity, and inclusion show that 61.4 percent of Canadian women participated in the labour force in June 2019, compared to 70.1 percent among men. In 2016, less than one fifth of all leadership roles were held by women, according to the federal statistics agency.

The Canadian Women's Foundation put it bluntly this way: "If you think we've achieved gender equality in Canada, think again."

According to the Toronto-headquartered organization, 1.9 million women in Canada live on a low income. As well, women are 60 percent less likely than men to move from middle management to executive ranks.

The Canadian Women's Foundation also notes that it costs Canada billions of dollars every year to deal with the effects of gender inequality.

"It's estimated that promoting gender equality could add $150 billion to Canada's GDP," the organization points out. As the CCPA's "Unfinished Business" report urges, "we can't be complacent." The report concluded, "There are reasons yet to march, gaps yet to be closed," *The CFNet Editorial Board*

Beyond Apology: A Call for Vigilance against Racism

By Eleanor R. Laquian

February 1, 2019 – In 1998, the University of British Columbia's Institute of Asian Research sponsored an international conference on Asian migration, local racism, and their implications for public policy in Canada. One of its conclusions was that discrimination against Asians exists in Canada.

Today, Asian immigrants have become targets of new forms of discrimination, insult, and abuse from a segment of the white population and other ethnic groups. This is truly lamentable and alarming, since Asian immigration has contributed to the many social, economic, and cultural achievements of Canada. It has served to blur the polarizing effect of the two-founding-nations concept and the bilingual and bicultural policies of the past.

Furthermore, it has helped to facilitate the advancement of Canada's official bilingual policy by de-linking it from the old bicultural scheme.

Litany of Apologies

For the past thirty years, Canada has apologized for certain "dark chapters" in its history dealing with Asian immigrants.

1. On September 22, 1988, Prime Minister Brian Mulroney delivered a formal apology to Japanese Canadians for internment during the Second World War. In 1942, over twenty-two thousand Japanese Canadians from British Columbia were evacuated

and interned in the name of "national security." Their properties were confiscated and sold to cover the costs of their internment.

2. On June 22, 2006, in the House of Commons for the first session of the thirty-ninth Parliament, Prime Minister Stephen Harper delivered an official apology to Chinese Canadians for the Chinese Head Tax levied on Chinese immigrants in Canada who had arrived between 1885 and 1923, and the *Chinese Exclusion Act* of 1923 that limited arrivals from the East Asian country.

3. While speaking at the thirteenth Annual Mela Gadri Babian Da in Surrey, BC on August 3, 2008, Prime Minister Harper also apologized for the Komagata Maru incident. South Asians roundly rejected the apology, saying it should have been done on the floor of the House of Commons.

4. Thus on May 18, 2016—nearly 102 years after the Komagata Maru sailed into Vancouver—Prime Minister Justin Trudeau offered a full apology in the House of Commons for the government's decision to turn away the ship, which was carrying hundreds of South Asian immigrants, most of whom were Sikhs. The ship was ultimately forced to return to India and was met by British soldiers. Twenty passengers were killed and others were jailed following an ensuing riot.

5. On November 7, 2018, Prime Minister Trudeau apologized in Parliament for Canada's refusal to admit Jewish refugees fleeing Nazi Germany just months before the outbreak of World War II. The ocean liner MS *St. Louis* departed Germany on May 15, 1939 and crossed the Atlantic with 907 German Jews aboard, desperate for refuge from persecution, but were turned away by Canada.

Only in Canada: Charter of Rights Protection

Canada is unique among nations of the world in having in its *Charter of Rights and Freedoms*, Section 27, which states: "The Charter shall be interpreted in a manner consistent with the preservation and enhancement of the multicultural heritage of Canadians."

Thus Section 27 acknowledges the fact that Canada today is composed not only of stereotypical white, blue-eyed Anglo-Saxon blonds, but of people of different ethnicities coming from many countries in the world, each with its own ethnic background, culture, and religion.

Formal Apologies are Not Antidotes to Racism

While formal apologies are reminders of past struggles suffered by Asian and other Canadian immigrants, and Section 27 of the Charter is a firm reassurance of Canada's commitment to the ideals of multiculturalism, they have not been antidotes to racism.

Today, Asian immigrants continue to be targets of new forms of discrimination because of their race. The Canadian government itself sets them apart from its white population by referring to them as a "visible minority," which in itself is a racist term because it is based on color.

A visible minority (French: minorité visible) is defined by the Government of Canada as "persons, other than Aboriginal peoples, who are non-Caucasian in race or non-white in colour."

Even when they comprise the majority in certain parts of Canada, Asian immigrants are still referred to as "visible minority" mainly because of the colour of their skin. It's about time that the Government of Canada retire this racist term

Racism is defined as the exclusion of individuals or groups from full participation in society because of prejudice—which is an unsubstantiated, negative pre-judgment of individuals or groups, usually because of ethnicity, religion, or race. Because of racism, Asian immigrants continue to be under-represented in the media, police departments, political office, and the public service.

Although Filipino immigrants enjoyed an employment rate (88.5 per cent) higher than their Canada-born counterparts (84 per cent) and even higher than other immigrants (78.9 per cent) according to the 2017 Statistics Canada report, the majority of them are temporary foreign workers, including caregivers, with part-time and low-paying jobs. They are in danger of becoming a permanent underclass and burdens in Canadian society if not given opportunities for upward mobility.

These low-paid Filipino workers are immediately employed, because they would rather take whatever lowly job is available than go on welfare, which would bring dishonour to their family.

Thirty years ago, racism among polite Canadians was a silent debate. They were reticent to discuss race and ethnicity in public, for fear of being branded racists or bigots, but racism was always in their consciousness.

With increased Asian immigration came a rise in racism. And today, what was a silent debate is no longer silent or subtle. Immigration and racism have become important issues for public discussion and debate because there is a need to openly discuss the relationship between immigration and racism and the costs and benefits of immigration.

A Call to Protect Our New Multicultural Canadian Identity

Nearly half a century ago, Canada de-emphasized the concept of "two founding nations" and championed a new policy of multiculturalism in a bilingual Canada. Since then, it has made steady progress, until about half a decade ago.

Countries in Europe and North America, Canada included, began to see increasing anti-immigrant virulence, explicit and implied, coming from some politicians, including leaders of certain political parties, such as the People's Party in Canada. It is no doubt caused, to a significant degree, by mass migration and irregular border crossings as a result of poverty, civil wars, and conflicts in developing parts of the world.

Thus, the need for vigilance and timely response whenever anti-immigrant views surface is self-evident. Indeed, it behooves all Canadians—particularly leaders at all levels of government--to weigh in and speak up against racial discrimination, to show Canada's genuine sense of wisdom and compassion. Only then can we stem this rising tide of racism in Canada and sustain our enviable and newfound multicultural Canadian identity.

Foreign Domestic Workers/Caregivers: Able and Available to Meet Canada's Labour Needs

By Eleanor R. Laquian

March 16, 2020 – To celebrate International Women's Day this year, thousands of women took to the streets in major urban centres, including Toronto and Vancouver, demanding gender equality and proclaiming women's rights.

These marches called to global attention the fact that there's still a lot to be done to advance women's rights all over the world, including in Canada, where undervalued women do housework and provide child and elderly care every day in many Canadian homes.

Female Family Members as Caregivers

In general, female family members—from wives, mothers, grandmothers to aunts, nieces, sisters—do a lot more housework and caring for the young and old than any male member of the family.

Foreign Domestic Workers and Caregivers in Canadian Life

Foreign domestic workers and caregivers have been coming to Canada for over a hundred years. In the 1800s, European women came to be household helpers. There were no restrictions on their becoming permanent residents or citizens in Canada. In fact, they were invited to immigrate and become full-pledged Canadians.

The last fifty years have changed the source countries for this vital labour force. Canada's Foreign Domestic Movement, established in 1981, targeted Caribbean women primarily, and its successor, the Live-In Caregiver Program, started in 1992, attracted Asian women. Both groups are women of colour who were not given an easy access to permanent residency and citizenship as European women who came to do the same work.

*Domestic workers and caregivers make it possible for ageing
Canadians to be cared for at home. © Can Stock Photo / Lighthunter*

Current Demographic Characteristics

The educational level of LCP principal applicants has increased steadily over the years and is now very high. An updated study of domestic workers and caregivers in Canada shows their current characteristics:

- In 2009, 63 percent of applicants held a bachelor's degree or higher. This is a remarkably high proportion, and far exceeds the proportion of principal applicants in "economic" categories of immigration who have university degrees (39.5 percent) [CIC Facts and Figures, 2009: p.42)
- From 1993 to 2009, 444 principal applicants had master's
- degrees and 48 had earned doctorates.
- The majority of principal applicants are aged twenty to forty.
- Principal applicants are more likely to be married.
- The overwhelming majority are women.
- Over 90 percent have come from the Philippines and are proficient in English.

From the lens of the Federal Skilled Worker Program.

If LCP applicants were evaluated under Canada's Comprehensive Ranking System or "points system" based on skills, education, language ability, work experience, and other factors such as age, most would easily score sixty-seven points or higher out of a hundred to qualify to immigrate to Canada under the Federal Skilled Worker Program.

Needs and Socioeconomic Implications of Canada's Ageing Society

With low fertility rates and more Canadian couples getting married at a later age and having fewer children, the number of those who are sixty-five years or older is expected to double in less than two decades, from 5.0 million to 10.4 million in 2036 as per the following calculations:.

- In 2014, over six million Canadians were aged sixty-five or older, representing 15.6 percent of Canada's population.
- By 2015, one in four Canadians was sixty-five or older. For the first time, there were more Canadians over the age of sixty-five than under the age of fifteen.
- By 2030—just ten years from today—seniors will number over 9.5 million, making up 23 percent of Canadians.

The greying of Canada's population carries the following socioeconomic implications:

- an increasing need for caregivers;
- less revenue for the government; and
- rising healthcare costs.

A 2002 study conducted by Health Canada found that 44 percent of family caregivers paid out-of-pocket expenses; 40 percent spent one to three hundred dollars a month on caregiving, and another 25 percent spent in excess of three hundred dollars.

The Costs of Caring for Ageing Parents

The cost of elderly care amounts to thirty-three billion dollars a year in out-of-pocket expenses and time taken from work and is expected to grow, according to a report by CIBC economists); average $11,635for those 65 and increase to as much as $21,150 for those 80 and older according to the Canadian Institute for Health Information (CIHI).

In Canada, the government only pays 70 percent of healthcare costs. The other 30 percent is left for seniors or their family members to pay.

After the age of sixty-five, Canadians expect to spend an average of $5,391 every year on out-of-pocket medical expenses. Family caregivers spend an average of $3,300 a year on these expenses.

Family members who cared for ailing children or older relatives reported more health and psychological problems, mainly because of the intensity of care they provided. Those who cared for an ailing spouse also experienced financial difficulties as a result of their caregiving responsibilities and loss of spousal income.

Without caregivers employed by families to look after their ailing spouses or parents or grandparents, the government will have to spend billions of dollars to provide institutional care where needed. Even at that, most nursing homes have been found by families to be wanting.

Consensus

The best place for ailing old people is at home, in the compassionate care of competent caregivers privately paid for and supervised by family members.

This is how the government can ensure the proper care of Canadian seniors and, at the same time, save money in institutional care and healthcare costs. Also, this approach would generate more revenue for the government, because more women will be able to work outside the home.

The services provided by foreign domestic caregivers and workers are essential and the need for them will be heightened with the rapidly increasing number of ageing Canadians.

The Philippines has been the dominant source of foreign domestic workers and caregivers (not only for Canada but also for the US, Spain, Israel, etc.) because Filipino caregivers are well educated, have a facility for one of Canada's official languages (English), share similar cultural and religious values with Christian Canadians, are committed to hard work and industry, and are imbued with a deep sense of caring for others.

Conclusion

Although the LCP was discontinued in 2014, there are about twenty-four thousand caregivers and family members of theirs who came under this program and are still struggling to get permanent residency, reunite the family, and secure a decent future in Canada. Due to certain restrictions of the LCP, years of family separation have caused familial conflicts, resulting in many family breakdowns and marriage failures.

These caregivers and their family members have suffered long enough. The current immigration pilot projects are mere band-aid solutions to LCP-caused problems that only prolong their uncertainty and insecurity. It is time for this social injustice to end. These care workers should be allowed to become permanent residents without being made to jump through hoops. This is the only just solution to this social injustice— landed status now.

Because they are qualified as skilled workers, future caregiver applicants should be admitted as regular immigrants with permanent resident status on arrival and the same right as other immigrants to seek a better life and a brighter future for their children in Canada. Because they provide an essential service to Canadian families, the processing of their applications as landed immigrants should be expedited so that they are able to arrive in Canada within two years upon application. Giving them the opportunity to improve their future would truly advance all women's rights in Canada and show appreciation of their work and contribution to Canada's development and progress.

Stereotyping and Racialization: A Constant Canadian Filipino Struggle

By Carlo Javier

May 1, 2018 – I'm a twenty-four-year-old Filipino immigrant, a graduate of Capilano University's Bachelor of Communication Studies program, and the outgoing editor-in-chief of the campus's official newspaper.

In my twelve years in Canada, I've experienced my fair share of racialization. Filipinos in Canada have long been intrinsically linked to the Live-In Caregiver Program, and that stereotype has expanded itself to custodianship.

A quick look at the union's posters and campaign flyers reinforced my case. The janitors at the university are predominantly Filipinos—exactly twenty-two of the twenty-nine are.

One of the individuals I spoke with during my research for this article was Leo Alejandria of Service Employees International Union Local 2. For over twenty years, Mr. Alejandria worked as a cleaner in a host of Vancouver schools. He estimates that 60 percent of cleaners in the Lower Mainland are Filipinos.

The numbers are shocking, but they made perfect sense to me. I know too many Filipinos in the cleaning industry. It is an honest job and should not be looked down upon—but it does sting when you're college-educated who may have built an impressive professional career in the Philippines, to find yourself cleaning toilets and tables at schools, offices, and malls.

Eymard Caravana is a Filipino cleaner who cleans the entire building where I work by himself. Mr. Caravana told me about maintaining the utmost level of professionalism in his job—no matter what his job is. I was impressed that he was proud of what many would consider a lowly job. But if there are some positives from all the racialized identities that have seen built for Filipinos in Canada, then I'd be proud of professionalism too.

Filipinos do indeed work well and hard—even if it's a job we never thought we would end up with, in a country where we came in pursuit of a better life.

Everyone Should Try to Avert a Climate Meltdown

September 1, 2019 – As the world warms up with the activities of its global population of more than seven billion, extreme weather events are becoming more frequent and intense, sea levels are rising, prolonged droughts are putting pressure on food crops, and many animal and plant species are being driven to extinction. Since climate change is primarily manmade, we, as individuals, can do something to resolve a problem of this scale and severity.

Climate change occurs when changes in the Earth's climate system result in new weather patterns that last for at least a few decades—and maybe for millions of years. Other telltale signs of climate change, aside from sea levels rising, are ocean warming and acidification, sea-ice and glacier melt, and extreme weather, which has left a trail of devastation on all continents, according to the World Meteorological Organization.

Seven of the ten deadly storms in the Philippines resulted in more than a thousand casualties. Five of the ten occurred between 2006 and 2019. But the deadliest storm on record in the Philippines was Typhoon Haiyan in 2013, known locally as Typhoon Yolanda, which was responsible for more than sixty-three hundred lost lives, four million displaced citizens, and two billion dollars in damages.

About twenty tropical cyclones enter Philippine waters each year, with eight or nine making landfall. Over the past decade, these tropical storms have struck the nation more often and more severely, most scientists believe because of climate change.

The Global Climate Risk Index 2015 listed the Philippines as the number-one most affected country by climate change, using 2013's data. Sea-level rise, a detrimental effect of climate change, can be exacerbated by the storm surge from tropical storms. Sea levels in the Philippines are rising at about twice the global average.

When especially strong storms like Typhoon Haiyan make landfall, the higher sea level contributes to a storm surge that can rise upward of fifteen to twenty feet, displacing thousands or even millions of citizens in coastal communities.

The Intergovernmental Panel on Climate Change Report on Global Warming of 1.5°C said that this target was physically possible, but would require unprecedented changes in our lifestyle, energy, and transport systems to achieve. It showed how keeping temperature increases below 2°C would reduce the risks to human well-being, ecosystems, and sustainable development.

Heat Waves, Droughts, Wildfires, and Floodings

According to the IPCC, human-caused global warming is driving climate changes that impact both human and natural systems on all continents and across the oceans. Human-caused global warming results from the increased use of fossil fuels in transportation, manufacturing, and communications.

British Columbia broke its record for the most area burned in a wildfire season for two successive years. California suffered devastating wildfires, with November's Camp Fire being the deadliest fire in over a century for the USA. The spring and summer of 2019 brought unprecedented tornadoes to Ottawa, flooding to Québec, and earthquakes to Northern BC and Southern California.

The Devastating Effects of Climate Change on Earth are Real.

There are people who deny that climate change is caused by human activities. They claim that increased hurricane activity and other extreme weather events are a result of natural weather patterns, not human-caused climate change. However, a 2013 review of over eleven thousand peer-reviewed studies published from 1991 to 2011 found that 97 percent of the studies expressing a position on the issue endorsed the idea that humans are causing global warming.

Whether climate change is caused by humans or natural weather patterns or a combination of both, the fact remains that there is now less snow in places where there used to be lots and more heat where there used to be less.

The decision to mitigate unprecedented climate change is within everybody's reach—like driving and flying less, switching to a "green" energy provider, and changing what we eat and buy daily. Let us work together to save the only planet we have.

The CFNet Editorial Board

Safeguard our Collective Multicultural Identity

By Eleanor R. Laquian

July 1, 2019 – Canada is among the few countries in the world that still accepts high levels of immigration. Canadians follow the rule of law, which makes Canada an ideal destination for prospective immigrants. A sense of being secure is what attracts people to Canada.

But for many, Canada's biggest asset is its diversity, which makes it such a model of civility—a model that is envied and admired all over the world. **Prime Minister Pierre Elliot Trudeau's single most important statement as he introduced his new policy of multiculturalism in 1971 may have been that "no singular culture could or would define Canada."**

In 1971, for the first time, the majority of new immigrants were of non-European ancestry—a trend that has persisted ever since. The 2011 Canadian Census recorded more than two hundred different ethnic origins in Canada. In fact, the 2016 Census revealed that the Philippine-based Tagalog—not English or French—had been the fastest-growing language in Canada since 2011. One fifth of the population had a mother tongue that was not English or French, with 64 percent of Canadians claiming to speak Tagalog at home. In 2016, newcomers accounted for two thirds of the country's population growth, with more than half coming from Asia.

The *Canadian Multiculturalism Act* became law in 1988, making Canada the first country in the world to adopt multiculturalism as an official policy. Multiculturalism "takes into account the contribution[s] made by other ethnic groups to the cultural enrichment of Canada."

It ensures that every individual is equal before and under the law and has the right to equal protection and equal benefit of the law without discrimination and, in particular, without discrimination based on race, national or ethnic origin, colour, religion, sex, age, or mental or physical disability.

The General Social Survey of 2013 reported that the overwhelming majority of Canadians shared the values of human rights (92 percent), respect for the law (92 percent), and gender equality (91 percent). They also value diversity, tolerance, compassion, and understanding.

As recently as March 2017, the Canadian Studies Association reported that Canadians were increasingly comfortable with diversity. Intermarriage rates are growing—a strong index of racial and cultural integration

Before 1971, Canada was defined primarily by the partnership of its two founding nations, France and Britain, and dominated by a bilingualism and biculturalism policy to preserve and safeguard the French and British contributions to Canada's cultural enrichment.

Multiculturalism, however, has so evolved that now, Canadians define themselves as citizens of a multi-ethnic, multireligious society. While Canada would remain a bilingual nation, it would pursue multiculturalism rather than biculturalism.

Multiculturalism respects the cultural freedom of all individuals and recognizes their cultural contributions to Canadian society while respecting the founding nations' Western cultures and Christian beliefs. It blurs the effect of biculturalism because it encourages people to look at society and culture from the viewpoint of a global perspective and develops the need to examine other cultures from a neutral—rather than Western— point of view.

Learning to accept and live with many different cultures helps Canadians understand each other and discourage hatred and violence. Learning one of the official languages helps them to adapt.

Excelling in Arts and Sports

It is widely recognized that immigrants are a source of diverse knowledge and experience. They increase innovation, creativity, and prosperity in society. New residents enrich the cultural fabric by introducing new foods, music, traditions, beliefs, and interests. Immigrants win more prestigious literary and performing arts awards than native born Canadians. In sports, unlike the mostly all-white Canadian hockey teams, the ethnically diverse Toronto Raptors reflects Canada's diversity. They united all Canadians in cheering them to victory in game six of the NBA Eastern Conference Finals in 2019.

Other benefits of immigration as listed in a recent immigration study are . . .

- Ethnic restaurants, grocery stores, and clothing stores add flavour and colour to communities, attracting new residents and tourists, and adding to community vitality.
- As more immigrants become settled, communities benefit from new cultural celebrations and more diverse cultural foods, music, and arts at local festivals.
- Schools develop cross-cultural curriculum, as in Alberta and Manitoba, which broadens all children's understanding of the world and their neighbours.
- Communities earn a reputation as fun, festive, and welcoming when their immigrant population is visibly celebrated and accepted.
- Skilled immigrants are a key source of information for Canadian companies in the new global economy.
- Immigrants can open doors to investment opportunities overseas and help attract foreign investment in Canada.
- Newcomers bring new education and work experience and an understanding of a global business context.

Our new multicultural identity is a precious legacy of liberal immigration policies that have welcomed people of diverse ethnic backgrounds to live in Canada while keeping their ethnic culture.

When the Canadian constitution was patriated by Prime Minister Elliot Trudeau in 1982, one of its constituent documents was the *Charter of*

Rights and Freedoms. Section 27 of the Charter stipulates that the rights laid out in the document are to be interpreted in a manner consistent with multiculturalism. On November 13, 2002, the Liberal government of Prime Minister Chrétien designated, by Royal Proclamation, June 27 of each year Canadian Multiculturalism Day. Celebrate it every day.

Why are Canadian Filipinos Underrepresented in Canadian Politics?

By Prod Laquian

July 9, 2016 – Filipinos in their home country are passionately engaged in politics. This is in sharp contrast to the seeming apathy among Canadian Filipinos toward Canadian politics, as noted by Tony Carpio, who studies and researches Canadian Filipinos.

In a recent presentation on Filipino migration to Canada at the University of British Columbia, Carpio calculated that with eight hundred thousand Filipinos in Canada, there should be at least six Filipino MPs in the House of Commons. However, since the 1960s, there has been only one Filipino MP, Dr. Rey Pagtakhan.

Pagtakhan started his political career in 1986 as the first Filipino in Manitoba to be elected school trustee. From there, he was elected to the House of Commons in 1988, and held that office until 2004.

Sadly, Pagtakhan's eighteen illustrious years in politics ended in 2004 because many Filipino voters in his riding still viewed politics as a patronage game. They felt that he spent too much time in Ottawa as an MP and "had not done enough on specific Filipino requests." Supporters of Pagtakhan said that "even though some Filipinos had lived long in Canada, they still saw politics as a means of exacting personal favours and rewards in exchange for their votes."

According to Pagtakhan in a telephone interview, "No politician has ever escaped criticism, but some critics are simply partisan and do not care to know the truth."

Asked why Filipinos are so inadequately represented in Canadian politics today, Maria Aguirre, an entrepreneur who has set up enterprises in several Canadian provinces said that, upon arrival, most Filipinos are too engrossed with making a living to care about politics. "Besides, some have a dim view of politics back home." She recalled one person telling her, "In Canada, I do not need a political patron to make it. I can succeed on my own."

Jeffrey Almeda agrees with Aguirre that most Filipinos who come as economic migrants are not too interested in politics. "Also, they are not united," he said, "Just think of the hundreds of Filipinos in BC who cannot work together behind a candidate. Besides, they do not congregate in specific ridings—there are no Pinoy Towns in Canadian cities that can serve as political bailiwicks."

Almeda hopes that in the future, second- and third-generation Filipinos may get more involved in politics. "The young ones are more economically mobile, and if they remain conscious of their identity, they [will] probably become more political," he said. "However," he quickly added, "this may not happen in our lifetime."

Marissa Roque from Toronto reiterates the divisiveness among Filipinos. She reported that in the last election, a number of Filipino candidates in Canada's largest city threw their hats into the ring, but they were not successful. She observed that Filipinos "are not as cohesive as other ethnic groups." She noted, however, that Filipinos in Winnipeg have been more successful, by supporting local candidates like Flor Marcelino and her brother-in-law, Ted Marcelino, who were both elected MLAs in 2011.

Tony Peña, a retired businessman, said some Canadian Filipino politicians had approached him for financial help. "I helped them because I like to see Filipinos become more successful in politics," he said. "However, I do not vote for candidates just because they are Filipinos. I think most Canadian Filipinos think that way. They are often critical of some Filipinos who run for office. They want to make sure that they are not running just for selfish reasons—but that they really wish to serve the community."

Peña also observed that some Filipinos are "too much in a hurry." He said that "some of them run for top-level positions right away. To succeed in Canadian politics, you may have to start at lower-level posts like the school board or parks board. You cannot be a star right away."

Professor Cesi Cruz, who teaches political science at UBC, thinks that political practices in the Philippines are very different from those in Canada. Back home, politics is "personalistic" and people vote for candidates they closely identify with. In Canada, people tend to vote on the basis of policies and programs contained in political party platforms. Lacking the emotional identification with candidates, Professor Cruz says Canadian Filipinos don't get too excited about Canadian politics.

Finally, Rafael Fabregas, a Filipino Canadian immigration lawyer who narrowly missed being nominated as the Liberal Party candidate for an MP position in a Toronto suburb, said that getting into Canadian politics is "awesome." However, "to win an election is not as easy as it seems to be."

There are probably many other reasons why Canadian Filipinos are underrepresented in Canadian national politics. There may also be many ways to remedy the situation and get more Filipinos involved in national and local elections, and find out why it is difficult for Canadian Filipinos to win.

Sorting Out Ticklish Situations in the Political Engagement of Canadian Filipinos

May 1, 2017 – Much has been said about the low level of Filipino representation in Canadian politics. It's only right to keep up the public discourse about this condition.

That's because only a few have prevailed at the ballot box since Conrado Santos, in Manitoba, became the first Canadian Filipino elected to public office in 1981.

With the community growing in numbers and political consciousness across the country on the rise, it seems easy to think that more political victories are coming. However, things aren't that straightforward. Engagement in electoral politics is a lot more complex. There are delicate situations that arise at times, simply because politics, in its essence, is a cold, calculating game.

Let's start with the common practice of established political parties of pumping up their diversity credentials during elections. One convenient way of doing this is by running Filipinos and other ethnic minorities in a number of unwinnable ridings.

It doesn't matter that a number of these candidates do not stand a chance. In fact, the candidates actually know it. They are often dismissed by others as stooges who are only too willing to do the bidding of their political masters, for perhaps the supposed prospect of future gain. As Filipinos are wont to say in the vernacular, "*nagpapagamit*" ("allowed oneself to be used).

This may be true in some cases, but it doesn't apply to everyone and every situation. It may be the case for some candidates that they are sincere in their attempt to win elected public office. They want to serve, and they're hoping for an upset.

It can also be argued that by running even in no-win ridings, candidates, as well as their supporters in the community, are able to gain valuable experience and insight into how things work.

These are assets that contribute to building the political memory and ability of the community, which can be deployed in future battles. It's practice, a sort of dry run for bigger engagements.

Another delicate situation that is sometimes practiced is that of mainstream political parties of pitting members of the same ethnic minority group against each other. For example:

Things get especially touchy when someone from the community comes up to challenge an incumbent who hails from the same ethnic group. Immediately, that candidate gets branded by the incumbent's camp as an opportunist. Among many Filipinos, it's almost an unforgivable sin. One can surely expect to hear the candidate described, typically behind the individual's back, as someone with no *delicadeza* (sense of decency).

Again, that may be true in some cases. There are other ridings to run in, and why should someone choose to go up against a compatriot in the first place? As in the case of a young Filipino who ran against a popular incumbent Filipino in the same riding. The upstart Filipino lost, of course. However, it can also be asked: Why should somebody get scorned for exercising the right guaranteed by the Canadian Charter to run for public office?

It can be argued that what is often forgotten is the fact that ethnic minority groups do not cast a monolithic vote based on racial affinity. An incumbent elected official does not have and cannot claim all the voters in that individual's community. And neither can the challenger.

This is why political parties sometimes field a community member against another. They recognize that the ethnic vote splits, and everything is fair game.

It can be said that also thrown out the window is the reality that Filipinos and other ethnic minorities are concerned more than just about their racial identities. Like other Canadians, they are also concerned about things such as jobs, safety, and other issues, which factor in their choices on who to vote for.

There's no question that ethnic identity is a huge part of people's lives, but that is not all that matters at the ballot box. That's why it should not be surprising that Filipinos are members of different and competing parties at the federal, provincial, and municipal levels. They're found everywhere, because they choose parties that identify with the personal values they hold dear to their hearts.

The CFNet Editorial Board

Filipino Food: Why Has It Not Gone Mainstream?

March 1, 2017 – Traditional, homecooked Filipino food is tasty and delectable. Even non-Filipinos have been captivated by it. However, with many more Filipinos in Canada today than Malays, Thais, and Vietnamese combined, why has Filipino cuisine not gone mainstream the way Malaysian, Thai, and Vietnamese foods have?

Why are Filipino restaurants in Canada short-lived? What can be done to make traditional, authentic Filipino food more popular? Is Filipino food good only for shared family meals at home, but too cheap and ordinary for restaurant fare?

Almost every country in Asia has a distinctive cuisine featuring a unique taste that comes from a peculiar combination of ingredients and cooking styles.

Filipino food is as rich and varied as other cuisines because many countries have influenced Philippine food throughout the country's history. Yet it embodies particular characteristics that distinguish it from other cuisines.

Sinigang na hipon (above) or baboy uses kamias, guavas or sampalok for its sour broth.

Its uniqueness comes from the unusual blending of native and Western ingredients in a mixture of Asian and predominantly Spanish flavours. It combines the sweet and the savoury, with no overpowering spices to dominate its salty-sour or sweet-sour taste.

This uniqueness of traditional Filipino food, however, is often lost when cooks add a modern twist to reinvent the national cuisine to attract foreign diners. The results of their innovations (*sisig* with sour cream and cheese or a taco filled with *longanisa*, cheddar cheese, and avocado) are not always palatable, because they are neither Western nor authentic Filipino food.

Fortunately, a Filipino restaurant serving homecooked traditional Filipino food was considered the best new restaurant in America in 2016. The Washington DC-based restaurant Bad Saint was *Bon Appetit* magazine's number-two choice among the ten best new restaurants in America for 2016. The restaurant's name is derived from Saint Malo, Louisiana, the first Filipino settlement in the US, established in 1763 by Filipino deserters from Spanish ships during the Manila Galleon trade.

A Filipino restaurant in Toronto, Lamesa, serves chick-silog.

Bad Saint's menu includes simple homey Filipino foods, with no attempts to westernize them. No artistic plating with blank space artfully drizzled with sauce surrounding the food. Instead, the home-cooked dishes are presented family style, with all dishes served at the same time for diners to choose which dishes to try first and in what combination.

The food simply goes from wok to plate to table, with no pretensions of looking expensive or fancy.

The success of Bad Saint shows that there is nothing wrong with traditional, simple, everyday Filipino food, if cooked as it should be. But it may take grandmothers who have perfected traditional Filipino cooking to take charge of modern Filipino restaurant kitchens in order to introduce authentic Filipino home cooking to appreciative mainstream diners.

The CFNet Editorial Board

Heart in Two Places: An Immigrant's Joy and Sorrow

May 31, 2018 – Home is where the heart is. We have all heard this phrase, and even without pausing to think about it, we know what it means.

Home is, of course, more than just a house, or the physical place where we live. As someone said, "it's the place where, when you come, they have to let you in."

Home is where we love and are loved. It's where we feel safe and connected. It's where we have people who care for us, understand us, and appreciate us for what we are. In most cases, it's where we find family.

Mobility is part of most people's lives. It's a natural cycle for many. You grow up at home, build friendships in the community, and, at a certain time, you move out. You settle in a new place, get a job, find a spouse, raise a family, and put down new roots.

You may subsequently move to other places, go through different homes and communities, but surely you will always have the softest spot for where you originally came from.

Mobility takes on an entirely different level when it comes to international migration. It means going to a foreign land, and most often, taking on a new citizenship.

For many immigrants, including Filipinos, leaving one's country of birth doesn't mean a final goodbye. It's "till next time." It's because we all know that there is always a piece of us that stays behind. We know that we will come back another time. Maybe not to return for good, but to visit and rekindle good memories with the folks we know. Memories are tied to places, and there's nothing like the place of one's birth, which evokes such powerful emotions and associations.

Immigrants like Canadian Filipinos are sometimes wedged in a state where they are mistakenly regarded with perpetual suspicion. They will not love Canada enough, and never will dol, because their true loyalties lie elsewhere. Yet on the other hand, they're also seen as having ceased to care much about their country of origin, because otherwise, they wouldn't have left.

We shouldn't be bothered by such erroneous thinking. It's not an either-or choice in the first place, as shown in a paper released in 2016 by Statistics Canada. Titled "Patterns and Determinants of Immigrants' Sense of Belonging to Canada and Their Source Country," the study drew data from the 2013 general social survey on Canadians' perceptions of national identity.

According to the paper, 93 percent of immigrants have a very strong or a strong sense of belonging to Canada. "Furthermore, a strong sense of belonging to the receiving country is not necessarily incompatible with a sense of belonging to the source country.

"About 69 percent of all immigrants had strong sense of belonging to both Canada and their source country," reads the study, prepared by Feng Hou and Grant Schellenberg of Statistics Canada and John Berry of Queen's University.

The authors noted that based on a huge body of psychological and sociological research, there are two "fundamental dimensions underlying immigrants' sociocultural-psychological integration: cultural maintenance (the importance of retaining own-group heritage culture) and participation in the receiving society." They wrote, "These two dimensions are independent, yet not necessarily incompatible with each other."

In one of the daily bulletins released by Statistics Canada that talked about the 2013 survey on perceptions of national identity, the federal agency noted that immigrants overall were "consistently more likely to hold strong beliefs in the importance of national symbols and the existence of a set of shared values."

In another bulletin, Statistics Canada observed that in 2013, immigrants (67 percent) were more likely than non-immigrants (62 percent) to describe their sense of belonging to Canada as "very strong."

June is an important month for Filipinos across the world. It's the time we celebrate our heritage as freedom-loving people. As we commemorate Philippine Independence Day in Canada, we may feel some sadness that we're now far away from the place we first called home. But we should consider ourselves fortunate. We know in our heart that we have not one but two homes. Our heart is big enough to love both our two homes.

The CFNet Editorial Board

Chapter 10:

FILIPINOS IN CANADA AS NATIONAL, TRANSNATIONAL, AND GLOBAL CITIZENS

By Prof. Leonora C. Angeles, University of British Columbia

There are nationalists, transnationalists, and postnationalists. They differ in their analytical positions, perspectives, and emphases. Both challenge the limitations of nationalist projects. Nationalists view the nation-state's interests and people's national identities as the most important elements shaping our lives. Transnationalists focus on increasing ties and relations across geographic and political borders of nation-states. Postnationalists promote the universalization of human rights and other values, thus eclipsing the state-centric view of citizenship rights (Bloemraad 2004). Postnational and denationalized citizenship forms arising out of transnationalisms and revived cosmopolitanism. Postnationalism is strengthened by the rise of deterritorialized global cultures (Sassen 2002ab).

These perspectives have implications for our individual, community, and international development. Filipino post/nationals have taken up dual citizenships in Canada and other countries. Canadians, of Filipino ancestry or not, could acquire Special Investor's Resident and Special Resident Retiree's Visas (SIRV/SRRV) in the Philippines. These post-national Filipino-Canadians, many of whom you have met in this book, interrogate and/or intensify economic and cultural globalization. They engage in dense transnational activities as citizens, migrants, workers, and temporary or permanent settlers in foreign lands. Thus, their identities, sense of nationalisms, attachments, and loyalties are also changing. I am interested in these changes.

Why Canada and the Philippines?

The Philippines and Canada have no historical colonial ties. For this reason alone, Filipino nationalists often—not always—look more favourably on Canada and Canadians compared to the United States and Americans. They are often more suspicious of American policies towards the Philippines, given their enduring history of surplus extraction, economic oppression, military aggression, and sovereignty transgression.

Still, there are historical and contemporary features of Philippine-Canada transnational linkages that reek of old-style colonial economic relations. But in a more complex modern world, punctuated by more complicated and multiple transnational feedback loops. Canada is the third-largest source of overseas remittances to the Philippines. It has also been among the top ten sources of foreign direct investment, commodity imports, and development aid to the Philippines since the early 2000s. These linkages grew because of temporary and permanent migration to Canada. The second-largest Filipino diaspora in the world, after the United States, is now in Canada. There were more than eight hundred thousand people identifying the Philippines as country of origin or ancestry in the 2016 Canada Census. They now rank Canada's third-largest visible immigrant group.

As Filipinos play out their citizenship rights and dynamics at various scales—local, regional, national, global—nationalism alone remains inadequate in explaining probable possibilities for the future of the Philippines and Filipinos in an increasingly transnational world.

What We Already Know

Links between development aid from donor countries and migration from recipient countries are related goals (DeWind and Kinley 1988). This nexus manifests in two ways. First, donors like Canada use foreign aid to serve immigration. They target migrant-sending areas to increase development and decrease the demand for entry into the donor country. Second, migrants living in donor countries like Canada lobby for additional aid for their homeland (Bermeo and Leblang 2015, 627). Bilateral aid influences migration jointly and positively in three ways. One, aid provides information about labour market conditions in the destination country (the attraction effect); two, it increases local spending and wages in countries of origin (the push effect); three, aid workers shape the outcomes of bilateral aid (the networking effect) (Berthélemy, Beuran, and Maurel 2009, 1576). In the European Union, foreign aid is used to influence migration choices and stem migration flows into donor countries (Lanati and Thiele 2018ab). Non-developmental aid is less effective than developmental aid. "Quality donor aid" with "development-oriented motives" helps foster economic growth (Kilbey and Deher 2010). Canada, like other donors, uses aid to promote democratization or reward countries stepping in a democratic direction (Bermeo 2011).

There are policy implications and development planning significance of these growing bilateral Canada-Philippine relations. Their past relations have shaped the current and future trajectory of their intricate transnational linkages. Scholars and popular media often use "uneven development," "reverse transfer of technology," and "brain drain" to describe bilateral relations between donor and recipient countries. In September 2008, for example, segments on CBC radio shows *The Current* and *Dispatches* highlighted the Philippine government's aggressive export of contract labourers. They also pointed to Canada's complicity in recruiting Filipino nurses, caregivers, and other temporary workers to meet its labour market needs, contributing to the collapse of the Philippine public health system.

However, a political or economic lens alone could not fully explain the dynamics of intricate transnational relations between Canada and the Philippines given the absence of historic colonial ties. Development assistance, trade, investments, and labour move both ways, producing complex structures and complicated spin-off effects. For example, labour and aid mobility have created new investment niches, such as nursing and caregiver training schools, immigration consulting, employment agencies, remittance sending and receiving offices, and development-oriented philanthropy and volunteerism in both Canada and the Philippines (Angeles 2008).

Philippine-Canadian aid and migration linkages are substantive in volume and scale compared to trade, foreign direct investment, and military aid. Canadian exports to the Philippines, composed mainly of agrifood products, amounted to almost $459,000,000, while its imports from the Philippines, mostly mechanical and electrical products, amounted to $765,000,000 in 2007. The amount of Canadian direct investment in the Philippines in 2007, $392,000,000, dwarfed the Philippines' $7,000,000 foreign direct investment in Canada in the same year. In 2000, Canada exported $5,240,000 worth of ammunitions, part of the total $6,083,000 Canadian military exports to the Philippines. Canadian development assistance to the Philippines has steadily increased from 1986 to 2016, particularly through the former Canadian International Development Agency and the International Development Research Centre. CIDA's total disbursement for 2006–2007 alone was $24,500,000; the estimate for 1986–2005 is $120,000,000.

CIDA supported many Canadian and international volunteer-sending organizations with headquarters in both countries, such as the Volunteer Services Organization and the Canadian Urban Institute. Canadian development aid compares well with the volume of human capital investments brought by Filipinos into Canada, who are healthy, well educated, skilled, and culturally adaptable. Conservative estimates of cumulative effects of immigration to Canada in 2001 was 0.33 percent of the GDP, or $3,594, million (Grady 2006).

The biggest strategic importance of the Philippines to Canadian national interests are its people. Labour as the source of all value, borrowing from classical economic thought, is at the heart of Canada's national industrial development policy. Canada needs heathy, educated, and skilled labour from the Philippines and elsewhere.

Canadian parents, on average, spend an estimated $13,388 annually or $240,588 over eighteen years to raise a child (Racco 2017). This amount is roughly equivalent to Canada's gain for every healthy and educated eighteen-year-old Filipino new immigrant. *MoneySense* estimated costs at $12,824 a year in 2011, or $243,656 over eighteen years, and updated this in 2015 to reflect inflation, and the yearly average rose to $13,366 (Racco 2017). On the other hand, a typical Filipino income-earner in Canada with family and kin obligations remits an average of five to ten thousand dollars per year to the Philippines (Angeles 2008). Both economies heavily invest in these transnational exchanges, with multiplier effects of remittances, human capital, and brain drain/gain (Yang 2003, Yang and Martinez 2005, Yang and Choi 2007).

The political economy of aid, trade, migration, and investment occurs within social realms, particularly in major cities, where their linkages are most dense and abundant. Development assistance and labour migration flows would not materialize without the creation and expansion of transnational social spaces and city-based transnational "cultural politics of contact zones" (Yeoh and Willis 2005), with their unique and interesting patterns of translocal and transnational communication in spaces that enable people, goods, services, and ideas to circulate between the two countries, particularly in their metropolitan cities.

Critical aspects we need to examine more are dual citizens, transnational actors, and agencies expanding trade-investment-development assistance-labour mobility linkages. Of particular interest is examining the patterns, mechanisms, and dynamics of transnational communication flows, or how opportunities, policies, and regulatory frameworks governing these fields (trade, investment, development assistance, and labour mobility) are communicated to and by relevant stakeholders, including NGOs, universities, and other institutions of higher education. This will help us understand the patterns in the sources, usage, and circulation of information, particularly how messages in/about these fields—especially those related to costs, benefits, consequences, risks, regulations, etc.—are designed, packaged, distributed, and circulated in formal and informal networks within and between these two countries.

Migrant stocks in donor countries affect not just trade and investment but also aid allocation (Berthélemy et al. 2009). We do not have adequate assessments of Canada's policy coherence in its aid, migration, trade, and investment policies toward the Philippines, or how they converge in coherent, contradictory, complex ways within transnational social spaces manifested in cities. Cities are critical to expanding transnational social spaces because of their density and roles in the agglomeration, concentration, and proximity of interaction between transnational actors. Cities, however, are not just spatial containers of flows, capital, bodies, and practices. They are points of transnational contact. Cities are transnational contact zones between actors and agencies with diverse assets and resources. Filipino-Canadians in cities carry communication codes, values, and norms as they interact in the course of aid, trade, and labour exchanges.

Canada-Philippine relations shaping the flows of development assistance and labour migration are not only political and economic in nature. They embed within social formations and social relations that stretch over transnational geographic space that constitutes "social space" (Massey 1984, 333). This "transnational social space" involves communications, social learning, networking, and other discursive practices that span across nation-state boundaries (Angeles 2003). They facilitate and mediate the material and non-material flows of capital, people, goods, ideas, information, imagery, and representations, and their discursive constructions and concurrent practices.

These material (i.e., development aid, gendered bodies qua human capital), ideological (i.e., ideas, discourses), and representational (i.e., media, artistic productions) flows are embedded within contingent social processes and working through power relations at multiple levels and scales of analyses and human experiences (i.e., individual, household, village, city, nation, and region). The transnational social spaces shaping the aid-migration nexus develop interesting patterns of translocal and transnational communication. They enable—or sometimes disable—people, goods, services and ideas to circulate between the two countries and their metropolitan city areas.

What We Still Don't Know and Why

Canada's relation with smaller developing countries like the Philippines is under-researched compared to bigger allies and trade partners in the Americas and Europe. Likewise, there is more attention on the Philippines' economic and political relationship with US and Japan, its former colonizers, and with important trade partners, aid sources, and hosts to large Filipino diasporas, such as the US, Korea, Singapore, Hong Kong, Saudi Arabia, and Australia (Choy 2003; Espiritu 1995, 2003; Kim and Mejia

1976; Okamura 1998; Root 1997; Tyner 1999, 2010). This neglect is perhaps due to the absence of Philippine studies or Philippine-Canadian studies programs at major Canadian universities, scholarship often embedded in Southeast Asia, Asian or Migration studies, and the overall decline of area studies.

The Philippines has waned in international and geopolitical importance since the end of the Cold War and formal American military bases closure in 1992. However, it regained strategic significance when Southeast Asia was declared "the second front" in the war against terrorism after 9/11 (Putzel 2003; Tyner 2005, 2006).

To date, scholars still rely on works by Martin Rudner (1990) on Philippine-Canada bilateral relations. Since the 2003 promulgation of the Philippine *Dual Citizenship Law* (*RA 9225*), there has been no major academic research on Philippine-Canada bilateral relations and transnational linkages. There are interesting shifts and inflections in Canadian governments' policies towards the Philippines from Conservative Premier Brian Mulroney in the 1980s to Liberal Premier Justin Trudeau. It is equally important to examine their fifty-year period of bilateral relations and transnational linkages of interest to this study in the context of political economic changes from an authoritarian dictatorship in the 1970s under President Marcos to the populist rule of President Duterte since 2016. Development-related bilateral relations are understudied compared to the history and outcomes of Filipino migration to Canada (see Chen 1990, 1998; Laquian 1973; Laquian and Laquian 2008, Lindsay 2007); the employment and lived experiences of Filipino domestic workers (see Brigham 1998; Grandea 1995; Grandea and Kerr 1998; PWC 1999; Stasiulis and Bakan 1997, 2005; Santos 2005); Filipina "mail-order brides" (see Langevin and Belleau 2000, PWC 2000); resettlement and family reunification issues (Pratt 2001); identity formation and struggles of Filipino-Canadian youth (see Pratt 2002; Farrales and Pratt 2009; Kelly 2014, 2015); patterns of employment, class, health outcomes (Farrales and Chapman 1999; Kelly; Kelly Garcia and Esguerra 2009; Kelly 2012); and remittances, philanthropy, and volunteerism (Angeles 2008, Silva 2006).

Related documentaries produced on Filipinos in Canada were on the plight of live-in domestic workers (*Brown Women, Blond Babies*, 1991), mail-order brides (*Say I Do*, 2002), family reunification and youth dis-placement issues (*When Strangers Unite*, 1999), and Canadian aid workers in post-disaster contexts such as that of Typhoon Haiyan (*When the Storm Fades*, 2018). These studies contextualize findings within political economy but are often silent on their implications for postnational citizen-ship, development aid, trade, investments, and migration. More research can uncover the intricate underlying (international) political economy of Canada-Philippine bilateral relations bolstered by postnationalist citizen-ship forms and their (community/ international) development planning implications for governments, business, and civil society organizations.

How to Approach Canada-Philippine Relations

Aid, migration, trade, and investment are predominantly studied from modernization or neoliberal perspectives (Aryeetey and Dinello 2007, Goldin and Reinert 2007). Canada-Philippines bilateral relations could be studied from critical development studies, postnationalist, and trans-nationalist perspectives. Postnationalism studies universalization and globalization trends beyond traditional nation-state boundaries, such as the rise of post-national citizenship based on identities and culture (Sosyal 1994, 2001). Transnationalism, an analytical perspective, emerged out of Marxist and postmodern critiques of global capitalism, disputes and dis-solves dichotomies (e.g., centre/periphery, local/global). It proposes com-plicated and contingent analyses of historical and geographic linkages in the increasing circulation of goods, money, services, people, and politics (Basch et al. 1994, Hyndman 2000).

Transnationalist migration studies, in particular, concentrate on activi-ties of ordinary, non-instituted individuals (e.g. domestic workers, enter-tainers, diplomatic wives, brides) who participate in transnational mobil-ity (Mahler and Pessar 2001, Parrenas 2005, Pratt 2001, Yeoh et al. 2000). Transnational studies on diasporas focus on various aspects of cultural assimilation, economic integration, and the creation of a "transnational habitus" (Kelly and Lusis 2005). This happens when immigrants maintain multi-stranded linkages between their home villages, cities, and countries, which continue to shape their lives in their places of resettlement and their places of origin (Basch et al. 1994, Lusis 2006, Parrenas 2005, Silva 2006). Transnationalism has been applied to understanding various forms and strands of connection, such as identity formation, representation, cross-border political organizing, entrepreneurship, diaspora remittances, and other flows and exchanges (Portes 2001, Portes et al. 1999, Pratt and Yeoh 2003). Transnationalism grounds globalization in particular places, practices, discourses, and histories. Transnational Filipinos increasingly face postnational memberships living in post-familial nations as family units are rearranged by transnational migration (Tolentino 2005).

We need future research on transnational processes (i.e., aid extension and bilateral relations) and spaces of relations (i.e., Canada, the Philippines) to attend to context, circumstances, and social structures shaping the transnational processes, relations, and activities in question. We need to examine expanding transnational connectivity, such as development assistance-labour mobility linkages or the aid-migration nexus. Trade and investments, linked to development assistance, facilitate labour mobility, which, in turn, shapes new patterns and forms of development aid, particularly dual citizens' investments, and diaspora remittances (i.e., economic and social), philanthropy and volunteerism contributing to Canadian and Philippine communities.

Filipino temporary workers and permanent residents were predicted to go to secondary cities, small towns, and less populated provinces under Provincial Nominee Programs and labour agreements entered by Canadian provinces with the Philippine government (Laquian and Laquian 2008). This trend could have positive outcomes conducive to the early and easier adjustment of Filipinos to life in Canada. Statistics Canada shows new immigrants in small towns and secondary cities tend to have higher incomes and lower unemployment rates and are more socially integrated than those in metropolitan cities like Toronto, Montréal, and Vancouver.

However, there is little research on Filipino-Canadian experiences in small towns and secondary cities, the communication dimension of trade-investment-migration. We know little about the sources, usage, and evaluation of information, and how messages around costs, benefits, consequences (intended and unintended), risks and regulations are designed, packaged, and distributed in both formal and informal networks, especially within large and secondary cities where transnational flows, processes, practices, and experiences occur and converge. Thus, Philippine presence in Canada and Canadian presence in the Philippines through the post-/ transnational activities of their citizens, three levels of government, NGOs, universities, and colleges deserve closer examination than their current cursory treatment. Tease out the policy, governance, and planning implications of postnational citizenship forms emerging from conceptual, normative, and operational linkages between bilateral fields of trade, investment, development aid, and labour mobility.

Future research can aid Canadian and Philippine policymakers, businesses, and civil society leaders in their mutual understanding of their growing ties and inter-dependencies in ways that speak to their societies' common values, agendas, and visions, informed by their residents' increasing forms of postnationalist citizenship. There are policy and development planning implications for the Philippine and Canadian governments and civil society organizations of the past, present and potential future patterns of growing transnational relations between Canada and the Philippines in the last fifty-year period (1970–2020).

Some questions we could address include: How are Dual Citizen Filipinos and Canadians on SIRV/SRRV, in particular, contributing to Philippine-Canada bilateral relations and forms of postnational citizenship? How have increased Canada-Philippine transnational linkages and postnational citizenship activities of their residents, shaped their bilateral relations, particularly in the related fields of trade, investment, development assistance, and labour mobility? How are these trends affecting both countries? What are the factors and mechanisms shaping the acceleration of trade-investment-aid-migration-development nexus, particularly dual-citizenship arrangements, including diaspora social and economic remittances?

To the extent national citizenship still matters in a world of global migration (Bloemraad and Shear 2017), who then claims dual citizenship among Filipinos in Canada? Who claims the Special Resident Visitor Visa among Canadians in the Philippines, and how are they contributing to trade, investments, development assistance, and labour mobility? How are old, new, and shifting opportunities, policies, and regulatory frameworks—especially dual citizenships, governing trade, investment, development assistance, and labour mobility—communicated to relevant stakeholders? What are the patterns in the actors and agencies' usage and sources of information? How are messages around costs, benefits, consequences (intended and unintended), risks, and regulations designed, packaged, distributed, and circulated within and between these two countries' formal and informal networks implicated in the aid-migration nexus? What new patterns and forms of Philippine-Canada bilateral relations can emerge from the knowledge generated? What about communication, financing and other patterns and outcomes of democracy-inspired development assistance on recipients? And how have these changed under different regimes and government administrations in Canada and the Philippines?

The lives of noteworthy Filipino-Canadians you have met in this book, to a large extent, have been living the answers to these questions. It is exciting and stimulating to witness a new generation of Filipino-Canadians inspired by the diversity of their own voices, perspectives, and contributions to Canada and the Philippines as transnational subjects.

References

Ami,Arlene, dir.2002. *Say I Do: Unveiling the Stories of Mail-Order Brides.* Vancouver:Red Storm Productions.

Angeles, Leonora. 2003. "Creating Social Spaces for Transnational Feminist Advocacy: The Canadian International Development Agency, the National Commission on the Role of Filipino Women and Philippine Women's NGOs." *The Canadian Geographer* 4 (October), 283–302.

Angeles, Leonora. 2008. *Filipino-Canadian Volunteering and Philanthropy: Implications and Lessons for Volunteer Sending Organizations.* Research Report submitted to Volunteer Service Overseas (VSO-Ottawa) and the Gordon Foundation.

Aryeetey, Ernest and Natalia E. Dinello. 2007. *Testing Global Interdependence: Issues on Trade, Aid, Migration, and Development.* Cheltenham, UK:Edward Elgar, .

Basch, Linda, Nina Glick-Schiller, and Christina Szanton. *Nations Unbound: Transnational Projects, Postcolonial Predicaments, and Deterritorialized Nation States.* Langhorne, PA: Gordon and Breach, 1994.

Bermeo, Sarah Blodgett. 2011. "Foreign Aid and Regime change: A Role for Donor Intent." *World Development* 39 (11): 2021–31.

Bermeo, Sarah Blodgett and David Leblang. 2015. "Migration and Foreign Aid." *International Organization* 69 (3): 627–57.

Berthélemy, Jean Claude, Beuran, Monica, and MathildeMaurel. 2009. "Aid and Migration: Substitutes or Complements?" *World Development* 37(10),1589–99.

Bloemraad, Irene. 2004. "Who Claims Dual Citizenship? The Limits of Postnationalism, the Possibilities of Transnationalism, and the Persistence of Traditional Citizenship.'" *International Migration Review* 38 (2): 389–426.

Bloemraad, Irene and Alicia Sheares.2017. "Understanding Membership in a World of Global Migration :(How) Does Citizenship Matter?" *International Migration Review* 51 (4): 823–67.

Boti, Marie and Florchita Bautista, dir. *Brown Women, Blond Babies.* 1991.Montréal: Productions Multi-Monde/Le Vidéographie.

Boti, Marie and Florchita Bautista, dir. 1999. *When Strangers Unite.* Montréal: Productions Multi-Monde and National Film Board.

Brigham, Susan. 1998.*The Perceptions and Experiences of Immigrant Filipino Caregivers: A Study of Their Integration into Canadian Society.* Ottawa: National Library of Canada.

Chen, Anita Beltran. 1990. "Studies on Filipinos in Canada: State of the Art." *Canadian Ethnic Studies* 22 (1), 83–100.

Chen, Anita B.1998. *From Sunbelt to Snowbelt: Filipinos in Canada.* Calgary: Canadian Ethnic Studies Association.

Choy, Catherine Ceniza. 2003.*Empire of Care: Nursing and Migration in Filipino American History.* Durham: Duke University Press.

Devlin, Sean and Chris Ferguson,dir. 2018.*When the Storm Fades.*Ottawa: Telefilm Canada and Canada Council for the Arts.

DeWind, Josh, and David H. Kinley. 1998.*Aiding Migration: The Impact of International Development Assistance on Haiti.* Boulder: Westview Press.

Espiritu, Yen Le. 1995. *Filipino American Lives.* Philadelphia: Temple University Press.

Espiritu, Yen Le. 2003. *Home Bound: Filipino American Lives across Cultures, Communities, and Countries.* Berkeley: University of California Press.

Farrales, Lynn and Gwen Chapman. 1999. "Filipino Women Living in Canada: Constructing Meanings of Body, Food, and Health." *Health Care for Women International* 22 (2), 179–94.

Goldin, Ian, Kenneth A. Reinert, World Bank, Open Knowledge Repository, and World Bank e-Library. 2006.*Globalization for Development: Trade, Finance, Aid, Migration, and Policy.* 2007, Rev. Ed. Basingstoke; New York; Washington, DC; World Bank.

Grady, Patrick. 2006. "The Economic Impact on Canada of Immigration."Global Economics. Global Economics, Ltd.. http:// global-economics.ca/immigrationsurplus.htm.

Grandea, Nona. 1996.*Uneven Gains: Filipina Domestic Workers in Canada.* Ottawa: Philippines-Canada Human Resource Development Program.

Grandea, Nona and Joanna Kerr. 1998. "Frustrated and Displaced Filipina Domestic Workers in Canada." *Gender and Development* 6 (1), 7–12.

Hyndman, Jennifer. 2000. *Managing Displacement: Refugees and the Politics of Humanitarianism*. Minneapolis: University of Minnesota Press.

Kelly, Philip and Sylvia D'Addario. 2004. "Understanding Labour Market Segmentation: Filipina Healthcare Workers in Transnational Toronto."**Atlantic Metropolis Conference, November 19, 2004.** Halifax, Nova Scotia: Metropolis Canada Atlantic Chapter.

Kelly, Phillip and Tom Lusis. 2006. "Migration and the Transnational Habitus: Evidence from Canada and the Philippines." *Environment and Planning* 38, 831–47.

Kelly, Philip F., Garcia Mila A. and EnricoEsguerra. 2009. Explaining the Deprofessionalized Filipino: Why Filipino Immigrants Get Low-Paying Jobs in Toronto. CERIS Working Paper No. 75. Toronto: CERIS-The Ontario Metropolis Centre.

Kelly, Philip F. 2012. "Migration, Transnationalism, and the Spaces of Class Identity."*Philippine Studies: Historical and Ethnographic Viewpoints* (2012): 153–85.

Kelly, Philip F. 2014. "Understanding Intergenerational Social Mobility: Filipino Youth in Canada."*IRPP Study* 45 Montreal: Institute for Research on Public Policy

Kelly, Philip F. 2015. "Transnationalism, Emotion and Second-Generation Social Mobility in the Filipino-Canadian Diaspora."*Singapore Journal of Tropical Geography* 36 (3): 280–329.

Kim, Hyung-Chan and Cynthia C. Mejia. 1976.*The Filipinos in America, 1898–1974: A Chronology and Fact Book.* Dobbs Ferry, NY: Oceana Publications.

Lanati, Mauro and Rainer Thiele. 2018a. "Foreign Assistance and Migration Choices: Disentangling the Channels."*Economics Letters*172: 148–51.

Lanati, Mauro and Rainer Thiele. 2018b. "The Impact of Foreign Aid on Migration Revisited."*World Development* 111: 59–74.

Laquian, Eleanor and AprodicioLaquian. 2008. *Filipinos in Canada.* Manila: Anvil Press.

Langevin, Louise and Marie-Claire Belleau. 2000.*Trafficking in Women in Canada: A Critical Analysis of the Legal Framework Governing Immigrant Live-in Caregivers and Mail-Order Brides.*Québec: Faculty of Law, Université Laval.

Lusis, Tom. 2006. "Class Identity and Filipino Transnationalism: The Toronto-Tagbilaran Connection." Master'sthesis, York University, Toronto, Ontario, Canada .

Mahler, Sarah J. and Patricia R. Pessar. 2001. "Gendered Geographies of Power: Analyzing Gender across Transnational Spaces." *Identities: Global Studies in Culture and Power* 7(4):441–59.

Okamura, Jonathan Y. 1998. *Imagining the Filipino American Diaspora: Transnational Relations, Identities, and Communities.* New York: Garland Publishers.

Parrenas, Rachel S. 2005.*Children of Global Migration: Transnational Families and Gender Woes.* Stanford: Stanford University Press.

Portes, Alejandro. 2001. "Introduction: The Debates and Significance of Immigrant Transnationalism." *Global Networks* 1 (3): 181–94.

Portes, Alejandro, Guarnizo, L.E., and P. Landolt. 1999. "The Study of Transnationalism: Pitfalls and Promise of an Emergent Research Field." *Ethnic and Racial Studies*22 (2): 217–37.

Pratt, Geraldine and Brenda Yeoh. 2003. "Transnational (Counter) Topographies." *Gender, Place and Culture* 10 (2): 159–66.

Pratt, Geraldine. 2001.*Filipino Domestic Workers and Geographies of Rights in Canada.* London: University of Reading.

Pratt, Geraldine. 2002. "Between Homes: Displacement and Belonging for Second Generation Filipino-Canadian Youths." *Metropolis Working Paper Series*No. 02-13. Ottawa: Metropolis Canada. http://www.riim. metropolis.net/Virtual%20Library/2002/wp02-13.pdf.

Pratt, Geraldine. 2009. "Circulating Sadness: Witnessing Filipina Mothers'Stories of Family Separation." *Gender, Place and Culture*16 (1): 3–22.

Pratt, Geraldine. 2012.*Families Apart: Migrant Mothers and the Conflicts ofLabourand Love.* University of Minnesota Press.

Putzel, James. 2004. "Political Islam in Southeast Asia and the US-Philippine Alliance." In *Global Responses to Terrorism: 9-11, Afghanistan and Beyond,* edited byMary Buckley and Rick Fawn, 176-187. London; New York: Routledge.

Philippine Women Centre of BC. 1997. "Trapped: Holding on to the Knife's Edge." *Economic Violence against Filipino Migrant/Immigrant Women.* Vancouver, BC: Philippine Women's Centre.

Philippine Women Centre of BC. 2000. *Canada: The New Frontier for Filipino Mail-Order Brides.* Ottawa: Status of Women Canada.

Racco, Marilisa. 2017. "How Much Does It Cost to Raise a Kid in Canada?"*Global News.* January 12, 2017. https://globalnews.ca/news/3172459/how-much-does-it-cost-to-raise-a-kid-in-canada/.

Root, Maria P.P. (Ed.). 1997.*Filipino Americans: Transformation and Identity.* Thousand Oaks: Sage Publications, 1997.

Rudner, Martin. *Canada and the Philippines: The Dimensions of a Developing Relationship.* Ottawa: Asian Pacific Research and Resource Centre, Carleton University; North York, ON: Captus Press, 1990.

Sassen, Saskia. 2002a. "Towards Post-National and Denationalized Citizenship." In *Handbook of Citizenship Studies,* edited byEngin F.Isin and Brian S. Turner, 277–92. London: Sage Publications.

Sassen, Saskia. 2002b. *De-Nationalization Territory, Authority and Rights in a Global Digital Age. Princeton.* NJ: Princeton University Press.

Silva, Jon. 2006. "Engaging Diaspora Community in Development: An Investigation of Filipino Hometown Associations in Canada." Master's Thesis in Public Policy, Simon Fraser University, Vancouver, BC, Canada. http://www.sfu.ca/mpp/pdf_news/Capstone/Silva_Jon.pdf.

Santos, Maria Deanna. *Human Rights and Migrant Domestic Work: A Comparative Analysis of the Socio-Legal Status of Domestic Workers in Canada and Hong Kong.* Leiden; Boston, MA: MartinusNijhoff Publishers, 2005.

Soysal, Yasemin Nohuglu. *Limits of Citizenship: Migrants and Postnational Membership in Europe.* Chicago: University of Chicago Press, 1994.

Soysal, Yasemin. 2001. "Postnational citizenship: Reconfiguring the Familiar Terrain." *The Blackwell Companion to Political Sociology,* ed. Kate Nash and Alan Scott, 333–41. Oxford, UK: Blackwell Publishing.

Stasiulis, Daiva and Abigail Bakan. 1997. "Negotiating Citizenship: The Case of Foreign Domestic Workers in Canada." *Feminist Review* 57 (1): 112–39.

Stasiulis, Daiva and Abigail Bakan. 2005.*Negotiating Citizenship: Migrant Women in Canada and the Global System.* Toronto: University of Toronto Press.

Tolentino, Rolando B. 2003. "PostnationalFamily/PostfamilialNation: Family, Small Town and Nation talk in Marcos and Brocka." *Inter-Asia Cultural Studies* 4 (1), 77–92.

Tyner, James A. 1999. "The Global Context of GenderedLabourMigration from the Philippines to the United States." *The American Behavioral Scientist* 42 (4): 671–89.

Tyner, James A. 2005. *Iraq, Terror, and the Philippines'Will to War.* Rowman and Littlefield.

Tyner, James A. 2006. *America's Strategy in Southeast Asia: From Cold War to Terror War.* Rowman and Littlefield Publishers.

Tyner, James A. 2010. *The Philippines: Mobilities, Identities, Globalization.* New York, NY: Routledge.

Yang, Dean. 2003. "Remittances and Human Capital Investment: Child Schooling and Child Labour in the Origin Households of Overseas Filipino Workers."Unpublished manuscript from the Gerarld Ford

School of Public Policy and Department of Economics, University of Michigan, Ann Arbor.

Yang, Dean and Claudia A. Martinez. 2005. "Remittances and Poverty in Migrants' Home Areas: Evidence from the Philippines."In *International Migration Remittances, and the Brian Drain*, edited byCaglarOzden and Maurice Schiff.Washington, D.C.: World Bank: 81–121.

Yang, Dean and HwaJung Choi. 2007. "Are Remittances Insurance? Evidence from Rainfall Shocks in the Philippines." *The World Bank Economic Review* 21 (2): 219–248.

Yeoh, Brenda S.A., Huang, S., and K. Willis. 2000. "Global Cities, Transnational Flows, and Gender Dimensions: The View from Singapore." *TijdschriftvoorEconomischeenSocialeGeografie* 91(2): 147–58.

Yeoh, Brenda S. A., and Katie Willis. 2005. "Singaporean and British Transmigrants in China and the Cultural Politics of 'Contact Zones.'" *Journal of Ethnic and Migration Studies* 31 (2): 269–85.

Appendix A

The *CanadianFilipino.Net* (CFNet) Team

President/CEO of Maple Bamboo Network Society (MBNS), and Founding editor of *CanadianFilipino.Net* (CFNet)

Prod Laquian is professor emeritus of community and regional planning at the University of British Columbia. He was a former director of the UBC Centre for Human Settlements. After retiring from the university in 2000, Laquian served as acting director of the Massachusetts Institute of Technology's special program in urban and regional studies in Cambridge. He was also resident scholar at the Woodrow Wilson Center for International Scholars in Washington, DC, a consultant at the Asian Development Bank in China, and a coordinator for a study of basic urban services in seven hundred cities and towns in sixteen Asia-Pacific countries, which was funded by United Cities and Local Governments (UCLG) in Barcelona, Spain. Laquian has a BA degree in public administration, cum laude, from the University of the Philippines and a PhD in political science with a major in urban studies from MIT. He has authored twenty books and numerous articles on urban planning, governance, and delivery of urban infrastructure and services (water, sewerage, transport, sustainable energy, solid waste management, and affordable housing).

Vice-President and Director of MBNS and Current Editor of *CanadianFilipino.Net*

Eleanor R. Laquian has written four bestselling books and co-authored four others with her husband, Prod Laquian. Over ten years, she served in various capacities at the University of British Columbia's Institute of Asian Research: as manager of administration and programs, editor and chair of the publications committee, and primary researcher of the Asian Immigration to Canada project. She did her BA degree in journalism at Maryknoll College in the Philippines, a master's degree in public administration at the University of the Philippines, and postgraduate studies at the School of Public Communications at Boston University in the US. Before coming to Canada, she worked with the UN Food and Agriculture Organization, the World Health Organization, and the UN Information Center. She was a researcher and bureau manager of *The New York Times* in Beijing, China from 1984 to 1990. She was the first and only Filipino to conduct a nationwide survey of Filipinos in Canada, in 1972, for her master's thesis at UP. It was published as *A Study of Filipino Immigrants in Canada, 1952–1972*. She updated the survey in 2005 for a book, co-authored with her husband Prod: *Seeking a Better Life Abroad: A Study of Filipinos in Canada, 1957–2007*,published by Anvil Publishing in Manila. She and Prod have visited over a hundred countries for work and pleasure. They immigrated to Canada in 1969.

Director Responsible for Fundraising and Fund Development at MBNS and Social Media Manager of *CanadianFilipino.Net*

Emmy Buccat is a donor relations professional at the University of British Columbia's Development and Alumni Engagement Office. She supports the communications, stewardship, and events team in keeping donors informed, involved, and engaged. She moved to Canada in 2008, with ten years of experience in marketing communications, public relations, and event management for brands Fuji Xerox and Speedo. She has a degree in journalism from the University of Santo Tomas, Asia's oldest university, a certificate in integrated marketing strategy from UBC's Sauder School of Business, and an associate certificate in fundraising management from BCIT.

Adviser to the MBNS Board

Eleanor Guerrero-Campbell is a city planner, community champion, and writer. She came to Canada in 1977 with a degree in English and comparative literature and a master's degree in urban and regional planning, both from the University of the Philippines. She went on to work as a planner-manager in Edmonton in Alberta, and Surrey, Richmond, and Vancouver in British Columbia. Guerrero-Campbell co-founded the Multicultural Helping House Society, where, as executive director, she established programs to assist newcomers in Canada. As chief executive of the Minerva Foundation for BC Women, she managed leadership programs for women at various stages of their careers. She currently co-convenes the City of Vancouver's Immigrant Partnership Program Committee on Access to Services. Her first novel, *Stumbling Through Paradise: A Feast of Mercy for Manuel del Mundo*, depicts the struggles of a Filipino family's immigrant journey in Canada through three generations. Eleanor is a recipient of many awards, including the Vancouver Civic Merit Award (she is the only Canadian Filipino to receive this award thus far) and the Queen Elizabeth Diamond Jubilee Medal for community service. Read more about Eleanor and her novel at *EleanorGuerreroCampbell.com*.

Honorary Legal Counsel

Melissa Briones, barrister and solicitor, is a lawyer licensed to practice law in British Columbia and the Philippines. A graduate of the University of the Philippines College of Law, she also received a degree in HR management at Ashton College (with honours) and obtained a Chartered Professional in Human Resources designation. As a lawyer for the ABS-CBN broadcasting corporation, when she arrived in Canada, she became the first editor-in-chief of *Philippine Canadian Inquirer*, a nationwide publication that focused on the Filipino diaspora. She is a director and member of the Rotary Club of Vancouver Mountainview and a former UPAABC president. She practises corporate, employment, real estate, wills and estates, and family law at her Vancouver law firm, Northam Law Corporation, in Vancouver.

Founding Member of the Board for Maple Bamboo Network Society

Carlito Pablo, in addition to being a founding member of the Board of Maple Bamboo Network Society, was a staff writer with Canada's biggest urban weekly, the *Georgia Straight* paper of Vancouver, from 2006 to 2022. He has also been editorial consultant for Metro Vancouver-based Filipino community newspaper, *Philippine Asian News Today*, since 2005. He was a national reporter with the *Philippine Daily Inquirer* before coming to Canada in 2005. He started as a journalist for *Ang Pahayagang Malaya* in the Philippines.

Managing Editor

Rachel Ramos-Reid started writing for magazines and newspapers when she was still a junior in the University of the Philippines' communications degree program, majoring in journalism. She continued to write in a public relations/corporate communications capacity for private and government offices until moving out of the country in 1997 to work as programme officer for the arts and culture branch of the Southeast Asian Ministers of Education Organization in Bangkok, Thailand. At the end of her term, she immigrated to Canada in 2000 and again searched for new beginnings. She is a governance professional at a small community college on Vancouver Island.

Webmaster

Arlene Wright is an independent website designer. She has developed sites for various companies over the last ten years. She is responsible for the CFNet's new look for 2022, which makes the website more accessible to mobile device users.

Social Media and Newsletter Coordinator

Iona Santos-Fresnoza has worked in government, IT, academe, and the non-profit sector. She specializes in program and community development, communication strategy, and advocacy. She believes in diversity and inclusion. A relentless learner, she is also a fair-trade coffee advocate.

Contributors

Jo Leuterio Flach, a graduate of the University of the Philippines, came to Canada to attend the University of Toronto's graduate school. She adores her family, which includes seven grandchildren, and loves books, food, and travel. A regular contributor, she is in charge of lifestyle trends for CFNet.

Dr. Mike Rayel—author, entrepreneur, and psychiatrist—has helped many individuals and families with their mental health and family issues. Aside from his clinical practice, he has dedicated his time to writing articles and books, such as the *Shrink* series, publishing webinars on mental health and emotional intelligence, and creating educational games and products to promote emotional health. Certified in psychiatry, with a sub-specialty in geriatric psychiatry and psychosomatic medicine, he has written a number of psychiatry review books designed for the American Board of Psychiatry and Neurology certification examination. He loves the great outdoors, sports, music, politics, and photography. For details about Dr. Rayel, visit *DrRayel.com*.

Mary Ann Reyes-Mandap has over three decades of experience in journalism, public relations, and corporate communications work, and was a staff member and writer for *Mr. and Ms.* magazine, *Malaya*, and *The Philippines Free Press* in the Philippines. While living in San Francisco in 2003–07, she worked as associate editor of *Philippine News*, the oldest and most widely circulated Filipino newspaper in the United States, and as editor of the *Filipino Insider* magazine. In Vancouver, she worked as community news editor of *Philippine Canadian Inquirer*, and was associate editor of *Dahong Pilipino*. She has authored a book, *Lakbay:Immigrant Seniors Find Their True North*. She has a BA in communications (with a major in journalism) and an MA in Asian studies from the University of the Philippines (and was granted scholarships by the Japan Foundation and the Local Scholarship Program of the Philippine Civil Service Commission. She also earned the California Health Journalism Fellowship from the Annenberg School, University of Southern California.

Adelaida Lacaba-Bago, PhD, is a retired professor of De La Salle University, Manila, where she served as Director of Research and concurrently Vice Dean. She has published four books on curriculum development, supervision of instruction, and the social dimensions of Philippine education. Her latest is *ThesisWriting with Confidence*.

A youth program coordinator at the Multicultural Helping House Society in Vancouver, BC from 2006–07, **MariaVeronica "Vernie" G. Caparas** wrote a syndicated column for three bilingual newspapers circulated on the West Coast. Her articles focused on South Asian newcomer youth and their families. She moved to Edmonton, where she taught English as a Second Language at the University of Alberta and eventually joined the Alberta Children and Youth Services. Her curiosity in the plight of skilled immigrants from Canada's top three source countries (China, India, and the Philippines) led her to a research journey that—through her critical theory lens - uncovered plots of Canada's undelivered promises; where international immigrants, however, successfully navigate their way around social mazes and "do their home countries proud." She finished her PhD in educational policy studies (theoretical, cultural, and international studies in education) at the University of Alberta on a full Social Sciences and Humanities Research Council – Bombardier scholarship, with the Presidential Prize of Distinction and GRA Rice Scholarship in Communications. She taught for over two decades at the University of the Philippines in Diliman, where she retired with the rank of professor.

Dulce Amba Cuenca, a lawyer in British Columbia was also admitted to the Philippine Bar prior to immigrating to Canada in 1996. She has worked in the field of human rights and employment and labour law since 2006, travelling across BC and the Yukon, representing workers and human rights complainants. She is a grateful immigrant who got her first job in Canada in 1996 by volunteering. She is passionate about civic engagement and contributing to the community. She served as trustee of the Richmond Public Library Board for eight years, and was a member of the board of Richmond Cares Richmond Gives. She also volunteers with Access Pro Bono. She believes that volunteerism completes any immigrant's integration in the community and unites people from diverse backgrounds to work toward a common goal.

Meyen "Marilynn" Quigley has a bachelor's degree in English from the University of the Philippines. In Victoria, she has worked for BC public services and in programs for persons with mental health and substance abuse issues and persons experiencing homelessness. She has a master's degree in intercultural administration from the School for International Training in Vermont and a graduate certificate in professional communications management from Royal Roads University.

Leonora "Nora" Angeles is cross-appointed faculty at the University of British Columbia School of Community and Regional Planning and Institute for Gender, Race, Sexuality and Social Justice. She taught at Queen's University, where she did her doctoral studies, University of Regina, and University of Saskatchewan before moving to Vancouver. She waspresident of the National Pilipino Canadian Cultural Centre for 2020, vice president of the University of the Philippines Alumni Association of BC, and member of the Company Erasga Dance board of directors and Critical Asian Studies editorial advisory board. She also helped convene the Daloy-Puso Youth Network and the Filipino-Canadian Futures: Education, Leadership and Capacity-Building.

Mel Tobias was a movie critic, lifestyle and entertainment editor, author, foreign correspondent, broadcaster, amateur actor, festivalier, impresario for the arts, proprietor of a vintage collectibles boutique, frustrated saloon singer, gourmet who knew where all the good eating places were, an avid collector of esoteric and nostalgia recordings and books, and a fundraiser for charitable causes. He passed away in October 2017.

Leonardo B. Cunanan was the founding editor of *Dahong Pilipino*, the only Filipino-Canadian community and business directory in Canada. Started in 1991, it is the only such directory that has published annually for almost thirty years. When Cunanan became an Immigration and Refugee Board member (1997–2005), his son Leo Jr. took over the publication, but he remained editor. He passed away in June 2022. In keeping with the technological advances of the time, Leo Jr. transformed the directory in 2011 from a traditional print publication to a modern digital directory but continues to distribute printed copies to advertisers (*DahongPilipino.ca*).

Emmie Joaquin and colleagues Rey-ar Reyes and Paul Morrow established The Pilipino Express, Inc., and began publishing the *Pilipino Express News Magazine* in Winnipeg. Joaquin is currently the company's president and the news magazine's editor-in-chief. Joaquin was a recipient of the Queen

Elizabeth II Golden Jubilee Medal in 2002, and the Queen Elizabeth II Diamond Jubilee Medal in 2012 for media and community service. She earned her degree in broadcast communication from the University of the Philippines. She worked in media and public relations before immigrating to Canada in 1988. In Winnipeg, Joaquin produced and co-hosted the daily morning drive-time show *Good Morning Philippines* on CKJS Radio 810 AM. She also produced and hosted the daily weekday afternoon show *Manila Sound* and the Saturday show *Tunog Pinoy Pang Sabado*. After almost fifteen years in radio broadcasting, Emmie left CKJS in December 2003 to serve as special assistant for communications for then federal minister of Western economic diversification, Dr. Rey Pagtakhan. She had a brief stint as executive assistant to deputy mayor and councillor Mike Pagtakhan on the City Council of Winnipeg.

Dr. Rey D. Pagtakhan, PC, OM, LLD, ScD, MD, MSc, is a retired lung specialist, professor of child health, author of articles and chapters in medical journals and textbooks, former health critic, parliamentary secretary to the prime minister, cabinet minister as Secretary of State for Science, Research and Development. He graduated from the University of the Philippines, did postgraduate training and studies at the children's hospitals of Washington University in St. Louis and the University of Manitoba in Winnipeg, and spent a sabbatical year as visiting professor at the University of Arizona Medical Center. In June 2003, he spoke on "The Global Threat of Infectious Diseases" at the G-8 Science Ministers/Advisors Carnegie Group Meeting in Berlin. His ongoing series on the COVID-19 pandemic, which started in February 2020, is published by *Pilipino Express* in Manitoba and by *CanadianFilipino.Net* in BC.

Joe Zagala is an active participant in Greater Toronto's Filipino community. He is a past president of the University of the Philippines Alumni Association (Toronto), former vice president of the Kalayaan Cultural

Community Centre, a former (and the only Asian) director of the Riverwood Conservancy, and one of the original organizers and a past presidents of the Philippine Chamber of Commerce in Toronto. He is a

holder of chemical engineering degree and a business administration degree from the University of the Philippines. He held high positions at large corporations in Canada, including as vice president for global business at CipherSoft, Inc. He is managing director of Lily Framarc Management Consultants, based in Mississauga, Ontario.

Rose Tijam lives in Toronto. She is a founding member of the Philippine Press Club of Ontario. She served her second term as president of the press club in 2016. She is a former president of the University of the Philippines Alumni Association Toronto. She was associate editor of two community publications. She worked for twenty-five years at a social work setting for women and continues to do so on a part-time basis at a crisis line service for women. She graduated from the University of the Philippines with a master's degree in communications. She speaks Spanish and French.

Carissa Duenas moved to Canada in 2006, leaving behind a career in the management technology consulting space. She pursued her master's in business administration at Queen's University in 2008 and has since worked in various finance and marketing positions for companies based in Toronto, Manila, and Hong Kong. Despite being rooted in the corporate world, she has always maintained a passion for writing. She writes essays in her spare time that delve into everyday life experiences. Her work has been published in the *Philippine Daily Inquirer* and the *Globe and Mail*. More of her writing pieces can be found at *CarissaDuenas.com*. She hopes to complete her book of personal essays soon.

Jaime A. FlorCruz is a veteran China-watcher and foreign correspondent in China. He was CNN's Beijing bureau chief and correspondent, (2001–2014), *TIME* magazine's Beijing bureau chief and correspondent (1982–2000) and *Newsweek's* Beijing reporter (1981). Twice he served concurrently as the China chairman of the Fortune Global Forum, a meeting of global business and political leaders in Beijing in 2005 and in 2013 in Chengdu. In 2017, he again served as China chairman of the Fortune Global Forum in Guangzhou. He was considered the dean of the foreign press corps in Beijing, having been the longest-serving foreign correspondent in China until his retirement in 2015. He was a two-term president of the four-hundred-member Foreign Correspondents' Club of China (1988–90 and 1996–99). He is the founding president of the Peking University International Students' Alumni Association (2010–present). In November 2017, he was elected for a four-year term as one of the vice chairs of the Peking University Alumni Association, the first-ever foreign alumnus elected to the position. He is the co-author of *Massacre at Beijing* (Warner Books, 1989), a book about the crackdown in Tiananmen Square and *Not On Our Watch* (2012), a book about campus journalists during the martial law years in the Philippines. He is fluent in English, Filipino, and Mandarin Chinese. He has retired and now lives in Manila.

Ellen T. Tordesillas is trustee and writer for VERA Files (*VeraFiles.org*), a group that undertakes in-depth reporting on current issues and does fact-checking to fight disinformation. She writes opinion columns that appear in *Malaya Business Insight*, ABS-CBN online and VERA Files. As a reporter, she covered education, health and science, the PCGG and foreign affairs beats, before she was assigned to cover politics. She has covered all Philippine elections since the 1986 snap elections that triggered the ousting of Ferdinand Marcos. She continues to watch anything relevant to the Filipino people closely.

Manolo Abella, a Filipino economist, was formerly the director of the International Migration Programme of the International Labor Office based in Geneva and a member of the Advisory Board of the Centre for Migration Policy and Society at the University of Oxford. He also served on the board of the Migrating out of Poverty Programme of Sussex University. He has been actively involved in international efforts to develop a multilateral framework for the management of labour migration and spent many years writing, speaking, and rendering advice to governments on policies and best practices. He heads the working group that developed, under the World Bank and the ILO's auspices, the methodology for measuring what workers pay to migrate, which is envisaged for inclusion as one of UN's Millennium Development Goals. He now lives in Vancouver, BC.

Appendix B

The Maple Bamboo Network Society, Publisher of *CanadianFilipino.Net*

WHO WE ARE

We are a group of Canadian Filipinos passionate about raising the profile of Filipinos in Canada by providing news and views about Canadian Filipino communities across the country.

WHY CANADIANFILIPINO.NET?

The number of Canadians of Filipino ancestry is approaching a million. The Philippines has become the top source country for recent immigrants to Canada.

Since the first wave of Filipino migrants came in the mid-1960s, the community has grown to include a second generation of young adults, who were born in the Philippines and raised in Canada, and a fast-growing third generation, born and raised in Canada. Canadian Filipino communities are found not only in big cities but also in small towns.

Through this website, we want to share stories and engage in a dialogue among Canadian Filipinos all over the country and across generations. With this information-sharing, we hope to start a buzz among and about Canadian Filipinos, inspiring our community to take its rightful place in Canadian society.

WHY THE TERM CANADIAN FILIPINO?

Why do we use Canadian Filipino and not the more common hyphenated Filipino-Canadian? Our goal is to promote Canadian engagement in Canadian affairs by Filipinos, and for Filipinos to make an impact in Canada. With this term, we emphasize the Filipino as Canadian and the Filipino's experience in Canada.We use the term 'Canadian' to describe Filipinos as Canadians—but although we have become Canadians, we are still Filipinos at core, with our Philippine values and traditions intact.

OUR VISION

A self-aware and connected Canadian Filipino community fully engaged in Canadian society.

OUR MISSION

To inform, engage and facilitate inter-actions among Canadian Filipinos coast to coast, and Canadians in general.

OUR MANDATE

To provide a platform for the different Filipino issues in a nationwide dialogue about Canadian Filipino concerns, needs, views, activities and contributions to Canadian progress and prosperity. In addition, to share this information with other Canadians in order to promote understanding and collaboration throughout Canada's diverse population.

HOW WE OPERATE

CanadianFilipino.Net is owned, managed, and operated by the Maple Bamboo Network Society, a non-profit society with the purpose of fully engaging Canadian Filipinos in Canadian society. We are all volunteers.

CFNet Google Analytics reports

Online readership grows every year.

Year 1 (2016–2017)	1,435,226 hits
Year 2 (2017–2018)	1,500,000 hits
Year 3 (2018–2019)	3,187,706 hits
Year 4 (2019–2020)	4,161,377 hits.
Year 5 (2020–2021)	5,271,251 hits

The CFNet team. Seated: Emmy Buccat, and Eleanor and Prod Laquian. Standing: Eleanor Guerrero-Campbell, Clay Campbell, Laura Ocampo, Paolo and, Iona Fresnoza, and Arlene Wright.

CFNet Social Media Handles:

 @iamcanadianfil

Twitter

 @canadianfilipinonet

Facebook

 @CanadianFilipinoNet

Instagram

 @canadianfilipinonet

LinkedIn

Contact Us: info@canadianfilipino.net

Funded by the
Government
of Canada

INDEX

1.5 generations... 4, 6, 18, 38, 118, 163-167, 173-174, 250, 289

accidental entrepreneurs... 11, 244

Adelaida Lacaba-Bago... 84, 87, 210, 326

affordable housing and childcare... 33, 64, 113, 320,

ageing... 204, 208, 228, 239, 240, 257, 283-285

Alberta Council for Global Cooperation... 157-158

Alberta Premier Rachel Notley... 102

All Saints' Day... 82-83, 231

All Souls' Day... 83, 231

Allan Cho... 241

Andy Naval... 127

Angela Rai... 164-165

Ann Makosinski... 118, 124

Anna Maramba... 21, 99,119, 133

Anthony A. L. Mandap... 265, 271

anti-Asian racism... 201

Antonio "Tony" and Marissa Peña... 118, 127-129

Antonio and Ross Baisas... 21

Aprodicio "Prod" A. Laquian... 4, 6, 9, 22, 25, 29, 34, 47, 54, 61, 64, 71, 88, 103, 109, 114, 164, 172, 205, 244, 247, 293, 316, 320-321, 335

Archbishop Christian Lepine of Montréal... 217

Archbishop Michael Miller... 80, 90, 92, 215-216

Archbishop Terrence Prendergast of Ottawa... 216

Archdiocese of Vancouver... 79-80, 90, 213-215

Asian HeritageMonth... 76

assisted suicide... 216-217

Audie Banania... 149

Audielicious Restaurant... 149

AVCommunications... 133-135

Bad Saint... 299

Baldwin Village Inn... 161-162

balikbayan... 15, 71, 264, 266

bayanihan... 47, 53, 71-72, 74, 76, 199, 253, 255-257

Beijing Declaration... 277

Belen... 87-89, 184

Ben Pires... 252

Benson Flores... 8

Bernette Ho... 19, 160

bilingual... 174, 278, 281, 291, 326

Bishop Douglas Crosby... 216-217

Bishop Noël Simard... 217

brain drain... 272, 304, 306

Brian Mulroney... 308

Business ImprovementProgram... 147

Cambio and Co.... 257-259

Canada Council for the Arts... 159, 314

Canada Pension Plan... 208, 240

Canada's diverse society... 4,17, 56, 72, 81, 165, 173, 262

Canada's Emergency Response Benefits... 46

Canada's Immigration Policy... 24-25, 30, 35, 43

Canadian International Development Agency... 305, 312

Cannes International Film Festival... 77, 132

Cardinal Gerald Lacroix... 217

Carissa Duenas... 4, 185, 187, 226, 330

Carlo Javier... 287

Carlos Bolosan Theatre... 118

Catherine Hernandez... 232, 241-242

Catholic church... 71, 81, 83-84, 91, 204, 214-217
Catholic Filipinos... 86, 90, 212
Catholic funeral... 215-217
Catholic traditions... 214
CDWCR... 11, 75, 109, 237-238, 240
Cecilia Yuthasastrakosol... 208, 210
Celso Gatchalian... 20, 160
Cesar's Cakes and Café... 248-249
Cesi Cruz... 295
Chandra Arya... 101
Charter of Rights andFreedoms... 26, 30, 44, 46, 52, 215, 279, 292-293
Chinese Exclusion Act... 279
Chinese Head Tax... 279
citizenship... 3, 5, 25, 38, 43, 234, 264-271, 274
Citizenship Retention Act... 265
Civic Merit Award of City of Vancouver... 105
Clay Campbell... 123, 335
climate change... 107, 157, 201, 288-290
Coffee AID... 97-98
Commission on Overseas Filipinos... 263
Committee for Domestic Workers and Caregivers Rights... 11, 109, 232, 237-238
Conrado Santos... 295
Consul Edwin Mendoza... 73,
cost of elderly care... 284
cost of preparing a will... 225
Court of Appeal... 19, 20, 105, 160
cultural globalization... 5, 302
cultural institutions... 180
cultural traditions... 81, 167
cultural traits... 65-67, 173
culture and identity... 170
Dahong Pilipino... 71, 76, 105-107, 184, 215, 247, 326, 328
David Lametti... 105, 160
Dawson Creek... 73, 150
death... 79-80, 189, 192, 201, 204, 212-219, 222-227, 231
Delia Laglagaron... 103

development aid... 303, 305, 307, 309-311
Diamond Jubilee Medal... 105, 123, 322, 329
diaspora... 169, 176, 258, 309-311, 315-317
Dimasalang group... 75, 127
discrimination... 38, 201, 269, 278, 280-281, 291
diversity... 8, 22, 26, 30, 32, 38, 40, 52, 76, 98, 118-119, 139, 168-170, 177, 181-182, 184, 233, 261, 273, 275, 277, 290-292, 296, 312, 324
doctor assisted suicide... 215-216
domestic workers and caregivers... 10-11, 16, 55, 117-118, 237, 261, 282-283, 285
Dominique Bautista... 170, 172
Dorothy Uytengsu... 132
double taxation... 269
Doug McCallum... 74
Dr. Barbara Perry... 31
Dr. Eileen de Villa... 19, 103, 109
Dr. Jon Malek... 5
Dr. Rey D. Pagtakhan... 1, 18, 24-26, 100, 103, 115-116-117, 124, 188-189, 191, 293, 329
dual citizenship... 48-49, 264-271, 311-312
Dual Citizenship Law... 264-265, 267, 308
Dulce Amba Cuenca... 20, 49, 51, 327
Dying with Dignity... 217
Edgardo Lantin... 127
eDrink Mug... 124-125
Edwin Empinado... 140
Eleanor Guerrero-Campbell... 24, 26, 65, 67, 118, 122, 132, 232, 241-242, 250, 322, 335
Eleanor R. Laquian... 4, 25, 29-30, 34-35, 43, 54, 56, 74, 82, 87, 108, 160, 205, 215, 228, 233, 237, 247, 263, 278, 282, 290, 321
Ellie Flagg... 165
Emma Navarro... 122
Emmie Joaquin... 118, 123, 328
Emmy Buccat... 153, 155, 321, 335

end-of-life choice... 217-218
English as a Second Language... 166, 326
Epic Grill... 148-149
Estela Aguilar Chow... 141
ethnicity... 38, 183, 280-281
euthanasia... 215-218
executor of will... 222, 225
Eymard Caravana... 287
Fely Villasin... 103, 117
Filipino associations... 13, 71-72, 74-76, 109, 143, 256
Filipino businesses... 106, 244-245, 247
Filipino Canadian Associations... 232, 252-254, 256
Filipino Canadian Cultural Heritage Society... 74, 155
Filipino channel... 105, 167
Filipino children... 58, 167
Filipino cultural values... 71
Filipino culture... 3, 52, 69, 77, 95, 102, 155, 179, 181, 253, 262
Filipino diaspora... 8, 77, 169, 180, 226, 242, 303, 307, 323
Filipino entrepreneurs... 11, 232, 244-247, 275
Filipino food... 63, 148, 177, 179, 253, 256, 298-299
Filipino heritage... 6, 20, 101, 112-113, 115, 120, 137, 143, 165, 176, 259-261
Filipino Heritage Month... 6, 99-103, 118, 120-121, 260
Filipino hospitality... 53, 57, 95, 98, 161, 235, 275
Filipino household... 153, 183
Filipino identity... 16, 44, 175-178, 181
Filipino immigrants... 10, 12-13, 18, 20-21, 23, 34, 45, 48, 54-55, 109, 118, 136, 138, 144, 205, 232, 243, 252, 272, 274-275, 280, 315, 321
Filipino migration... 2-3, 6, 8-9, 48, 293, 308
Filipino movies... 76-78
Filipino nuclear family... 210
Filipino overseas contractworkers... 201

Filipino restaurants... 47, 63, 71-72, 179, 298-299
Filipino Seniors... 75, 204, 229-231
Filipino service workers... 201, 203
Filipino traits... 53, 56-57, 65, 95, 136
Filipino values... 6, 46, 99, 165, 174, 232-233, 275
First Nations... 53, 144
Flor Marcelino... 118, 125-126, 294
Forbes's "Thirty Under Thirty" list... 124
foreign direct investment... 303, 305
Foreign Domestic Movement... 10, 55, 202, 239, 282
Foreign Investment Act of 1991... 268
Fort St. John Women's Resource Society... 149
frontline workers... 45, 47, 189, 203
funeral expenses... 214
funeral homes... 213-214
Gail L. Gatchalian... 19, 160
Gardian Cardeno... 145
Garry Tanuan... 151
Gelaine Santiago... 232, 257, 259
Gemma Dalayoan... 156
gender equality... 139, 261, 276-278, 282, 291
Georgie Award... 250
Geraldine Pratt... 166
global citizens... 4, 49, 175, 263, 302
Global Climate Risk Index... 288
Global Pinoy Food Store... 233, 249
global warming... 289
Good Friday... 80, 207
Governor General's Gold Medal... 107
Greg V. Barcelon... 75
Gregg Apolonio... 74
Harper government... 23, 26
health sciences ... 110, 204, 238
healthcare professionals... 202, 215, 219
healthcare workers... 137, 188, 190, 232, 272, 315
herd immunity... 193-195
home-cooked meals... 64, 185, 299

House of Commons... 25, 42, 101, 115, 120, 137, 279, 293
human rights... 30, 51, 105, 139, 160, 254, 264, 291, 302, 318, 327
immigrant entrepreneurs... 247
immigrant parents... 4, 19, 137, 163, 172-173, 183
immigrant youth... 113, 133, 165
Immigration and Refugee Board... 107, 215, 328
immigration policy... 24-26
Immigration, Refugees and Citizenship Canada... 43, 239
Indigenous identities... 70
Indigenous nations... 168-169
Indigenous peoples... 31, 68, 70
inheritance... 55, 221-222
Institute of Asian Research... 34, 108-109, 278, 321
INTERCEDE... 75, 117-118
International Development Research Centre... 108, 305
International Women's Day... 276, 282
interracial marriages... 206
Iona Santos-Fresnoza... 96, 98, 324
Irving K. Barber Learning Centre... 127
Japan Foundation... 184, 326
Japanese Canadians... 278
Jay-R and Rose Lacsamana... 233, 249
Jeffrey Almeda... 294
Jérôme Gagnon-Voyer... 258-259
Jess Hipolito... 127
Jim Chong-Wu... 243
Jim Wong-Chu... 241
Jo Leuterio Flach... 58, 92, 134, 161, 195, 198, 220, 325
Jocelyn Curteanu... 143
Jojo Alpuerto... 73-74
Joselito and Dorothy de Leon... 148-149
Joseph Planta... 177, 179
Julie Diesta... 238
Junifer Torralba... 146
Justin Trudeau... 26, 53, 140, 215, 276, 308

Justine Abigail Yu... 167, 170
Kababayan Academic Mentorship Program... 128
Kababayan Community Centre... 118, 135
kababayans... 71, 242, 244, 271
Kapisanan Philippine Centre...118
Kathara Society... 180
Kaye Banez... 95
Kevin Laxamana... 157-158
Kimwell Del Rosario... 238
Knights of Rizal... 13, 75
Komagata Maru... 25, 279
Krisha Quiambao... 157-158
labour force... 36, 202, 232, 277, 282
labour market... 27-29, 35, 37, 41, 242, 304, 315
labour migration... 40, 306-307, 332
labour mobility... 306, 310-312
labour mobility linkages... 306, 310
Lady Luck Restaurant and Buffet... 141
LCP... 10, 202, 238-240, 283, 286
Lea Salonga... 111
lechon... 92-93
Leo Alejandria... 287
Leo Cunanan Jr.... 127
Leonardo B. Cunanan... 78, 103, 106, 212, 215, 247, 328
Leonora C. Angeles... 3, 68, 70, 103-104, 200, 302, 312, 327
Leylah Annie Fernandez... 118, 121-122
LGBTQ... 30-31
life expectancy... 206
Lisa Abarquez Bower... 142
LiterASIAN... 241
Live-In Caregiver Program... 10, 23, 48, 202, 239, 282, 287
Lorina Serafico... 238
Lota Banate Coroza... 105
Lower Mainland... 113, 171, 213, 216, 287
Lucille Nolasco... 72
Luz del Rosario... 151
Ma-Anne Dionisio... 103, 110
Mable Elmore... 103, 112
Macario "Tobi" Reyes... 232, 250

Maharlika Award...155, 256
Makotronics Enterprises... 124-125
Manila North Cemetery... 82-83
Manitoba Association of Filipino
  Teachers, Inc.... 156
Manolo I. Abella... 35, 40, 332
Maple Bamboo Network Society... 64,
  109, 115, 123, 261, 320, 323, 333-334
Maria Aguirre... 294
Maria Apelo Cruz... 127
Maria Veronica G. Caparas... 271, 326
Marichu Antonio... 118-120
Marie Kondo... 223
Mario Hernandez... 74
Marissa Roque... 294
Marites Sison... 73
Marvi Yap... 21, 99, 119, 133
Marvin Flancman... 58
Mary Ann Reyes-Mandap... 182, 184,
  235, 325
May Farrales... 166
Mayrose Salvador... 118, 129
Meals on Wheels... 209
Media Noche... 92
medical assistance in dying... 215-219
Medisina at Politika... 1, 116, 188-189
Mel Tobias... 76, 78, 119, 131-132
Mel Tobias Plaza... 133
Melissa Remulla-Briones... 20, 223,
  225, 323
mercy killing... 215, 217
mestizos or mixed-race... 174
Michael Parillas... 153
Michaelangelo Dacudao... 132
Michelle Elliot... 103, 111
Midnight Mass... 86, 90, 92
Migrante... 73, 121
Mila Bongco-Philipzig... 153
millennials... 183
Minerva Falcon... 76
Minerva Foundation for BC Women... 67,
  123, 322
minimum-wage... 11, 166, 212, 240
mixed marriages... 58, 174

multicultural agency... 21, 134
Multicultural Helping House... 67, 118,
  122, 241, 322, 326
multicultural moguls... 21, 100, 119, 133
multiculturalism... 9, 25, 26, 30, 32, 35,
  52, 112, 119, 126, 168-169, 182, 261,
  264, 280-281, 290-291, 293
Multiculturalism Act... 26, 52, 290
National Household Survey... 165, 183
national identity... 6, 41, 182, 301
National Pilipino Canadian Cultural
  Centre... 70, 104, 328
national security... 41, 279
Neil Ferrer... 76
new immigrants... 35, 135-136, 209-210,
  233, 241, 249, 254, 261, 290, 310
newly arrived Filipinos... 76, 128, 135, 181
Next Day Better... 181-182
Nobel Prize... 162, 227
Noel Trinidad... 127
Norma and Zosimo Salazar... 137
North American Free Trade Agreement
  (NAFTA)... 47
Northam Law Corporation... 226, 323
Northern Gateway project... 140
Ontario Court of Justice... 20, 105
Onyok Velasco... 154
Outstanding Filipinos... 99, 103-104,
  117-118, 256
Overseas Absentee Voting Law... 267
overseas contract workers... 201, 269
overseas remittances... 303
palliative care... 215, 218
pandesal... 145-147
Patrick Alcedo... 159
Paul Morrow... 123, 328
Paul Ong... 22
Paulina Corpuz... 100, 118, 120
Paz Antonio... 206
Peña Family Foundation... 128-129
people of colour... 33, 35, 188, 261
people power... 117
permanent residency... 28-29, 36, 169,
  185, 234, 239, 282, 286

Phebe Ferrer... 175, 177
Phil de Luna... 19, 103, 107
PhilHealth benefits... 212
Philippine Advancement Through Arts
    and Culture... 100, 120
Philippine Canadian Centre of
    Manitoba... 72
Philippine Civil Service Commission...
    184, 326
Philippine Consulate General... 9,
    159, 271
Philippine Consulate Outreach
    Services... 256
Philippine culture... 69, 76, 101, 165,
    173, 259
Philippine Educational Theatre
    Association... 253
Philippine Embassy... 13, 49, 71, 74, 265
Philippine Independence Day... 73, 75,
    101, 120, 301
Philippine Women's Centre... 166, 317
political parties... 14, 26, 42, 281, 295-297
PortLiving... 250-251
postnationalism... 5, 182, 302, 309, 313
Powers of attorney... 221
Prayer for a happy death... 212
Prayers for the dead... 214
pre-need funeral plans... 213
Prime Minister Brian Mulroney... 26, 278
Prime Minister Jean Chrétien... 116
Prime Minister Justin Trudeau... 22-24,
    52, 182, 279
Prime Minister Pierre Elliot Trudeau...
    26, 52, 290
Prime Minister Stephen Harper... 279
Prod and Eleanor Laquian... 4, 29,
    172, 247
Professional Regulation
    Commission... 266
Provincial Nominee Programs... 23,
    29, 310
public health... 4, 19, 109-110, 157,
    188-195, 202, 304
public office... 144, 266-268, 295-297

Pueblo Science... 118-119, 129-131
Pura Tolentino... 233, 248
quality of life... 32, 204, 206, 228-230
Queen Elizabeth II... 105, 117, 123,
    322, 328-329
RA 9225... 266-270, 308
Rachel Ramos-Reid...1, 17, 100, 145,
    149, 156-157, 159, 199-200, 241, 248,
    257, 324
racism... 23, 26, 31, 33, 109, 173, 201, 233,
    243, 261, 278, 280-281
Rafael Fabregas... 295
Rafael Joseph "RJ" Aquino... 179-180
RBC Top 25 Canadian Immigrants
    Awards... 257, 259
Rechie Valdez... 18, 119, 137
refugees... 9, 27, 30-34, 36-39, 42, 74, 239,
    279, 315
Registered Retirement Savings Plan...
    208, 225
RESPECT... 200
retirement... 14, 19, 55, 123, 204-206,
    208-210, 212, 229-230, 239, 331
Reverend Amador M. Abundo...
    78-81, 91
Rey Fortaleza... 153-155
Rey-ar Reyes... 123, 328
ReyFort Media Group... 155
Roberto Jalnaiz... 154
Rod Pedralba... 127
Rogie and Tess Concepcion... 161-162
Rommel Silverio... 151
Romy Mabilangan Coroza... 105
Roseni Alvero... 236-237
Rowena Santos... 142
Royal Ontario Museum... 162
Ruben Cusipag... 117
Salubong... 78, 81, 233
Sambayanang Pilipino... 90-92
Sammie Jo Rumbaua... 181-182
SARS-CoV-2... 190-191, 194-195
Scarborough... 100-101, 121, 232, 242-243

second generation Filipinos...2, 4, 6, 16,
    18, 55, 113, 118, 136, 163-165, 172-175,
    177, 182-184, 315-316, 333
Seeking a Better Life Abroad... 6, 25, 34,
    109, 164, 321
Simbang Gabi... 86, 90-91, 94, 233
Simeon Dee... 127
Sinta and Co.... 258-259
social distancing... 86, 195-196, 199
social justice... 16, 46, 70, 104, 112-113,
    117, 126, 264, 327
Social Sciences and Humanities Research
    Council... 5, 159, 326
Sofronio Ylanan Mendoza... 118, 126-127
Statistics Canada... 141, 174, 234, 246,
    261, 277, 280, 301, 310
Stephanie Valenzuela... 119, 136-137
Steve Coroza... 20, 103, 105-106
Stumbling Through Paradise... 123, 132,
    232, 241, 322
Taal Volcano... 72-74, 149
Tagalog... 47, 58, 69, 72-73, 78, 83, 86,
    90-91, 120, 134, 136, 147, 153, 166,
    170-171, 175-176, 233, 256, 290
Talisay Association of Manitoba... 72
Tara, kape tayo!... 98
Ted Marcelino... 294
temporary foreign workers... 9, 23-24,
    28-29, 36, 40, 42, 48, 112, 165, 249,
    256, 280
Temporary Foreign Workers Program...
    26, 28, 36, 40, 42-43, 48, 234
Terry McGee... 109

Time magazine's "Thirty Under Thirty"
    list... 124
Tolentino family... 248
Tony Carpio... 293
Tony Flores... 152
traditional Filipino family... 54
transnational... 5, 302-304, 306-313,
    315-316, 319
Typhoon Haiyan... 256, 288, 309
UBC Philippine Studies... 104, 180
UN Convention on Refugees ... 37
UN HABITAT... 115
UNESCO heritage site... 62-63
United Council of Filipino Associations in
    Canada... 109
United Nations... 110, 114, 157, 276
Vancouver Civic Merit Award... 123, 322
Vancouver General Hospital... 205
Vancouver School Board... 128, 166
Venket and Letty Rao... 58
Victoria Filipino Canadian Association...
    232, 252, 254
Victoria Francisco... 132
visible minorities... 10, 125, 144
Will-writing... 224-225
women's rights... 276-277, 282, 286
World Health Organization... 34, 108,
    189, 191, 321
World Meteorological Organization... 288
young generations of Filipinos... 4,
    55, 163
Yukon-Filipina community... 139
Yvonne Clark... 138-139

CPSIA information can be obtained
at www.ICGtesting.com
Printed in the USA
BVHW062305240323
661089BV00003B/16

9 781039 158993